AS MEDIA STUDIES FOR OCR

SECOND EDITION

Jacqueline Bennett, Tanya Jones
Consultant Editor: Peter Fraser

Hodder Arnold
A MEMBER OF THE HODDER HEADLINE GROUP

Orders: please contact Bookpoint Ltd, 130 Milton Park, Abingdon, Oxon OX14 4SB. Telephone: 44 (0)1235 827720. Fax: 44 (0)1235 400454. Lines are open from 9.00–6.00, Monday to Saturday, with a 24-hour message-answering service. You can also order through our website www.hoddereducation.co.uk

If you have any comments to make about this, or any of our other titles, please send them to educationenquiries@hodder.co.uk

British Library Cataloguing in Publication Data
A catalogue record for this title is available from the British Library

ISBN-10: 0 340 899 891
ISBN-13: 978 0 340 899 892

First Edition Published 2001
This Edition Published 2005
Impression number 10 9 8 7 6 5 4 3 2 1
Year 2009 2008 2007 2006 2005

Typeset by Fakenham Photosetting Ltd, Fakenham, Norfolk
Printed in Italy for Hodder Arnold, an imprint of Hodder Education, a member of the Hodder Headline Group, 338 Euston Road, London NW1 3BH

CONTENTS

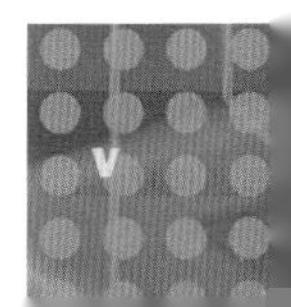
v

Acknowledgements

The authors and publishers would like to thank the following for permission to reproduce copyright illustrative material:

Andrew Cooper/Kobal, p. 61 (bottom); ARTISTS/THE KOBAL COLLECTION, p. 2; Associated Press, p. 216 (bottom); BBC, pp. 142, 143 (top), 191 (top left and bottom left), 210; British Film Institute, pp. 5, 70 (bottom left), 196, 201, 207, 208, 212, 213; bfi Stills, pp. 75, 75, 211; CHANNEL 4 PICTURE PUBLICITY/British Film Institute, p. 184; © Disney Enterprises, Inc. & Jerry Bruckheimer Inc./British Film Institute, p. 71; educationphotos.co.uk/westmore p. 19; Edmund Nagele, p. 29 (bottom right); © Essentials/IPC+Syndication, p. 94; Everett Collection/Rex Features p. 143 (bottom); IMAX p. 164; ITV Granada, p. 3; ITV/Rex Features p. 191 (bottom right); Joan Williams/Rex Features p. 11; Keith Hamshere/ Edmund Nagele p. 29 (bottom left); LUCASFILM/Moviestore Collection Ltd p. 70 (top right); Mirrorpix p. 107; movie store collection p. 68; NI Syndication, p. 108; © Now/IPC+Syndication, p. 93; Nguyen Kong/Associated Press, p. 216 (top); © Paramount/ Aquarius p. 62; Rex Features p. 191 (top right); Ronald Grant Archive pp. 9, 19, 61 (top); SABAH ARAR / Rex Features p. 217 (top); Sega, p. 7; Sipa Press / Rex Features p. 217 (bottom); Sony, p. 7; © Twentieth Century Fox /British Film Institute p. 74; WHITE / Rex Features p. 173; © Twentieth Century Fox/ The Ronald Grant Archive p. 77; © 2005 Universal Studios/British Film Institute, p. 29 (top left); © 2004 Warner Bros./ The Ronald Grant Archive p. 70 (bottom right); © WALT DISNEY PICTURES/PIXAR ANIMATION STUDIOS/ British Film Institute p. 158; Warner Bros/The Ronald Grant Archive p. 198; WORKING TITLE FILMS, STUDIO CANAL + & UNIVERSAL FILMS/ The Ronald Grant Archive p. 29 (top right).

The authors and publishers would like to thank the following for permission to reproduce copyright material:

© Guardian Newspapers Limited 2005, pp. 105, 156–158, 169, 174-175, 179-180, 182-183; www.computing.co.uk, pp. 155, 172, (reprinted with kind permission and may not be republished or used without the express permission of VNU Business Publications).

The publishers apologise if inadvertently any sources remain unacknowledged and will be glad to make the necessary arrangements at the earliest opportunity.

Preface

When I started teaching Media Studies over 20 years ago, the UK had only just acquired its fourth TV channel, the first personal computer made by Apple had just been released, home video had only recently taken off, mobile phones were a rarity, the first British multiplex cinema was about to open and none of us had heard of the Internet. Even then, people talked about the influence of the media and the idea of a media-saturated society, yet compared to media consumption today, it seems very little. Nowadays the media dominate our lives in ways that were unimaginable back then. The idea that we could access any information we want, instantly and without wires, from a computer which also plays music or films, or talk live on video with people in Australia, would have seemed like something out of *Thunderbirds*. The fact that we can be doing all these things at once, as well as catching the latest news as it happens and writing about our interests to post them live on a blog for others to read, illustrates just how far things have moved on.

These changes in the media have been increasingly reflected in Media Studies specifications and teaching. The single, expensive, heavy and poor quality Portapak video cameras that schools might have had in the mid-1980s have been replaced by a vast array of production facilities which are often easy to use, much more reliable and very flexible for the user. Many students are now producing media texts from websites to music videos that can easily be shown to appreciative audiences. This marks what is potentially a major change in the relationship between audience and media, as increasingly the consumer can become a producer.

All this points to the importance of Media Studies in the curriculum today. In choosing it as an AS level, students may be opting for a fourth subject alongside three which are more conventional, or may be seeing it as the first step towards a media career. Either way, they should find a subject which is lively, varied and engaging.

Media Studies offers an unusual space within the education system, bringing opportunities to discuss things students would choose to consume anyway – magazines, websites, music, films, games, radio and TV programmes. The OCR specification offers the chance to study examples from each of these media, to analyse them in depth and to find out more about how they are produced. With practical work, it also brings the chance to develop skills of teamwork, organisation and planning, as well as particular skills in the equipment used to produce media texts.

This book offers a clear and comprehensive framework for students taking the AS level. You will find clear explanations and applications of key terms – almost a working dictionary of the language you will need to use. Words which appear in bold text are explained in the glossary at the end of the book. There are sections on each of the course units, where the authors describe the range of possible options for the two exams and the coursework and provide helpful case studies as possible models for student work. The tips on production should enable you to produce better structured work which will be good enough to show to audiences and allow you to reflect on how media texts function. The range of case studies for the Textual Analysis unit will give you the basis for your own analysis of media texts and give you the confidence to approach the exam. The variety of articles for the Audiences and Institutions unit will introduce you to many of the issues involved and prepare you for the tasks in the exam.

This textbook will act as the foundation for your studies, as you will be pointed towards other resources

such as books, newspapers, video and particularly the web. Media Studies is a living and ever-changing subject, and keeping up to date is crucial for success.

Of the many good textbooks on Media Studies now available, this is the only one specifically aimed at the OCR course, the most popular of the AS level options. The first edition from 2001 has been updated here with some new options introduced, such as videogames for Unit 2731 and many new case studies on technology and ownership for Unit 2732, which reflect the changing nature of the media. The media texts referred to have been updated to include more contemporary examples of magazines, newspaper stories, sitcoms and action films.

Using this book

Although ideal as a whole-class textbook, this book is designed so that students can use it for independent study as they work through the course.

Section 1 covers the key concepts you will encounter throughout the course.

Section 2 offers clear guidance on the processes of production for the Foundation Production coursework briefs.

Section 3 covers textual analysis, both the Unseen Moving Image section (Action films) and the options from comparative analysis.

Section 4 deals with case studies for Audiences and Institutions in the two options (New Technologies and Ownership).

Section 5 looks in detail at how elements of the course can be related to Key Skills, though the material will also be of help in developing your understanding of the key concepts of Media Studies.

Throughout the book you will find a variety of clearly defined suggested activities, most of which can be undertaken on your own at any time. However, there are some areas of discussion where you will find it helpful to work with others.

If you are taking this course after Media Studies at GCSE, it will hopefully broaden and deepen your understanding and develop your skills; if it is a completely new course for you, it should open your mind to new ways of thinking about the media and introduce you to new practical skills. Whatever your situation, I hope you find this an enjoyable course that will encourage you to take your study further to A2 and perhaps beyond.

Pete Fraser (Chief Examiner 2005)

SECTION 1
THE KEY CONCEPTS OF MEDIA STUDIES

Introduction

Your Media Studies course will include various areas of study. You might focus on a particular film, television programme, print publication or piece of practical production work. You will build up not only critical analysis skills, but also an understanding of institution and production practices. In order for you to be able to make connections between the different elements of your course, you need to have a clear understanding of the Key Concepts within Media Studies. These concepts encourage you to discuss the wider implications of the media and provide you with a more comprehensive view of what the media are and how they work. This section will introduce you to the Key Concepts and explain how they relate to the OCR Media Studies specifications.

Part One

Media forms and conventions

Form

The term **form** can best be explained in relation to the shape, structure or skeleton of a text, and in this way is often linked to **narrative**. Narrative provides a basic shape to the media text. Indeed, structuralist analysts, such as Tzvetan Todorov, have argued that all stories told contain the same basic structure: the initial equilibrium of the story world is disrupted during the body of the story by opposing forces, but is re-established at the end as a new, revised equilibrium. Obviously, individual media texts will represent this basic structure in a way that is specific to them. For example, the form of soap operas necessitates continuous, multi-stranded storylines, with individual episodes frequently ending with a cliffhanger. On top of this basic structure are placed the elements that make the text even more distinctive.

Your discussions of the form of media texts will also include the analysis of the 'micro' elements of that text. In relation to visual texts such as TV programmes, adverts and films, consideration of textual form should include discussion of ***mise-en-scène,*** editing, cinematography and sound. The ways in which these elements help to provide a structure through which meaning is delivered to the text's audience will be an important consideration within your analyses. The use of *mise-en-scène* within a particular genre of film or TV programme, for example, which is recognisable to viewers as being part of the conventions of that genre, would become part of your discussions of form.

Style

Style refers to the distinctive 'look' of a media text. In film you can frequently identify the individual style of a particular director. He or she might use distinctive *mise-en-scène*, lighting, music, camera

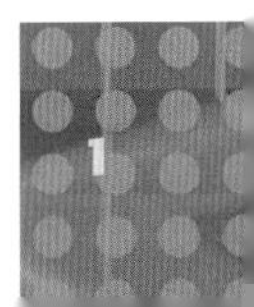

angles, movement, framing and editing. In print media such as magazines it might be said that particular texts have a house style. These can be identified by the use of colour, typography, graphic design, layout and tone of written text. The style of a media text is what distinguishes that text from any other text, even from those within the same genre.

Genre

A still typical of the Western genre

If a group of media texts has a similar form/structure or pattern of elements, then this might be due to a link in **genre**. Western films, for example, have common structural elements that make them recognisable as a specific genre: they often end with a final gunfight and resolution to the problems established at the beginning of the film. *Unforgiven* and *Once Upon a Time in the West* both have characteristics of form which define them as Westerns, but individual elements which make them distinct. Media texts of the same genre have distinctive characteristics or conventions. TV news programmes share a set of distinctive characteristics, as do soap operas and radio programmes.

Sub-genres are groups of media texts which come under the same main generic heading, but which can be further distinguished. These smaller groups of media texts are still part of the wider grouping, but might share particular characteristics which other texts under the broader heading don't. Horror, for example, is a very broad generic term and includes sub-genres, such as slasher films and zombie films. Hybrid genres are those which combine the conventions of different genres. The conventions used are recognisable as being from two (or more) different genres, but combine to present the audience with a new generic type: a hybrid. A docu-drama, for example, would use the two sets of conventions from a TV documentary and a TV drama together.

Conventions

A typical scene from a soap opera

In order to be able to identify media texts within particular categories or genres, you will need to analyse a text for the codes and conventions it uses. The characteristic 'ingredients' of a particular genre, and the elements which make it recognisable, can be defined as conventions. Conventions provide a common link between, for example, a group of films, television programmes or types of newspaper. These conventions may be connected to form, language, theme or visual elements. Tabloid newspapers share styles of language, composition, image and content which make them distinct from broadsheet newspapers. Horror films share styles of lighting, camera work, character profile and music which differentiate them from other genres.

Television soap operas all contain a series of conventions that help to distinguish them from other programmes, such as documentary programmes or news broadcasts. Soap operas contain, for example, rolling story lines, recognisable characters and consistent settings. They often tackle social issues, and will have a series of episodes which build towards climaxes. Soap operas are also set in small community areas, with defined meeting places.

Conventions are not always used in an obvious or literal way in media texts. They might be subverted or revised so that the creator can make a specific point. Modern horror films tend to end with the final female character confronting the force of evil which has eradicated the other characters: *Halloween* is a classic example of this. Many more recent horror films, however, have created final scenes which do more than merely pit the heroine against the killer. *The Blair Witch Project* has its final female character alone with a video camera, unable to confront what is frightening her and waiting to die.

Conventions provide recognisable elements for the audience to use as an indication of the intention and potential meanings evident within the text they are viewing, listening to or reading. Audiences have expectations of the conventions that they associate with particular genres and will bring these expectations to the viewing process. There is a need for the conventions expected within a particular genre to be evident to the audience member. However, there is also a need for audiences to experience conventions in new ways in order for their attention to be maintained.

To show your understanding of form, style, genre and conventions in analytical and practical work, try to concentrate on three areas:

- How form and style are used in each medium to generate meaning.
- What effects form and style have upon the audience.
- How media texts are organized in categories or genres.

Part Two

Media languages

Media languages can be written, verbal, non-verbal, visual and aural. Most texts that you study will include a range of media languages and will use them to generate different effects and responses.

Written language

The most obvious place for written language is within print-based media. Newspapers and magazines all have a particular style and presentation of language that is specific to their genre and audience. The language of print-based media is evident in the articles you read, but also in text such as the captions for photographs, mastheads (the title of the publication) and advertisements. Written language is also an essential element within silent films and works to 'fix' or anchor our reading of the visual elements in the same way that a caption does in a newspaper.

The text within print publications is often referred to as **copy**. It is carefully selected in order to create an identity for the particular publication, and as a means of engaging the particular target audience. The language chosen generates meaning as it helps to form our understanding of the ideological stance, intention and values of the particular publication. For example, a caption for a photograph will help to fix the way the audience looks at the image. Captions allow the publication to present the story in a particular way. By looking at the way the publication tries to shape our understanding of the image through the caption, we can understand more about the intention of the magazine or newspaper.

Verbal language

Verbal language is evident in many media areas such as films, television programmes and the radio. The choice, delivery and context of the language used are important factors in the way meaning is generated for the audience. A television news item, for example, will be delivered using language that creates a sense of the importance of the story in the mind of the viewer. This in turn might link with images shown in order to shape that importance further.

Non-verbal language

Non-verbal media language is often defined in terms of body language: gestures, stance and mannerisms. We can read meaning into a scene in a drama, for instance, by the way in which the actor uses his or her body. Silent films are perhaps the best example of a medium in which non-verbal language is essential. They include captions in order to help explain the action we see, but it is from the obvious and subtle movements, gestures and mannerisms of the actors that we understand fully what the scene is about.

Visual language

A film still from a silent film

Many of the media texts you will study as part of your course will be visual: for example, films or television programmes. In order to study them effectively you will need to be able to discuss **visual** language. An analysis of the visual elements of a film will include technical areas such as **camera work**, *mise-en-scène* and analytical readings using analytical frameworks such as **semiotics**. What you see on the film or television screen, or in the piece of photojournalism, has been chosen in order to generate a series of effects and meanings.

A film director, for example, when planning a particular scene, will choose to use certain camera angles and movements in order to tell the story of the scene. A **tracking shot** (sometimes called a **dolly shot** when the camera moves on a dolly around a scene) might be used to introduce the audience to the film's setting, and thus establish the setting as having an important role within the film.

A **point of view shot** (where the camera is placed in the scene as if it were one of the characters) might be used in order to position the audience within a scene and to allow them to experience some of the thoughts and emotions of a particular character.

Camera angles and positioning are technical devices that help construct the film or television programme. They are also used within videogames, which are becoming increasingly cinematic.

Another important area of study within visual language is *mise-en-scène*. Literally meaning, 'put into the shot or scene', *mise-en-scène* also includes lighting, props, location, costumes and set design. If you freeze-frame a film or television programme and analyse the constituent elements of the still, looking at all of the elements of *mise-en-scène*, you will then be able to make comments on the genre of the piece, its intention and the meanings it is attempting to produce. You might freeze-frame a film and notice the use of shadows and light. This might then help you to define the film in terms of its style. Examples of **film noir**, for instance, can often be identified by their distinctive visual style.

Semiotics

The term **semiotics** (the study of signs and symbols) can often be confusing, but at its simplest it is a way of discussing both the literal and the potential meanings of the images we see on the screen. It was Roland Barthes (see bibliography) who developed notions of signification in his analysis of the way signs work in culture. Barthes identified two orders of signification, **denotation** and **connotation**. **Denotation** is the term applied in Media Studies to indicate literal or obvious meaning. This can be referred to as a simple description of what is physically seen or heard.

Connotation is the term used to indicate potential or suggested meaning. A cross, for example, is a sign that has many different literal and potential meanings. Depending on the context in which it is placed it can be a literal indication of a mathematical plus sign or a crossroads. Given another visual context, the cross might become a crucifix, which is understood by most societies to indicate or **denote** Christianity. This is the literal level of the sign's meaning. The potential meanings of the crucifix, or its connotations, are more varied. It might conjure up images of suffering or oppression or sacrifice.

When you are discussing visual language remember to analyse all that you see and all that is implied on the screen or in the image. Look at the images, the composition and the colours that are in front of you, but also remember to identify what helps to construct the visual – the camera angle.

Aural language

Aural language is an important area for study within media texts. We have looked at written and visual language, but you also need to be able to discuss what you hear. Media texts often include a mixture of sounds, all of which help to generate meaning for a text. This includes spoken language, but also any sound within the world of the programme or film (**diegetic** sound) or on the soundtrack (**non-diegetic** sound). Radio is an interesting medium because it is purely aural. It cannot rely on images to help root (or **anchor**) the sounds we hear. In a film or a television programme we might hear the diegetic sounds of traffic or animals or the weather and this will help in our construction of environment, atmosphere and mood. If a city is saturated with sounds of cars, building work, radios and so on, this can create the impression that the setting is chaotic and oppressive. If a building is devoid of sound we might perceive it as isolated or isolating. The non-diegetic sound within media texts can be in the form of music or any other noise that is added in post-production. The aural language of a media text (both diegetic and non-diegetic) can help us also to define the genre of a piece. A horror film, for example, might include non-diegetic heartbeat sounds or chants in order to provoke a response in the audience.

Part Three

Media institutions

Definition

For the purposes of this Key Concept, try to think about media institutions in terms of the people who have a role in the production process of media texts, the companies/organisations they represent and the processes of production, distribution and marketing in which both are involved.

The roles within the media production process are many. Depending on the medium you are studying they may include, for example, directors, editors, producers, scriptwriters and screenwriters. A discussion of institutions may begin by identifying issues of ownership, and you will need to conduct research into who owns companies such as TimeWarner, Sony or Sega and what their area of production is.

The last area of importance within this Key Concept asks you to look at processes of production. You may look at a specific media product and analyse how it has been produced, what its distribution breadth is and what strategies are being used to market it. To show your understanding of institutions you will need to be able to discuss:

- Media texts as products of institutional, economic and industrial processes and how this affects the text produced.
- The production, distribution, exhibition and consumption of media texts.
- The advances in media technologies and how these affect the processes of production and consumption.

Any media text, whether it is a film, newspaper, television or radio programme, is produced within an institutional context. A television drama, for example, will begin life as a piece of either commissioned or non-commissioned work. Once the drama has been written, a production company will produce it. The production company will, in turn, offer the programme to a television station for broadcast. The process seems simple, but it is often lengthy and fraught with difficulties. If the drama has not been commissioned, the writer(s) will have to approach an appropriate production company. This is likely to be one that either has a history of producing this type of drama or is willing to speculate on the success of the product. (The insecurity of this stage can be bypassed if the writers or presenter of the programme own the production company.) Once the drama has been produced it has to be sold to a television station, and again the success of the sale will depend on factors such as the station's history of broadcasting this type of programme, audience desire for the product and even whether or not there is an available and appropriate scheduling slot.

Any new media product will have to prove itself in economic terms. If the production costs outweigh the potential return, in terms of either revenue or viewing figures (which make the profile of the institution more secure), then the product is unlikely to begin production. Generating financial backing for a product is often extremely difficult. Often funds have to be generated through asking investors to speculate on its potential success.

The industrial processes behind a media text are those which create it. A pop video, for example, will have been created using camera and editing technologies. With the advent of digital processes, most video production has left analogue methods behind. When you look at a media text, as well as considering what you see in front of you, try to consider what kinds of technology produced it. The type of industrial process used to create a media product will affect the text produced, because it will have an impact on the potential contexts in which the text can be consumed and the way the audience will be able to consume it.

As an extension to some of the points we have just looked at, the Key Concept of Media Institutions also asks you to study production and distribution. Production extends beyond the industrial considerations looked at above and includes research into the roles within the production process. For each of the media you study you will need to know the nature of each role and the place of that role within the production process. Also consider what technology each person is required to use, and the control they have over the 'look' of the final product. Production processes use people and technology together. A newspaper editor, for example, will liaise with advertising managers, art directors and the publisher to ensure that the product is cohesive. The technology that each of these people uses comes together to produce the final product. You will need to consider the production process as a unified whole. Economic, institutional and industrial concerns should also be considered fully within a discussion of the production process.

Distribution, consumption and exhibition

The **distribution** of a media text is a vital element in its success. The distributor of a product will need to consider issues such as the context(s) for the product's exposure and access to the target consumer. (For a film, the context in which it is screened is its **exhibition**.) For a film distributor, for example, choices will have to be made concerning where the film is first screened or premiered, whether the place in which it is screened allows for **consumption** by the target audience, or whether the film is worthy of cinema release or goes straight to video. The marketing of a media product is also an important consideration, and institutions have to consider such areas as posters, trailers, teaser campaigns, Internet sites and so on.

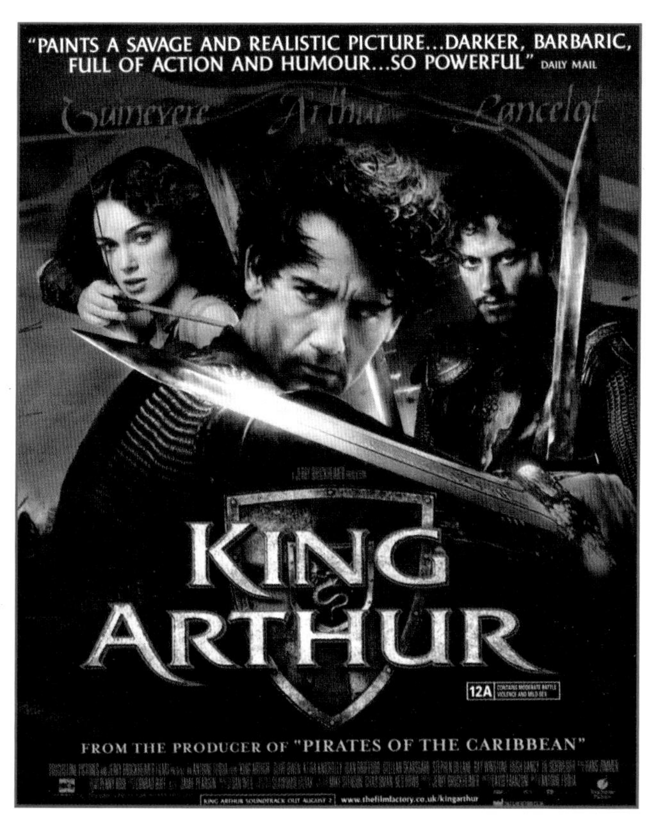

A poster advertising the film *King Arthur*

Media technology has advanced at an incredible rate and this has had an effect on both the texts produced and the way in which they can be consumed. We have already identified a shift in film editing from analogue processes to digital, but the digital explosion extends into most of the media you will study. Radio, television, the music business and print media can all now take advantage of digital technology. Most households are now saturated with new media technologies: mobile telephones, computers with Internet facilities and games consoles, to name but a few. We can watch a film on video, DVD or digital television. We can listen to music on CD or from an MP3 file downloaded from the Internet. The technology available and therefore the ways in which we can consume the media around us are more varied than they have ever been. As a media student, you will need to consider the effect of all this choice on the consumer. Does our mode of viewing, listening or reading change because there is so much choice? News stations such as CNN, and music television channels such as MTV, offer bite-sized chunks and do not demand consistent or continuous viewing. The question has to be asked: are we now used to more fragmented viewing practices? We now have greater access to information, but does this necessarily breed a greater understanding of the world around us?

Part Four

Media audiences

Definition

The audience for any media product is the group that consumes it. The target audience is the group at whom a product is specifically aimed. Some media texts will aim to engage a wide or **mass** audience, and others might aim at a specific or **niche** group. Each audience (and indeed individual member of an audience) will consume the media product in a different way. In order to be able to target the most appropriate audience, the producers of a media text will research using categories which include age, gender, socio-economic group, sexual orientation and consumption history or preference.

Media language and audiences

The various languages (discussed previously) that media texts use to generate meaning are chosen to provoke specific responses in the audience. Media products all have a target audience, which could be defined by many things, including age, gender and demographic group. We will explore the concept of an audience in more detail later in this section, but language is one of the ways in which a media product can shape audience responses. Different audiences and different individuals within the same audience will engage with and understand the language they are offered in varying ways.

To show your understanding of media audiences you will need to be able to discuss:

- The fact that all media texts have a target audience.
- The various ways in which both institutions and producers research and target the audience.
- The ways in which the audience responds to representation in media texts.
- The means by which individuals learn to consider their role within an audience.
- The consumption of media texts by the audience.

Whether you are studying a lifestyle magazine, a piece of animation, a chat show or any other media text, each has a defined target audience. When you are discussing the Key Concept of Audience you must show an awareness that these audiences are different and that a product has been constructed to be consumed by that particular audience.

In order to be able to target an audience effectively, media institutions and producers use various methods of research in order to discover the preferences and expectations of that audience. One useful way of defining research types is by categorising them as either **qualitative** or **quantitative**.

Qualitative research methods aim to discover the opinions and preferences of the target consumer, and one good example of this mode of research is the **focus group**. The producers of a product will select a group which has the profile of their target audience, and will show them the product. This can be done pre-release, or post-release if the product is not performing as successfully as anticipated. The producers then use the focus group's response to alter, completely rethink, or even confirm the look and content of the product.

Quantitative research concerns itself with numerical data. It can be used either by the producers of a product or by the institution which is selling it. Television companies use **BARB** (Broadcasters' Audience Research Board) data to analyse viewing figures, and radio stations use **RAJAR** (Radio Joint Audience Research) statistics to check listening figures. Qualitative and quantitative methods are used in parallel in order to research the habits and preferences of the target audience.

In order to define the profile of the audience, institutions and producers might look at existing demographic models (definitions based on socio-economic or lifestyle profiles), or they may try to construct a new audience for their product. Constructing a new audience is much harder to achieve and a producer will have to create a product which is attractive to those that feel there is a gap in their product market, or bring a group of individuals together who all aspire to a new social phenomenon.

Once a profile of the target audience has been established, the product producers will target the audience by using a carefully constructed campaign of promotion. The product might be advertised in magazines that the target consumer reads, on Internet sites which are popular with that group, or feature on a commercial between preferred programmes.

Reading a text

It would be a mistake to assume that audiences for media texts are passive consumers of what they see, hear or read. The text they are in the process of consuming might include a **preferred**, **oppositional**, or **negotiated** reading – or a combination of all three. There may also be an **aberrant** reading.

A **preferred** reading (or **dominant system of response**) is a way of understanding a text that is consistent with the ideas and intentions of the producer or creator of that product. This may lead to an acceptance of the dominant values within the text.

With a **negotiated** reading (or **subordinate response**) the individual has a choice as to whether or not they accept the preferred reading as their own. Audience members might read the text through a filter of their own personal agenda. Although there may be a general acceptance of dominant values and existing social structures, the individual might be prepared to argue that a particular social group may be unfairly represented.

In an **oppositional** reading (or **radical response**) individual members of an audience might reject completely the preferred reading of the dominant code and the social values that produced it.

An **aberrant** reading is where an entirely different meaning from that intended by the maker will be taken from a text. This could be when individual members of the audience do not share, in any way, the values of the maker of the text. A famous example of this was the television series *Till Death Us Do Part*. The character of Alf Garnett was created by Johnny Speight as a figure of fun. His extreme and bigoted views were, however, admired by some of the audience of this popular series: clearly aberrant readings of Speight's text.

Alf Garnett from *Till Death Us Do Part*

Just as audiences are often prepared to question information they receive or representations of social groups, individuals frequently consider their own place within a particular audience. For example, if an individual were to refer to himself or herself as a *Guardian* reader, they might also be considering what this indicates about their interests, political orientation, socio-economic status and educational experience. Some audience members might derive status from the audience group of which they consider themselves to be part. Some might feel a sense of social responsibility and others might use the defined group in which they place themselves to engender a feeling of community or security.

When you are discussing media audiences, remember that as individuals we often define ourselves through the groups within which we are included. Fans of different types of music will often define themselves in relation to their musical tastes. They may dress in a way which presents them as connected with a genre of music, or create a website or magazine/fanzine through which they contact other fans.

It is clear, therefore, that audiences consume the media texts with which they are presented in differing ways: they may accept, reject or negotiate a response to a preferred textual reading and will often be extremely active within the consumption process. The impact of a text on the target audience can come in many forms and we should not forget that analysis is often a secondary response. An audience will often respond emotionally to what they are consuming: it might repulse them or give them pleasure. These emotional responses should be considered as important factors in how the audience encounters a text. We might also have a particular ideological position that is being engaged by the media text. Remember that whether we read something from a dominant, negotiated or oppositional perspective, it is intrinsically linked to whatever personal experience or detail the text encourages us to reflect upon.

When discussing theories of audience consumption, you should try to refer to certain theorists to substantiate or explain points you are making. Australian researchers Hodge and Tripp, and British researcher David Buckingham, for example, have conducted extensive studies into the nature of children's consumption of television. Their findings point to an active model of consumption, within which children have the capacity to decode what they are seeing and form coping strategies to deal with problematic material. The active model of audience consumption is countered by American researchers, such as Donnerstein and Linz, and Bushman whose findings point towards passivity in the audience. The American theorists' model uses the case of media violence to promote the idea that an audience will be directly and negatively affected by watching violent images. Bushman conducted studies in which he sought to prove that exposure to violent images encourages violent behaviour. Whichever theorists you use within your own debate, remember that their arguments can be challenged!

Part Five

Media representations

Definition

The different modes of reading a text are important when considering how an audience tackles the issue of **representation**. Representation is the process by which images, words or sounds are used to indicate issues or debates beyond what they literally mean. The most common form of representation is that of social groups, and debates arise that analyse both the positive and negative aspects of representation. Of course, the notion of positive and negative representation is subjective, and different members of a social group might have opposing views of what is or isn't a positive/negative representation. Debates arise when a **stereotype** is either explored or exploited.

A film character, for example, has importance because of their place within the story world, but we could also extend their importance by defining the social, political or racial group of which they are part and then begin to discuss how that group is being treated within the film and society. Audiences will often respond to different representations actively and bring their own thoughts about society and the world to that response.

To show your understanding of media representations, you will need to be able to discuss the:

- processes through which representation occurs
- ways in which these representations can be analysed
- ways in which the media analyst or student can engage with the processes of representation in order to be able to analyse its use within media texts.

Media texts use representation to varying degrees and for various purposes. It might be the intention of a particular text to discuss the representation of a certain social group, or a text might contain representational debate almost unintentionally. In order to understand the processes through which representation occurs, we will look at two examples: the use of characters within soap operas and the use of photojournalistic images within newspapers.

The representational potential of a soap character can be established in a number of ways.

- If the character is of a different ethnic minority than others in the soap opera, or is part of an ethnic group, the issues concerning the depiction of ethnic minorities might be debated. As with all of these examples, you will need to remember that representation does not solely deal with *negative* stereotypes. *Positive* representations may also be constructed. It is essential to be aware of just who it is that deems the stereotypes on display as positive or negative.
- The focus of an episode or a series of episodes might be the sexuality of a particular character and might deal with the responses of other characters to that sexual orientation.
- The gender of a character might be highlighted in an episode by the experiences they have and the treatment they receive, thus encouraging the viewer to consider the depiction of men or women.
- A character's age might be a focus and their attitudes or behaviour contrasted with those of other age groups. From this we might consider the treatment of different age groups within society.
- Social class is another area of possible representational debate, and discussion may ensue from the problems characters have that are connected with their socio-economic status.

Discussions concerning issues of representation should include the profile of the character, the position they are given within the programme and how they link to wider social debate. Remember, however, that an individual character or group of characters does not have to be part of a minority in order to warrant representational debate.

If we now look at the processes of representation connected with an image within a newspaper, we can broaden our knowledge of the processes of representation. Any piece of photojournalism, even before it has been placed within a newspaper, will have potential representational qualities, but the discussion can be extended when we consider the factors below.

- The caption added to any image within a newspaper aims to fix the audience's potential reading of that image. The caption will help us to consider not only the basic representational qualities of the image, but also what the newspaper wishes us to understand from it.
- An image will be chosen to highlight a particular aspect of the story it has been chosen to illustrate, and we can use the text of the story to extend any discussion of the representational debate evident in the image.

- The specific newspaper in which we see the image is also important and should be remembered when discussing image representation. The newspaper's political or socio-economic leaning will have an impact on the way images are used within it and will therefore inform our consideration of representation.
- The position of the image on the page or within the newspaper is an essential factor to consider. Newspapers are composed through a hierarchy of importance, with the lead story on the front page. The importance of the image and, by extension, the representational debate that it explores, can be understood when this positioning is analysed.

These factors, alongside the content of the image, help us to consider not just what is being debated, but also how it is being debated.

We can analyse these processes of representation by considering all of the factors that surround an image, sound or word. Remember to consider where something has been placed, how it has been composed, the type of publication, programme or film which is its context, the media institution that has produced it, the current social debate surrounding it, and also your own response to the way in which something is being represented.

Part Six

Ideology

Definition

Ideology is often referred to as an unconscious set of ideas, values and beliefs that a group, society or an individual believe to be true or important, and which provide a framework for a particular view of the world. The values and beliefs perpetuated by the majority within a society may be described as the **dominant** ideologies. Within a society there might be different ideologies at play representing different sets of social interests, but powerful institutions such as religion, the family, education, government, the law and the mass media may influence dominant ideologies. Dominant ideologies may also be hidden in terms such as 'common sense' or the common-sense view. Such a consensus view of society is achieved with the consent or agreement of the majority of a particular society as a whole, and this consensus is referred to as **hegemony**. Hegemony is, however, subject to renegotiation and redefinition, and the consensus may be broken as the ideologies of subordinate groups come into direct conflict with dominant ideologies.

Within an analysis of a media text you will need to consider how people, places or things have been represented historically, and how/why that representation has changed. There will have been shifts in ideas, values and beliefs, which mean, for example, that a group now has a differing representation. Consider the way in which the police have been represented over the years and you can examine how this representation reflects the social and political attitude current at any given time. You might also discuss in groups how renegotiations in hegemony have been reflected in media representations of women, homosexuality, ethnic minorities and family in recent years.

Summary

As we have seen through this discussion, the Key Concepts of Media Studies exist in relation to each other. When you are analysing texts, consider not only what needs to be discussed for each one, but also how they can be discussed together. The key conceptual areas have been defined in order to help you to understand and explore all of the areas necessary to produce a comprehensive media analysis.

SECTION 2
FOUNDATION PRODUCTION

Introduction

Practical work is probably the main reason why students undertake a Media Studies course, but you will be spending a considerable amount of time learning about, amongst other things, 'reading' the media, institutions, audiences, ideology and representation. Then, when you undertake the production element of the course, there is suddenly a reason for it all and a chance to demonstrate skills, understanding and creativity.

This section is designed to help you prepare, organise, create, edit and analyse your work within the confines of an A Level specification.

In some ways it might be said that creating a practical project for an examination is an artificial exercise. After all, we know that Spielberg does not sit down and define all the character roles in a forthcoming movie according to academic theorists before the screenplay is completed. We also know that a television programme will be defined by its scheduling and by the channel on which it is broadcast, and that these can be highly significant factors from inception onwards. In other words, the institutional and audience factors are fundamental for all but the most art-house of pieces.

At the beginning of your first attempt at Foundation Production you will probably feel that you have plenty of time before your piece is due for completion and there is ample time for thinking and experimenting before you begin the real work. It is best to avoid this dangerous train of thought as it implies too much 'inspiration time' before any real work gets done. In this scenario everything becomes a rush job, everything is done at the last minute and the finished piece frequently does not do the student justice.

This section focuses on the six set briefs in the OCR specification and offers preparatory exercises to develop competence. These exercises will give you an opportunity to develop your creative skills in your chosen medium. There are suggestions for various ways to approach planning and research, construction and evaluation for the final projects, and some pointers are given for improving media texts along the way.

This section will focus on the four media specified for these briefs:

- moving image (film and television)
- print (newspapers and magazines)
- radio
- new media (websites, multimedia, interactive media, digital media).

Although the section is aimed primarily at the OCR A Level specification, the comments, suggestions and exercises are equally valid for all Media Studies A Level specifications with a production unit, since the principles of assessment for practical work remain constant across the various awarding bodies.

Context of Foundation Production

In the OCR AS Media Studies specification the purpose of the production module is defined as follows:

> 'The purpose of this unit is for candidates to demonstrate a range of technical skills and understanding of media concepts by the construction of a media text of their own production. Candidates also record and monitor the production process and demonstrate evaluation, from planning to outcome, in the Production Log.'

Original images

The Board considers original images to be those created by students and manipulated by them for inclusion in their projects. This does not include images obtained from other sources (e.g. downloaded from the Internet), however much such images have been manipulated by the student. The requirement is for at least three original images in print or new media production work and this should be supported by including copies of original photos in the research portfolio to demonstrate what pictures were taken and how they have been employed within the project.

Ways of approaching practical work

There is usually a series of stages for any project to go through, from the original idea to final production, but the most important factor when planning a project is to remember that production work usually takes far longer than you anticipate. Given that you also should allow 'fall-back' time when preparing for a project, the time soon evaporates – what seemed well organised, under control and on schedule can easily become a last-minute panic, resulting in disappointing work.

The availability of technical equipment will depend to a large extent upon the facilities at your school or college, although you may have access to your own or friends' equipment. Of course, the other significant limiting factor is technical expertise in the use of the equipment, which is why this is assessed as part of the project. Skilled work on low-tech equipment can often be far stronger than work done using sophisticated equipment but with limited technical competence. This is why preparatory exercises are suggested for each of the major media specified here, to allow you to gain competence before you begin the project. It is strongly recommended that you complete at least one of these tasks, and ideally all of them, before actually beginning the project itself. There is a world of difference between theory and practical work and you cannot develop your practical skills adequately without practical experience. It is common to discover that groups who have never used video cameras or non-linear editing facilities before, and thus cannot make creative use of the equipment, have made poor quality media texts for submission. Equally, there is usually a significant difference between the first web page produced using a particular software package and a later production, once greater technical competence has been developed. It is essential to practise basic competencies first so that your creativity will not be hampered.

Competency

For each of these media there is a list of specific competencies given in the specification. These are regarded as the basic skills you need to demonstrate in your practical work, to show that you have learnt how to work within that medium appropriately.

Students using production equipment

It is easy to see how to use these competencies in theory, but the trick comes in ensuring you have thought carefully about each aspect when making your media text. You might rightly argue that George Lucas does not think explicitly about whether he has demonstrated an ability to use appropriate framing for his shots when making the latest *Star Wars* epic. He will, however, automatically frame his shots (in conjunction with his team, of course) in an interesting, appropriate and varied way for each scene, because he is a skilled practitioner. Only by explicitly debating the best framing and *mise-en-scène* for a key shot, for example, can you hope to develop the kind of competence necessary for it to come naturally. Just as when you started to read, you started with little words and spelt them out slowly when you were not sure what they were, so you must now learn to communicate using this new vocabulary of moving image, print, audio or new media competence. At the beginning of your AS course you probably needed to learn how to 'read' the screen, audio track or printed page in detail. You learned to identify how the different elements were used to communicate to a reader/viewer on many levels and create a defined context in which the text could be interpreted. Now you must do the same in order to learn production skills.

Preliminary research

The principal difference between this unit and the other two units for AS Level is that this is practical. This may seem a ridiculously obvious statement to make, but the truth is a little more complex.

For the Textual Analysis unit the objective is for you to understand the key theories and debates relating to the texts that you study: to 'assess candidates' media textual analysis skills using a short unseen moving image extract and to assess their understanding of the concept of representation using two texts' (OCR Specifications). Your research may be conducted individually or in a group, the texts may be mainstream or *avant garde* and the institutional context significant or secondary, but the overall intention is that you should analyse existing texts.

The purpose of the Audience and Institutions case study is to develop your 'knowledge and understanding of media institutions, production processes, technologies and related issues concerning audience consumption and reception' (OCR Specifications).

The practical production unit allows you to reverse these procedures and become the creator, and allows you and others to construct (and also deconstruct) your creation. The danger with this unit is that you will either abandon all the theory and principles that you have so painstakingly learnt and construct an insubstantial piece fairly quickly, or produce a piece which is so complex and meticulously structured that it becomes self-indulgent and obscure. Just as the professionals do, you have to strike a balance and produce something that is marketable and credible.

Form

The form of your piece is largely dictated by the chosen brief. If you are creating an opening sequence for a film, the form of your piece is substantially different from the form of a series of television adverts, for example. This is a crucial starting point for your project. So to create an opening sequence you will need to research a number of appropriate texts and note the general principles about their form. For instance:

- How are characters introduced?
- How is the mood set?
- How is the sound used?
- How is the text structured? Look in particular at sequences which relate to your chosen brief (e.g. an opening sequence) and consider how they are structured to create meaning for an audience.

Style

Form and style cross over substantially, but you should ensure that for style you have also thought about the following:

- The type of shots used or the ways that layout or *mise-en-scène* create a sense of genre and meaning for the audience.
- Use of fonts in moving image opening sequences or in print adverts – what generic codes and conventions do they suggest, for example?
- The jingles for radio, which will always directly reflect the nature of the station and especially the context of the particular programme or element, e.g. traffic news.
- The language used, as this is a very clear signifier about the text itself – you would not expect to read an article in *The Sun* written in the style of *The Times*, for example, or an interview with Britney Spears written in the style of *Loaded* appearing in *Woman's Own*. This crosses over with content and theme, but is fundamental when defining the style of a media text.

Audience segmentation

In your studies on audience you will have learned that audiences can be 'segmented' or divided up in different ways and may be identified with different texts and different contexts. Some of these divisions are explicit. If your movie is classified as a 15 or 18, you are aware that there will be some language or actions in the movie that necessitated it being given its particular classification. Some of the divisions are implicit. If you like a particular style of music and follow local bands, for example, you are likely to be a member of a target audience for a new radio station playing that type of music and giving exposure to local bands. Newspapers and magazines are carefully constructed to appeal to a very particular audience, whether that is a fairly broad target audience or a niche audience.

Defining a project

Having prepared yourself by doing some detailed relevant research, you need to start preparing for your chosen project. **For OCR AS Media Studies the MAXIMUM number allowed for a group is four**.

It may be best to apportion specific jobs to each member of the group from the beginning. Not only does it make the organisation much easier if tasks can be allocated among the group, but it also allows group members to develop a speciality very quickly and to have a specific focus for their production report. Since it is essential for evidence to be available to show the individual contribution of each member of a group, and your teacher will be expected to identify your individual role in the group work, it will be far easier for you to justify your work if you have planned, worked and evaluated from a specific perspective from the very beginning. However, it is important that everyone in the group contributes at all stages, so do not have someone sitting around insisting that they are not going to participate until the editing phase begins.

Having a clear media institutional context

All media texts are produced by individual media institutions and the institution that creates a text is usually a defining factor in the end result. A celebrity interview programme to be shown on prime time BBC1 is likely to be a very different type of programme to a celebrity interview programme shown late at night on cable or satellite. You must define the type of institution for your media text early on and allow this to have some bearing on the resulting text, to show that you understand how much influence the institutional context has.

Having an identifiable audience

As with the institutional context, no text is made in isolation. The audience should be an integral part of the decision making at all stages. One of the most common mistakes in media production exercises is that groups become so wrapped up in the artistic integrity of their piece that they forget that the primary objective is to appeal to an audience. As mentioned earlier, audiences are usually segmented – even highly popular television programmes such as *EastEnders* tend to have defined target audiences, even if they are very large in numbers, and most films define a very tight audience to target from the very beginning.

Creative opportunities

It is worth remembering when you are thinking about your project that you have a great deal of freedom of choice, even though your main brief is prescribed. Although you are working in an assumed institutional context, you are not constrained by these factors. Your constraints are probably the technology to which you have access and the range of experience within your group.

You can be creative and original with your approaches and solutions to the problems that you face, but beware of the temptation to allow the technology to dominate your choices. While an extensive use of filters, intricate transitions and other special effects may seem an effective way of demonstrating technical expertise, they may not be appropriate for your product. It is a difficult balance to strike – on the one hand you want to demonstrate your skills and your control of your medium, on the other hand material that is too 'creative' and uses unnecessary trickery can fall into the trap of being self-indulgent and thus lose its supposed audience appeal. Only you or your group can make the final decision about

what is appropriate for your product, but remember that originality for originality's sake is rarely successful. True creativity is tempered with restraint and the most difficult skill to learn is to be creative while tweaking the edges of commercial culture, not straying so far away from the designated context that your text loses its plausibility as a media text rather than a piece of fine art.

Is it viable as a project?

You must be practical with your intended content. If you plan a project that is too long or too challenging you will inevitably be disappointed with the result and the outcome will probably be less successful than a piece which is tightly constructed. Editing all media products is far more likely to involve editing out or dropping material than scrabbling around for additional material.

The key constraints to bear in mind here are:

- Time/length – if there is a length of time recommended in your particular brief it is because it is unlikely that you will produce something of high enough quality if you create something longer. If the brief states 2–3 minutes, stick with it. Two minutes of well shot, tightly edited thriller is far more convincing and appropriate than a five-minute extended opening that is repetitive and loosely edited. If you are creating a new website, by all means indicate on a navigation bar what other areas might be available, but if three pages per group member in addition to the homepage are specified, you will not get as much credit for twenty mundane pages as you will for twelve high-quality pages (assuming a group of four) reflecting industry codes and conventions and creating an exciting and innovative media text.
- Technical facilities – if you have access to a single camera and limited access to an editing suite, deciding to create an effects-laden sequence to match *The Matrix* trilogy may be over-ambitious. Excellent work can be achieved with a single camera and simple facilities – after all, when you are planning your 'shoot', you will probably not be taking your shots in narrative order anyway. You therefore have the opportunity to retake the same shot from different angles, so that you can choose the best one for your completed narrative. Indeed, if you have the patience, excellent results can be achieved by creating an animated piece (although be prepared for the amount of time this requires). One simple way is to use a digital camera and upload each shot on the camera to become a 'frame' in your narrative – or you could use an ordinary camera or even drawings and scan them into the computer, then edit them using your editing software just as you might do with conventional analogue or digital video material.
- Experience – it may be that members of your group have a great deal of experience in the use of your chosen technology. If, however, you decide to add a multi-layered exploding title as the opener to your movie without having the experience to produce this particular sequence, the process of learning the skills for this may detract from the project itself and thus you might ask yourselves whether a more straightforward effect might suffice.
- Institutional context – if you have decided to produce a music programme for a local radio station with a youth-oriented target audience, your programme needs to reflect this audience. If you decide to create a 'spoof charity campaign' (and remember that spoofs are especially difficult to create effectively), this will have substantial implications for the form and structure of your piece. Creating a piece which did not fit your specified institutional context would clearly be viewed as less successful than a piece which did fit the specified context.

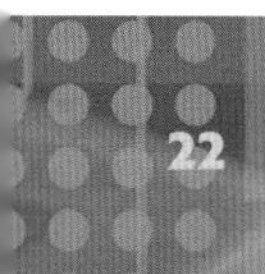

- Audience – this is closely related to the institutional context you define for your project. If your audience is defined as 'under 5s', for example, this will impact on the discourse used, *mise-en-scène* and length of project or segments of the project. If you are creating a website for a new band whose audience is primarily high-income, middle-aged professionals, the design, discourse and content will be very different to a website aimed at teenagers.

Planning a production

Organisation of time, people and equipment

By now you have got a pretty good idea of what you want to create. Now you need to think about the practicalities. Start by drawing up a plan to show how much time you can give to the project. Map out on this plan deadlines for the completion of the pre-production, production and post-production phases, remembering to allow time for evaluating and keeping your production report. Always allow a little extra time for 'contingencies' as well – equipment may break down, the weather may be too bad for outside filming or a group member may be ill, for example.

You will then need to decide what equipment you will need and map this on to the plan, making note of exactly when you will require particular pieces of equipment. It may be a good idea to book all the equipment you will require for particular sessions at this stage. That way you can be sure that you will have access to the necessary equipment when you need it. In the real world, of course, not only does equipment have to be booked a long time in advance but it also has to be paid for, even if it is not used. So planning when you will need access to a recording studio to complete your radio broadcast, for example, or the high-quality printers to print off your final adverts is essential.

If you are using people as actors, such as the studio host or as interviewees for a radio documentary or actors in a film, they also need to know well in advance when they will be required, for how long and what clothes or other props they might need to bring with them. It is no good filming some shots one day and then catching your main actor in the corridor another morning and asking if they can find the same clothes so you can carry on filming that afternoon. Performers in your film do not count towards the total number of people permitted for group work. Choose the best performers available to you. They do not have to be part of your Media Studies group.

Designing the product

The methods you employ to plan your original designs will depend upon your chosen medium. Time-based media such as film sequences/trailers and television adverts are usually planned using a storyboard. New media work can be planned with a storyboard, but diagrams may be more appropriate to show interactivity. Radio work is usually planned using an annotated script and schedule, and print work with flat-plans and mock-ups. Not only does the specification require that you include evidence that you have planned your media text efficiently, but it is essential to plan the text properly if you are to be able to engage fully with the requirements and opportunities.

The production process

Once you have decided on your role(s) in the project, you need to start keeping a production report and to be researching/producing/reflecting at all times. This report is your evidence of your

contribution to the project. Use it to demonstrate the aspects of your work that might not be immediately obvious to an outsider. For example, evidence of detailed research might be annotated print adverts for similar products taken from magazines, showing how you have deconstructed the products. Evidence for audio work might include transcripts of commercial programmes you have researched, with analysis of their style, structure and form. Make a note of the decisions you make as you go along, and the reasons for them. All this will help you when you come to write up your production report.

Audience research

There is a balance to be struck here. While there is no substitute for first-hand research about your media text, it would not be appropriate to conduct a full-scale research exercise, such as collecting information from 200 questionnaires, in the time available for your project. The most important aspects of audience research to bear in mind are:

- asking members of the sample audience about their experiences with similar products
- product testing on an audience sample, post-production.

In both cases a small sample – perhaps five to ten people from the designated target audience – would probably suffice as long as you remember that this is just a sample and not guaranteed to be fully representative.

Existing products and practice

No real producer would dream of establishing a new product in isolation. At times our world is described as being 'media-saturated' and one aspect of this is that all new products relate in some way to current and previous products. There is a vast range of media texts across all the media and it would be considered short-sighted of a producer to create a text without exploring the marketplace and assessing the competition. You need to be prepared to analyse at least two existing products that are relevant for your chosen media text. You might wish to include this analysis as an appendix to your evaluation so you can easily make reference to these texts as comparison in your evaluation. This will also count as supporting evidence of your research.

Whilst it is necessary to offer evidence of planning as required by the specifications, it is not necessary to include everything you have done in the material presented for external moderation. Your teacher must, however, see the stages of planning and research in order to give you an assessment, and he or she will help you decide what evidence you should include in your portfolio for the moderator.

Construction – general

There is a range of 'competencies' defined in the specification that are really the basic skills which we expect you to be able to use when working in your chosen medium. Your ability with these skills, thinking and planning, understanding what you can do, what is effective and – above all else – why you think that *your* way is the best way to communicate to your audience, will be deciding factors in assessing the quality of your final media text. Successful work will use these techniques and skills to good effect; less successful work will show an insecure grasp of these competencies and how they affect communication. It is worth writing out the list and keeping it with you while you are planning, particularly to ensure you have demonstrated your mastery of these areas.

There are also established forms and conventions assumed in each of the briefs given. For example, we conventionally expect to be told the name of the film in an opening sequence. It is assumed that material broadcast on radio is audible! We would not expect to hear a presenter say 'look at this', for example, unless it was immediately followed by an audio description. All this may seem very obvious, but it is surprising to examiners and moderators the extent to which these basic points are ignored. Institutional determinants, globalisation, media saturation and skilled marketing and advertising mean that the audience for any contemporary media product is explicit and clearly identified at the planning stage of development.

Evaluation – general

Finally, you should bear in mind that you have to provide an evaluation for your media text and that this is also assessed. We will look at the evaluation itself in more detail at the end of this section, but your planning stages are part of the production report – you are required to attach copies of your storyboards, flat-plans and so on to the production report to provide evidence of planning and process.

The production report is *not* a diary of events or a record of progress. Rather it is a summative and reflective document reflecting your working practice as a group and your individual contribution. As a record of your individual contribution to the group work the production report can be vital as it should show how you overcame hurdles, skills you have learnt, successes and failures during the pre-production and production stages, and how your media text is meeting the criteria you have defined for yourselves.

Part One

Approaches to Practical Skills Film and Television

Making the moving image

'I've always tried to be aware of what I say in my films, because all of us who make motion pictures are teachers, teachers with very loud voices.' George Lucas

Formal brief for OCR specification

Brief 1: Film

The opening sequence of a new thriller, including the titles (approximately two minutes duration) for a 15 or 18 certificate audience.

Brief 2: Television

The opening sequence of a new television programme, for children (aged 5–12) in a genre of your choice.

Preparatory exercises – moving image

ACTIVITIES

Try one or more of these suggested activites.

Create a ten-second video in which one of your group appears to perform a complex magic trick exceptionally well.

Recreate a clichéd comedy scene by shooting a sequence in which a ridiculous number of people seem to emerge (comfortably) from a small car or from behind a tree.

Record a 'chase' scene working in groups of three so you can organise a pursuer, victim and camera operator. If you have more people in your group, you have more opportunities to experiment with sound and lighting. Plan a storyboard and try to use the minimum number of shots, but also try to vary angles, framing and pacing. A good preparation for this exercise is to ask each group member to prepare a storyboard and reach a consensus regarding final storyboard before shooting. With a review afterwards, once the material has been edited, this can be a valuable 'trial run' for the actual project.

Visit http://www.bbctraining.com/onlineCourses.asp which is the BBC's free collection of online tutorials for freelancers and professionals. There is a range of tutorials you can work through there about preparing for video production, completing risk assessments, pre-production, post-production and, in particular, a useful range of tutorials about how to shoot high-quality DV material and how to edit it. You will need a good Internet connection and speakers or headphones to listen to the voiceover if you are to complete these tutorials.

Defining your project (Film and Television)

Start by examining a range of relevant film openings or children's television programmes in your chosen genre for similar products. For example, try to do a detailed analysis of three thriller openings or three children's programmes. For each text:

- analyse how the shots are organised and chosen
- analyse the use of *mise-en-scène*, representations and media language to create meaning and appeal to the target audience
- identify the target audience and consider how the text addresses them.

This should give you a good basis on which to draw up a set of conclusions about the form, style and content of your piece. On this basis you should be able to decide on the content of your text or texts and begin to plan your work.

Additional or alternative exercises

ACTIVITIES

Create a 30-second 'day in the life of' video of an individual, using as many brand names and close-ups of various products used by the person as possible.

Create an opening sequence or title sequence for a new consumer affairs programme.

Recreate an early soap powder advertisement in the style of advertisements from the 1950s, as a lead-in to an episode of a soap opera.

Preparation (Film and Television)

Part of your planning is the general logistics of creating a media text that were covered earlier in this chapter. Now you need to think specifically about the content of your text and plan how, what, where and when it will be created.

Remember that opening sequences are intended to hook a specified target audience and to engage them with the product. The opening of a text will be crucial to the audience's understanding and expectations. Careful thought must go into the setting up of characters, themes, setting and atmosphere.

Storyboards

Once the idea has been formulated it must be defined in detail, and this is done using a storyboard. Storyboarding is, in essence, drawing a cartoon of the video that you will make. Each shot in the movie is drawn and then labelled with movement notes, dialogue, sound effects and any other important information. It also gives you the opportunity to look at your text in detail and see if it is really going to work. In recent years, storyboarding has become more advanced as directors look for even better ways to plan their stories. Two examples of this are *Revenge of the Sith (Star Wars Episode III)* and *The Matrix* trilogy. For both movies, complex sequences were pre-filmed using models and representative figures. In *Revenge of the Sith*, the planning team used moveable figures and dioramas (painted scenes in which models are used and lit to create illusions of action) to plan and time complex sequences such as the speeder bikes. The planning team of *Jurassic Park*, however, took it further, filming the entire film first using claymation (like *Wallace and Gromit*) to watch every shot in the movie before investing in the kind of technology they needed to film it properly.

There is no getting away from storyboards – they are an essential part of planning a moving image piece and, properly used, will help you reflect critically on your media text before you begin actual filming. This will mean that you are confident about why you chose your *mise-en-scène*, framing, camera angle and shot length to create the required effect, and you will be clear about how you want to edit it together to make it successful.

There are many different ways of creating a storyboard, and varying degrees of detail are possible. Some film producers like to produce full colour illustrations for each shot, with annotations about camera angle, editing and so on, to produce almost a paper version of the film before they start. Others prefer

to keep a functional storyboard where the drawings are more basic but there is far more technical information regarding camera angle, shot length, editing, framing, lighting and *mise-en-scène*.

Once you have completed the storyboard you can create the shooting script. This is another essential document which defines all the technical aspects of each shot, lists equipment needed for each shot, and probably also lists the required personnel, props and so on.

The shooting script is usually broken up into shooting days. Filming is not done in chronological order – if you are shooting a series of television adverts for a product, you may decide to shoot all the close-ups of the product for the different adverts on one day, so you can control lighting, use the same prop and so forth. Equally, you may have to shoot particular scenes on one day, as that is the only day one of your actors can manage.

As part of the shooting script you can therefore list all the equipment you will need, to ensure you don't forget anything vital. You can make a note of continuity issues, such as clothes and hairstyles, and list all the props needed for a particular shot – in this way you will achieve more as you will be better prepared.

Holding a shot steady

The basic way of making sure that you hold a shot steady is to use a tripod. Whatever size camera you are using, your shots will be far more professional if they are steady. Aim to use a majority of shots where the camera is static.

Try to use the 'zoom' function as little as possible. While it is common in amateur work, zooms are rarely used in professional shooting unless it is for a particular effect. If you want to zoom in on a face to show a reaction to a piece of news, for example, that can be very effective. However, for most other shots, it is far better to shoot a sequence of short shots and avoid a zoom effect.

There may also be occasions where you don't want a steady shot, of course, such as when the camera is following someone running through some woods. If you choose to have a shaky shot, to establish a particular mood in your sequence, for example, then that is a valid decision – providing your audience can see the difference between these shaky shots and the fixed shots and can understand your reasons behind it.

Framing a shot

Only include what is necessary in the shot. There is a difference here between film and television: film tends to use a wider frame, even when not working in wide-screen; television tends to work more with close-ups. Close-ups are important in film as well, but are used more sparingly – a full-screen close-up of Julia Roberts on the screen at the multiplex can sometimes be very effective. Television uses more close-ups to create a greater sense of intimacy and communication between the audience and the programme.

The range of shot lengths that you can use is fairly extensive. There is a main set of five frame types that we refer to, and subsets of these that can be specified for particular effect. These are listed below, and some examples are given to show the effect of each.

Extreme long shot	Establishing shot – showing figure in its full context
Long shot	Focus on figure
Mid-shot (medium shot)	Common shot to link sections
Close-up	Important shot for actor often used to show strong feelings
Extreme close-up (big close-up)	Used for a particular effect

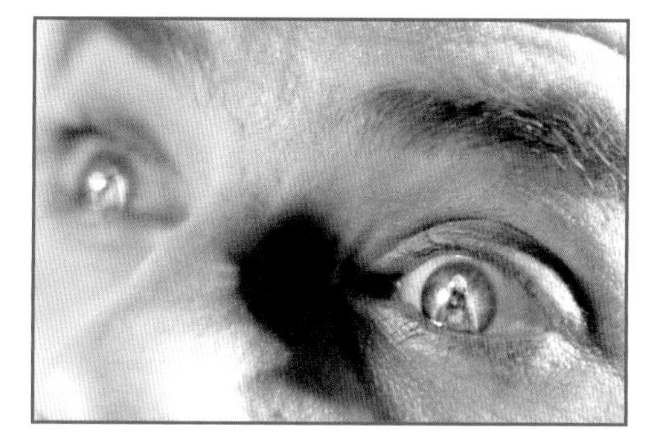

The convention when framing shots is the use of the rule of thirds, whereby you imagine four lines on the camera lens, dissecting the frame into nine sections (i.e. two vertical lines and two horizontal lines) – the resulting intersections are the points to which the human eye is naturally drawn. Thus you can bring greater attention to a character's face or an important object by placing it slightly off-centre. (This is why newsreaders, for example, are often placed slightly to the side of the screen with a logo or a blue screen to show images behind them.) An image that is centred in the frame is very stable, yet visually it is very inactive. You want your audience actively to watch and scan the image. By placing the images around the frame you encourage this concentration.

Using a variety of shot distances and camera angles

Variety is the spice of film as well as life. Once you have formed your basic plan and decided what shots might be appropriate, it is worth taking a step back and checking that you have made use of a range of shots – conventionally we start a sequence with an ELS (extreme long shot) as an **establishing shot** for the action to follow, and use a variety of CUs (close-up) and ECUs (extreme close-up) to focus on characters' faces during a conversation. You may want to use POV (point of view) shots to communicate a character's feelings or perspective, for example, if they are being chased, or an 'over-the-shoulder shot' to show reactions during a conversation while keeping both characters in focus.

It is easy, with a bit of planning, to make the same classroom seem welcoming, suitable for children or adults, threatening, evil, depressing or romantic. By controlling the *mise-en-scène* in this way the audience will usually accept your film more readily. It is difficult for the audience when you make little effort with the *mise-en-scène*. If nothing else, you can use lights to create long shadows – maybe even with a green or red filter – for a horror effect, or use a filter over a light to create a soft romantic light. You do need to produce a sequence that is clearly readable as the opening of a film in the thriller genre, or produce at least three adverts that meet the brief set.

Camera angles are also extremely important. The two most important angles are high angle and low angle. A high angle shot looks down on characters, reversing the effect of the high angle and making them seem small or weak. A low angle shot means that the camera looks up at the character, often making them seem powerful. To see mastery of the use of camera angles study Orson Welles's *Citizen Kane*. Less commonly, you may want to use a 'Dutch angle' (also referred to as a canted angle). This is achieved by tilting the camera slightly, and can convey a sense of urgency or fear to a scene, especially when it illustrates a character's reaction or shows the point of view of someone who is drunk.

There are a number of other ways to draw attention to key points in a frame. Among these are colour, light and movement. It is always important to make sure the main elements contrast slightly. In many early Westerns, filmed in black and white, the heroes frequently wore white hats to distinguish them on the screen and when fighting with a group of villains who would be wearing black hats. Think also of situations in films where a particular colour may have special significance – an obvious example would be the colour red in horror films.

A figure standing still while many other figures rush around them is a clear focal point. A slow pace of movement can enhance a mood of peace or romance or even menace. A whole style of film known as 'film noir' developed from careful use of light and dark to communicate emotion and atmosphere, with shadows across faces and scenes shot in low light conditions to establish mood and danger. Equally, you can use light and dark to indicate characters' feelings and situations – a wood is far more frightening in the dark, for example, than on a bright sunny day. If you don't have the facilities to film at night, try filming at dusk or manipulating the film during editing to make it darker for the same effect. Filming on a dull day and using a deep-blue filter can also give the impression of a night scene (this is called shooting 'day for night').

Whenever people are in your shot it is important to frame them properly. Your characters must have headroom, meaning that you can't have the top of their hair on or above the top edge of the frame as it makes them look cramped. You also need to think about what is behind them so they don't appear to have plants growing out of their heads! Similarly, you don't want too much room between the top edge and the character's head or it makes them look out of place and tiny. When a character moves within a frame it is always important to give them what is called 'lead room'. For example, if you're filming a character as he runs, frightened, down a wooded path, as you track alongside him you should give him enough room in front so that he looks as if he is running in the frame, not constantly on the verge of running out of it. If you don't, your audience may become more aware of the framing than the content and lose the impact of the piece.

When filming dialogue, or any other scene where you change between character perspectives, it is important to remember the 180° rule. According to this rule, there is a line in any given scene that splits it into two halves. When shooting a scene that switches back and forth between points of view, all shots must be made from the same side of the line otherwise the scene will look mismatched.

You must maintain the same arrangement that was in your establishing shot. If you suddenly 'cross the line', the character who was initially facing right is now facing left from the new perspective. Since the other character is still facing in the old direction you have two characters facing left, and if they try to talk to each other that could be very confusing for the audience.

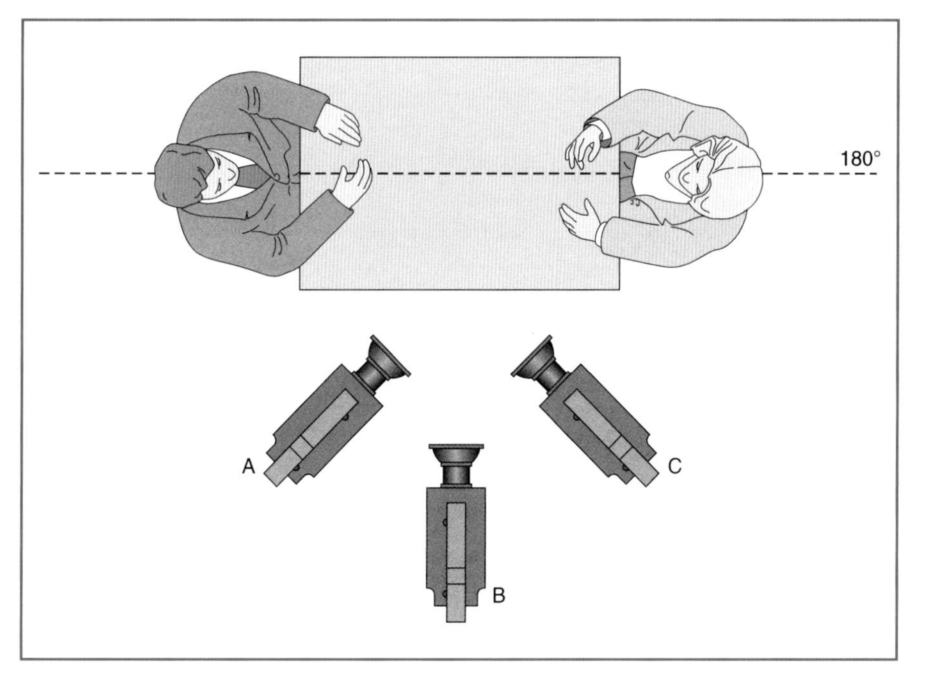

The 180° rule

Shooting material appropriate to the task set

Although this might seem obvious, there are certain tricks which can be useful. Probably not all your shots will need to be on location – a close-up on a hand going into a bag, for example, can be shot almost anywhere and slotted in. Equally, you may be lucky and be shooting outside at a time when the light is particularly effective or something happens that you can use. If in doubt, aim to shoot three times as much material as your final piece will last, without allowing for retakes. That way you will have enough material to reject some (possibly two-thirds or more) during editing and also give options to develop your material in various ways while you are editing.

As a part of this, it is worth remembering to think about continuity. If you are shooting a chase sequence in the woods over two days and your heroine appears in a different floaty dress on day two, it may not do much for the credibility of your final piece if her dress changes colour mid-chase! The same comments apply to lighting, both outside and in, and any other elements of the *mise-en-scène* that might be affected. This is why, on real shoots, a continuity person is employed to check things like whether Mel Gibson's hair is curling the same way on each day of shooting a particular scene. In reality a series of Polaroids is taken for every scene, so that continuity can be sure of repeating the same costumes, hair, and so on if a scene is shot over several days; but you should be able to rely on memory and notes!

Editing so that meaning is apparent to the viewer

There are various methods of editing material together, and all may have their uses. A few are explored here with examples. Part of the craft that you will be learning is to decide how to edit your material together as well as possible and how to use effects, control, cuts and other techniques to appropriate effect.

The most common type of transition used in film and television work is the cut between shots. Shots are usually between three and eight seconds long (depending on the tempo you are establishing) and the cut simply changes between shots. A **fade** can be useful to suggest a passing of time or change of place/action, and a **dissolve** is most commonly found at the beginning or end of a dream sequence, for example. A fade is where the image appears from or fades out to (usually) a black screen. A dissolve is where one image fades to be replaced by an emerging second image. **Wipes** and other transitions available on most non-linear editing systems are rarely used in film and television unless a particular effect is intended, such as implying an alien transport or a character descending into a nightmare. With all effects the simple rule is 'don't use them without a very good reason'.

When shots are being linked together there are various ways of suggesting continuity. Common structures can involve patterns such as establishing shot, action shot, bridging shot, reaction shot to create a sense of action – shot of woods, shot of victim running, close-up on knife, shot of pursuer, or the typical shot/reverse shot to show two people having a conversation. Editors sometimes refer to 'matching' shots – for example, they will make sure the eye line between shots is matched, or will match on movement (a popular convention is to match on walking). Alternatively an angle change on the same scene can be used to give a different perspective, or a bridging shot, such as a close-up or neutral shot, to give variety or add fresh information for the viewer or to cover problems such as crossing the line. In this situation we usually refer to the different shot in the middle as a 'cutaway', which can also be a valuable device either to change or build atmosphere or to disguise problems such as crossing the line or slightly different framing.

A good way of keeping the action continuous is to keep the soundtrack running underneath all the changes – for example, a conversation continuing as the shot/reverse shot happens, or a voice-over continuing over a close-up of a key prop.

Even simple actions take up a great deal of time on film. Imagine a sequence of a person getting dressed. In real life this process can take two or three minutes or more, but this would not make exciting footage to watch. Everything is edited, including 'fly-on-the-wall documentaries', to keep the action moving and keep it interesting. If that same person pulled clothes out of a wardrobe and in the next shot walked into the kitchen, the obvious conclusion the audience will make is that the person got dressed.

Editing can serve to create atmosphere. When viewing a scene the human eye does not remain stationary. If you were watching two people having a conversation you would automatically switch your focus from one to the other. Good editing mimics this, but controls your perspective and hence your opinion about the action. If you see Person 1 getting aggressive and Person 2 getting upset, your sympathies may lie with Person 2. If the editor shows you the letter that Person 1 is holding reveals that Person 2 has been convicted of murdering Person 1's parents, your sympathies may well be different.

Editing can also control atmosphere by use of rhythm and pacing. An example of this would be a fight sequence. As the two enemies approach each other the shots are long, keeping the pace slow. As tension builds, the shots become shorter, building energy. When the fight begins the shots become short and fast, giving the scene energy that the audience feels. Finally, one fighter falls to the ground and the shots lengthen again. The energy of the scene drops and the audience relaxes. The editing of shots has created a rhythm that heightens the power of the scene.

Alfred Hitchcock used the example of a scene where a group of people sitting around a dinner table was blown up by a time bomb. In a real-time version of the scene the people sit down at the table and the bomb goes off: end of scene, end of people. But no real suspense would be generated by this approach. In his second version the people gather, talk, and casually sit down at the dinner table. A shot of the bomb ticking away under the table is shown, revealing to the audience what is about to happen. Unaware of the bomb, the people continue their banal conversations. Close-up shots of the bomb are then inter-cut with the guests laughing and enjoying dinner. The inter-cutting continues (and speeds up) until the bomb finally blows the dinner party to bits. The latter version understandably creates far more tension and emotional impact.

Often, a function of editing is to suggest or explain cause. We may see a dead body on the living room floor during the opening sequence of a film, but who killed the person and why is not revealed until the very end. It makes a more interesting story – one that would be more likely to hold an audience – if we present the result first and reveal the cause gradually over time.

Careful editing can also imply cause, speeding up narratives. If we are shown a shot of someone with all the signs of being drunk (effect), we can probably safely assume they have been drinking (cause).

Example: A woman drives up to a house in a car. She gets out. She enters the house and goes upstairs. She walks towards a door. She hears noises coming from within. She pushes the door open.

If this sequence of actions were shown in real time it would take about five minutes and viewers would get bored. Editing allows the sequence to be cut down so that the focus is clearer and the tension built

more quickly. A shooting sequence for the same event is given in the example below. The time in seconds for each shot is given in brackets.

Example: Woman drives up to house (5), gets out and walks to door, looking for key (5), ELS (extreme long shot) of her walking up drive from perspective of neighbour mowing lawn (5), MS (medium shot) following gaze of neighbour to drawn curtains at bedroom window (3), MS of woman walking up stairs (3), ECU (extreme close-up) on door handle as woman reaches for it and pauses (2), MS of room from perspective of woman as she walks in (5).

This makes a total of seven shots and 28 seconds in screen time instead of up to five minutes in real time. Our imagination fills in the missing parts – the walk into the house, the history implied as known by the neighbour, her thoughts as she hears the noises, and so on.

Editing is the final control of meaning for your media text. Imagine the visual effect of arranging the shots described below in these sequences: 1–2–3, 3–2–1, 2–3–1, 2–1–3.

1. MS: A man jumps from an exploding car.
2. MS: A fire breaks out in the engine of the car.
3. LS: The car explodes.

Possible meanings for these different orders for the sequence might be:
1–2–3: A man jumps from a car seconds before it explodes.
3–2–1: A car explodes, forcing a man to jump away from the fire.
2–3–1: A man jumps from a car after a fire causes an explosion.
2–1–3: Because of a fire, a man jumps away just in time to escape.

Part Two

Print

Formal brief for OCR AS Specification

Brief 3: Print

You are asked to create one of the following:

Pages from a new teenage magazine, aimed at an audience aged 13–19 of either or both genders.

Individuals must produce the front cover and at least one double page spread, to include a minimum of three original images.

Groups must produce a minimum of the front cover and at least one double page spread per group member. The work must feature at least three original images per group member. There must be a clear sense of house style for all work produced by the group.

Brief 4: Print

- A series of advertisements from a campaign for health education or a charity, to include advertisements for magazines and/or newspapers, billboards and flyers/brochures.
- **Individuals** must use at least three original images. At least three advertisements in total.
- **Groups** must produce at least three original images per group member. At least three adverts per member of the group.

OR

- **Individuals** may choose to create the packaging and a magazine advert for a new console or computer game (PlayStation™, GameBoy, PC, etc.) to include at least three original images.

Preparatory exercises

You should try to undertake at least one of the tasks below and ideally at least four of them in the weeks preceding your work for the project or as part of your ongoing practical skills development during the terms leading up to the exam. As we have said before, you cannot expect to write copy and take pictures for the first time when undertaking this project, or learn how to use a DTP package as you go, without there being an impact on your final media text.

ACTIVITIES

Try one or more of these suggested activities:

Use an interview piece from a film or men's magazine and try rewriting it for a different audience and/or editing it down. This gives you a chance to develop copywriting skills and to learn to identify the most important sections of an article and to analyse how a particular voice is constructed for a particular magazine. For example: a *Vogue* piece rewritten for *Nuts!* or a 1000 word article in *GQ* reworked as a 400 word piece in *Loaded*.

Find a selection of adverts for different chocolate bars and see how far you can swap the text and the images before the identity of the chocolate bars is changed. Are any of these chocolate bars so easily recognised that this limits the changes? What can this tell us about the branding of these bars?

Choose a well-known national charity and deconstruct a selection of recent adverts taken from different places (e.g. leaflets, billboards, magazines, newspapers). Can you identify the elements which remain constant throughout the different media? Which elements change? Why is this? How far do the images and text reflect your assumptions about the charity? Is there a reason for this? Can you apply the AIDA (Attention, Interest, Desire, Action) principle to these adverts? What can you say about the way they are constructed?

Try deconstructing the layout of a newspaper article to identify house style and approach. Then remodel this to suit a different newspaper or magazine so that you can see how the layout of a particular newspaper/magazine affects the content decisions. For example, deconstruct a key article from the *Daily Mail* in terms of content and layout, and look for aspects which you could alter to make the article suitable for a different newspaper, such as *The Guardian*.

Take a range of photos of someone to use as the key image for an article to be published in *Cosmopolitan* and identify which shots would be most suitable for different themes, such as holidays or date rape or disability. Be prepared to justify your decisions to the rest of the group.

Analyse a range of teenage magazine front covers:

Target audience – who are they and how are they targeted?

Media institutions – what is revealed about the institution? What level of institutional knowledge is expected?

Reading the media – how is the magazine constructed visually to meet these aims? What language is employed to suit its context?

How does this impact? What representations are used? How might the ideology of this institution be perceived?

Planning your media text

- Know your market – define what your media text will be and be prepared to justify why you think it is credible and viable. For example, if you decide you want to produce a teenage magazine about skateboards, you need to be able to justify why you think this is a viable publication and how it will fit the audience profile.
- If you are producing the packaging for a new game and an advert, how will you ensure the packaging stands out on the shelves, clearly defines the product and appeals to the target audience?
- Once you have defined the general outline of your product you need to prioritise the content – what will the lead story be or the key image? If you are creating a series of adverts for a national charity, for example, what is the central piece of information or main theme that you want to get across in your campaign? What image might you use to signify your game?
- A magazine will probably not have a logo as such although it will usually have a masthead that works the same way. By defining the logo or masthead early on in planning a project, you start to define the magazine's identity, which helps keep your focus.
- You should also list the images which you will need to create, and decide on which is the central image to be used.
- Most publications have a limited style of photographs used and a limited colour palette (which may even be black and white for some niche market magazines). You need to define what your palette and image style is at this point so you know what images you will be constructing. Following on from this, you need to decide on appropriate fonts and heading/sub-heading/pull-quote to reflect the theme and style of your media text.

Use of IT to create a media text

- If you are going to use DTP to produce your media text you will need a level of competence with a DTP program – which might be as sophisticated as Adobe InDesign® or might be a simple program such as greenstreet® publisher. Both will allow you to produce good quality media texts. DTP programs allow you to put stories and pictures into boxes, which can be edited on the page, moved around and stacked at will. Frames and backgrounds can easily be added and a pasteboard facility allows for continued modifications. If you construct your media text in a word-processing program you will find it more difficult to manipulate your layout since word-processing programs do not like working with a large number of columns, pictures or boxes.

- You will need a degree of confidence with a picture-editing program which will allow you to manipulate the graphics necessary for your media text. Again, you may not have access to a high-end product such as Adobe Photoshop® but a program such as Paint Shop Pro®, would be more than adequate for the picture manipulation required and a lot simpler for a novice to learn.
- You will need a basic understanding of the design principles behind DTP work and will need to develop an understanding of the conventions of layout, graphics, colour and page design and learn how to work to a grid or template for every page. If you are using InDesign® or a similar program, you can make use of the master page layout to ensure your pages are the same and to avoid the necessity of pasting common elements onto each page in turn.

General print design principles

- Make bottom margins wider than the top as the eye is more comfortable with this.
- Keep pictures and text aligned – use guidelines to keep everything neat.
- Show awareness of the need for variety in fonts and text size.
- Do not use more than two fonts in a publication. Conventionally one serif font is used for the body text and one sans serif font for titles, etc. Make sure there is a clear contrast between the two fonts. If in doubt, make the contrast greater, not smaller.
- Group components on your page to keep it neater and more professional. Use a box to demarcate the central story on the page or explicitly to link a caption with a picture.
- Use WOB (white on black) for greater contrast – use shades of grey for the box if black is too harsh. This can be useful for black and white work in particular, and it is a favourite device on the front cover of tabloid newspapers, for example.

Appropriate images and text

If you have created a set of pages for inclusion in an upmarket magazine for investors, the use of cartoon clipart such as that given away free with computer magazines would probably be totally inappropriate – however appealing it might seem as an initial filler. If you are taking a picture of a 'film star' (friends and family are usually only too pleased to become 'stars' for a day!) to include with an article, the style of photo will also be dictated by the publication. The photo selected by the *News Of the World* would probably be different to that selected by *The Independent.*

Found images

See the notes earlier in this section about original images. It is a requirement that you produce a certain minimum number of original images in your publication. You can use more original images and make additional use of found images, but if you do use found images, you should acknowledge their source in your written evaluation. In general, taking your own photos is a much better option: getting

friends and family to dress up as 'characters' or 'celebrities' for your magazine or adverts gives you the opportunity to show your skill with the camera and subject matter.

Register and tone

It is important that the tone of your articles is relevant. The vocabulary used in *Zoo* is deliberately different from that used in *Glamour*. If you were to create an edition of one of these magazines that did not reflect the language of the publication, it would be inappropriate.

The **register** of a particular publication is also significant. The register of *Loaded* is different to that of GQ and, again, media texts that did not use an appropriate register would probably be largely unsuccessful.

> The **register** refers to the style of language employed by a publication. The registers you use when talking to your friends or when talking to a little baby are very different. We use these different registers or styles of language all the time, adapting and adjusting as we go. Print publications must decide on appropriate register and this becomes one of the defining features of the publication.

Use technical and symbolic codes effectively

Using technical codes to construct still images effectively simply means that you know how to frame shots and take shots that can be used in publication. The symbolic codes are mixed up in this but can be summarised as 'intention'. If you want the photograph of a politician to seem a positive portrayal you would frame it, catch an expression, construct the *mise-en-scène* and so on to present a positive impression. It is just as easy to use a photograph to create a negative impression.

Technical effects such as filters or effects which are available in most photo editing software can also be used to good effect – especially for advertising campaigns. However, you need to ensure that the focal product is not obscured in any way, unless that is an intentional part of the campaign message. For example, if you were advertising a brand of trainer and wanted to imply they would make a person run faster, you might want to use a motion blur effect to give an impression of speed. The blurring effect called a Gaussian blur can be used to soften an image and create a drop shadow or halo effect.

An example of Gaussian blur

To see the effect of the Gaussian blur and how to create it, access the website:

http://www.luminous-landscape.com/tutorials/gaussian.shtml

Other soft focus effects can add glamour to a portrait that has a hard edge to the image, for example, a 'vignette' filter.

It may be worthwhile accessing websites dedicated to your own photo editing software as these can give useful additional help and advice.

Some images are best presented separately; others may be most effective with text wrapped around them or used in a creative way. You need to be able to crop images, resize them, flip them or use a clipping path if you are to be able to manipulate them appropriately for your media text. In particular, you should usually try to crop images tightly – a tight focus on a face is far more effective than a long or mid-shot, as readers can then identify with the image more quickly. For example, if you were creating an advertising campaign for a product, your images of the product would probably need to be tightly cropped close-ups, not out-of-focus long shots.

Clipping paths – these are used so that you can isolate an image from its background. Advice on how to use this technique effectively, using either Adobe Photoshop® or Adobe InDesign®, can be found on the following websites:

http://desktoppub.about.com/library/tutorials/bl121302c-clippingpath.htmhttp://www.adobe.com/print/tips/illclippath/main.html

Alternatively, use a search engine and simply type in 'clipping path' to see what you come up with.

What is your purpose?

The function of your magazine, game packaging or adverts is the essence of your communication. If your magazine is intended as a fan magazine for a band, then that is your function. A precise and well-defined function is essential. If you do not define your function properly before you start, your media text will be unfocused.

Define your target audience

Whom is your message intended for? If you are targeting younger people to buy your game, your register and information level will have to be understandable to them. On the other hand, if you are targeting high income earners with your charity campaign, then your register will be more sophisticated. Define your target audience, because that will decide how your message is presented.

Make the flat-plan

How many pages or adverts are you going to make? What size will they be? Where will they be placed? How will these factors affect your designs? What will the balance be on these pages? For example, if you are producing a magazine, how much space on the pages will be taken up with advertising? Are you creating a glossy magazine? What proportion of text to image is appropriate for your publication? What is the average story length for your publication?

Develop your concept

The concept of 'theme' is the underlying creative idea of your media text. Even in a big advertising campaign, the theme will remain the same from one advertisement to another, and also across media. This is central to an ad campaign – the audience needs to be able to identify the theme quickly and easily so that it can begin to establish a brand loyalty. For a console game, there may well be a theme for the game and this will be reflected not only in the copy but also in the images, titles, layout, choice of adverts and general 'look' of the promotional materials.

The visual

Research indicates that 70 per cent of people will only glance at an advertisement and only 30 per cent will pause long enough to read the copy. It is not dissimilar when people are flicking through a newspaper. They will glance at the pictures and may look at an effective title, but will not read the copy unless they have been attracted by either the visual or the headline. It is better to use a photograph unless you have decided to use a graphic for a particular reason. The image should be the key focus of any page and should be effective and striking if it is to catch the attention of your target audience.

The hook

Your main headline should act as a 'hook'. The aim is to affect the reader emotionally, either by making them laugh, making them angry, making them curious or making them think.

Keep the headline short and snappy but strong. It can take time to think of a good line but it is usually worth it.

> Think of the AIDA principle again – **attract** the target audience, create **interest**, establish **desire** and then explain what **action** will fulfil the desire you have now created.

The copy

Keep the copy near your title where possible and try to create a visual continuity that will draw people to the important information or action you want them to read. Use a serif typeface for your copy whenever possible. Use subheads or pull-quotes to break up the columns of text and create interest, and use signposts through a long article if this is appropriate for your chosen publication. (Some magazines break up text with lots of images, pull-quotes etc.; others use long tranches of text.) However, the by-line and image of the writer are usually very prominent in these publications as they can be a key hook for the reader.

Finally

The single most common mistake is visual clutter. Don't be afraid of white space on your page – especially in advertising where the white space can help to focus the eye very quickly. Less is always better than more. If you're not certain whether something is worth including, then leave it out. If your ad or page layout is chaotic, people will simply turn the page, and your message will never be read.

It is always valuable to test your publication as well. For example, make a draft copy of your adverts and check that your target audience understands them and relates to them. Once you have a mock-up of one of the pages for your magazine you might want to lay it next to pages from a competing niche magazine to compare layout, approach and structure. You should also test-market these drafts on your target audience once you have done all this. Remember that the feedback from these tests can be very valuable for your evaluation.

Part Three

Audio

Formal brief for OCR Specification

Brief 5: Radio

Create a series of at least three advertisements for a local or regional event (sporting, musical, entertainment, community). The three advertisements may alternatively be for three separate local events. The total duration of the advertisements should be between 60 and 90 seconds. There should be demonstration of a mixture of sound sources evident across the advertisements.

Preparatory exercises

You should try to undertake at least one of these tasks and ideally all three of them in the weeks preceding your work for the project, or as part of your ongoing practical skills development during the terms leading up to the exam. You cannot expect to record an effective campaign for the first time when undertaking this project, or learn how to use recording equipment as you go, without there being a detrimental effect on your final media text.

ACTIVITIES

Record an audio version of a simple song or poem, using music and sound effects in the background – *Old McDonald's Farm* can work well.

Record 'a day in my life' with audio notes, recorded as you go through the day and edited into a five-minute summary of your day with appropriate music or sound effects to create interest.

Compose and record a 20-second jingle for your Media lessons.

Planning and designing your project

First you need to decide what event you are going to promote and what radio station you will be broadcasting on. As with television, your choice of station will affect your choice of content. You need to decide not only the type of event you are promoting but also whether to use regional or national advertising (the format and style are likely to be different and the budget may be very different).

You need to consider:

- station identity, scheduling and audience profile – how do these affect the form and style of the adverts?

- typical use of different sound sources
- integration and employment of speakers
- length of segments, number of adverts, jingles and SFX
- use of language and register, and balance of four codes of radio – talk, silence, music and sound effects. What is the impact of this arrangement?

Drafting your advertising campaign

Before planning your campaign you need to decide exactly what sort of adverts you are going to create, on which station they might be broadcast, and the format, style and content of the adverts.

You should define the target audience and identify three key ways in which your campaign will explicitly target them (for example, a jingle based on a song which they would be likely to know very well, or a celebrity endorsement using a celebrity who would appeal to a particular audience).

Once you have decided on the structure, form and content of your campaign you are ready to plan the construction. Start by breaking down the content for each advert in your campaign.

It is usually a good idea to write a complete script for a radio advert so the presenter(s) know what they need to say. 'Drying' (forgetting what you have to say next) on air is very obvious on radio and not as easily covered as it can be on television, so a script will be a valuable resource for those presenting. You may want to script specific elements such as 'vox pops' separately, and you may find that a list of questions is more effective than a script for an interview.

Once you have recorded these sections they can be added into the running order if you are working in a recording suite, or simply played from a different tape recorder as part of the recording process if you have to use a very low-tech approach. If you are working in a low-tech way, remember that your teachers and moderators will mark the quality of your work, not the quality of your equipment. As long as you have tried to work professionally, the quality of the recording tone, for example, will not be a factor when your work is being assessed. However, it must be audible!

When the script has been written, you should write a detailed cue sheet for each advert with accurate timings, so you know when the stand-alones, such as jingles, are going to be placed. It may be that you wish to leave some of the interviews or vox pops less scripted, to allow for 'real' responses, for example. This can be successful but may cause problems when you try to fit strong material into a short space of time, as people tend to speak for too long if not controlled.

Post-production

Radio production work can be done very simply, using a mix of live sounds (as basic as two microphones and some sound effects) and a second cassette recorder to provide a sound bed. However, the results from basic equipment like this are not always adequate, although if that is the only equipment available to you, it is important to highlight this in your production report. As previously stated, moderators will always look for the positive use of the technology you have available to you, not criticise a lack of technology, provided you explain to them what you do have and how you have used it.

However, if you can get access to some form of audio production facility, the quality of your final production will be technically far better. For example, you may be lucky enough to get access to facilities at a local radio station for a day, in which case you can make good use of excellent equipment. However, it is likely that you can get access to good quality computer-based editing software fairly easily.

You may already be familiar with using Adobe Premiere® to edit video, for example. It is perfectly possible to use Premiere to edit audio as well, simply by using the audio tracks without putting anything onto the video tracks and exporting audio only when the project is complete. This will give you access to reasonable audio editing tools in a software package which you are familiar with and will enable you to multi-track your sound sources (music, sound effects, presenter and vox pops, for example) very easily.

However, for production work which is closer to broadcast quality, you should use specialist digital audio editing software, to give you more flexibility and better results. If you use an audio editing package, it is far easier to mix sounds, control sound levels, add effects and balance volume, tone, pitch and so forth. Most of these packages are fairly simple to use and one of the best known is Adobe Audition®. This is the digital audio editing package used by the BBC to produce much of their output and, as with video production, they have produced a range of tutorials, showing you how to use Adobe Audition® to produce good quality radio. These can be accessed from the website below and provide useful simulations, showing you how to get audio source material into Adobe Audition®, edit it, make use of multi-track options and export your finished production.

http://www.bbctraining.com/radio.asp

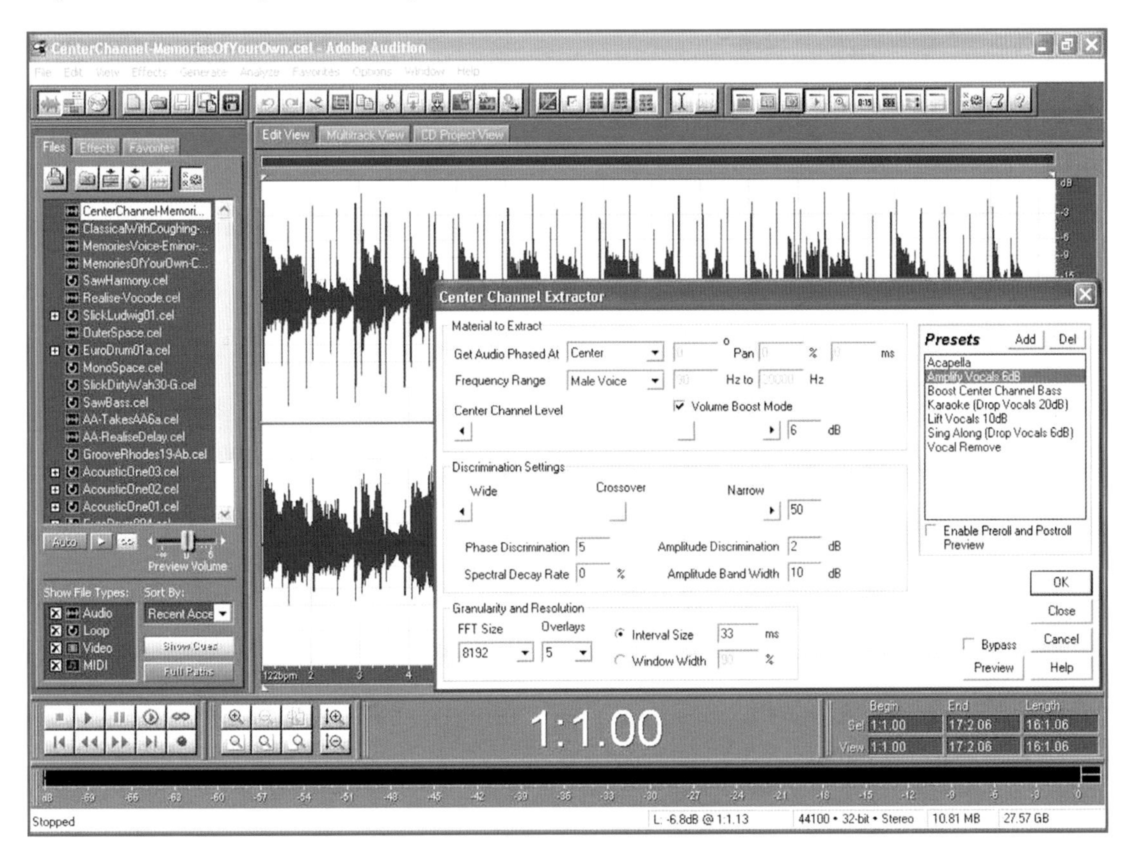

Adobe Audition®

Technical production issues

Always wear headphones when recording as you need to be able to monitor the sound quality and stop recording if things are not right. You don't want to spend all day recording and then discover that the time has been wasted.

Microphones

You are unlikely to have access to professional-quality microphones but you can do a lot to ensure the best possible sound quality. Put microphones about 10–15 cms away from the mouth of the person talking. Be careful about getting too close as you may pick up some sounds, such as 'p' or 's' too clearly, and this distracts from your material as well as sounding unprofessional. If you find it hard to get rid of these sounds, move the microphone slightly to the side of the speaker's mouth and see if that helps.

Preparation

- Always bring at least one extra set of batteries.
- Always have more than enough discs on hand.
- Always write-protect your discs after you finish an interview.
- Label and number your discs. If you are recording several 'takes' of a show and you don't label them carefully, or are not careful with the file names you choose, you will not be able to remember which is the final version and may end up submitting an early version which is not as good.

The BBC Training Online site contains a very useful tutorial which gives you a lot more insight into using handheld microphones and getting good sound quality for radio production work. This tutorial can be found at:

http://www.bbctraining.com/onlineCourse.asp?tID=2508&cat=2772

Tips and tricks

Always record two minutes of 'room noise' after finishing an interview or any part of a programme not recorded in the studio. When you start editing your documentary or current affairs programme, you can use this sound to make smooth transitions in and out of the scene and between the narrator's voice and the subject's voice. You can also record and use other material as backing material to add atmosphere or mood.

Interviewing tips

Conduct interviews in the quietest place possible. It is far easier to add sound tracks or additional sound played on a second cassette recorder during an interview or part of the studio presentation, than to try and hear speech with noise such as a television in the background. In addition, you cannot easily edit out the noise you do not want and may end up having to re-record to get better sound.

Start interviews or segments of the programme by asking questions and letting the answers serve as

introduction, for example, 'Who are you?' 'How old are you?' 'What do you do and how long have you been doing it?' or whatever introductory question is appropriate for the particular story.

Help interviewees to be more descriptive. For visually descriptive information, ask your subject to 'paint a picture with words' of whatever you need them to describe. In addition, emotional content works very well on radio. Questions like 'How does this make you feel?' tend to yield good tape.

The BBC Training Online site contains a useful tutorial about interviewing for radio, which features a good range of basic help with live studio interviews from Libby Purves, advice about recording and using vox pops, and some examples of when things don't always go according to plan. It can be found at:

http://www.bbctraining.com/onlineCourse.asp?tID=2555&cat=3

Finally

- Remember that you can keep re-recording your material until you get it right.
- Remember your audience all the time and keep asking yourself 'Will they want to listen to this?'
- Test your programme on a sample audience before submission to see if it works. Can they identify the branding of the programme/the style/ the content and so on? Do they feel they are part of the target audience?
- Make sure that the listener's attention is held throughout the programme. This can be done with frequent changes of activity (narrator, interview, jingle, traffic, adverts, jingle, news summary, narrator again) and the use of familiar items (e.g. jingles) coupled with fresh elements such as interview pieces.
- Keep to your time plan. Not only is radio always a pacy medium, but your original plan ensures frequent changes of noise and balance of elements to keep the audience's attention.
- Be aware that the project is defined as an extract from a longer programme, so you may choose to record the beginning, middle or end of the programme. A piece of this sort would normally be no longer than ten minutes. The Specifications suggest approximately five minutes. We have specifically excluded music programmes to help you avoid the 12 minutes of music and one minute of links approach that does not demonstrate much skill in the medium.
- Remember that this programme is designed to appeal to a target audience. What is its USP (Unique Selling Point)? Why should the audience tune in to this programme? Are you directly appealing to your target audience?

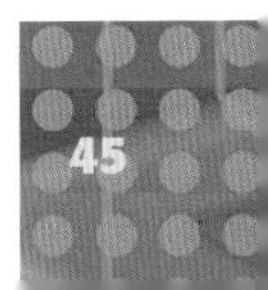

New media – ICT

Formal brief for OCR AS Specification

Brief 6: New media/ICT

Individual students need to produce a homepage and at least three linked pages (incorporating at least three original images) from a website for a new band.

Group members need to produce one homepage and at least three linked pages with at least three original images *per group member* from a website for a new band. For example, a group of four students must produce at least one home page and twelve linked pages.

Preparatory exercises

ACTIVITIES

Analyse a range of 'branded' sites to see how the branding affects the experience.

Do a detailed deconstruction of some very successful sites such as *BBC Online* or *The Onion* and some less successful sites. Visit www.websitesthatsuck.com for examples of bad design and be prepared to explain why these sites are effective or not effective.

Compare and contrast the online presence of key bands such as Coldplay with their other advertising and promotional methods. How central would you say their web presence is to their branding. Why is this?

As a practice run, design a basic homepage for yourself and include the following elements – title, an image of yourself centred and saved as a JPEG, some text in a table, anchors to scroll up and down the page and links to at least two external sites.

Design a basic site map layout for a local company and set out the basic pages with links to show how the site would work as a mesh, a hierarchy or a linear site.

Create an animated GIF that might be suitable as a logo on the entry page of a site trailing a new horror film. Present your animation to the rest of the group and explain how it reflects the chosen film. Note: If you have never created an animated GIF before, you may want to use a simple software package such as 'GIF Animator™' to help you. This can be downloaded from www.ulead.com/ga/runme.htm for a 30-day free trial, which (if you plan your time properly) should give you enough time to complete that aspect of your project.

Design three to four pages giving information about your Media course and post it up on the web to test it properly – use images, text and maybe sounds and video extracts.

Study at least three current websites for different bands across different musical styles and write a short report about the form and function of each one, with careful reference to how the site reflects the band's branding and musical style.

Defining your project

Planning

- Plan in detail and ensure your site is 'sticky'. A sticky site is one where there is enough interesting material on every page to make visitors want to stay with the site.
- Use a mesh or hierarchy to link the pages. Make sure you include links back to the homepage on every page and think about links to other sites as well.
- You may need to consider using frames to make your site look professional – for example, a navigation frame.

Basic planning

- Can the end user immediately understand what the site is for? Are the titles easy to understand and readily visible?
- Can the user follow the links between the different sections and understand the structure of the site? Hidden links may seem clever but can be really irritating. If the list is complicated, why not use a picture or a series of pictures to set the links up?
- Is it easy to find the way back to the homepage or opening page? (It is a good idea to use a home icon or a suitable piece of text on each page to aid this.)
- Does each entire page fit inside the user's computer window so they do not miss anything or need to scroll the page? There are occasions when a scrolling page is appropriate, such as a more text-based page, but it should never require more than four clicks to jump up or down the page. If you have more information it is generally better to create more pages and link them.
- Is the page too cluttered with too many links? Or too many graphics? Or too many moving parts that don't stop? (Remember – that cute animated GIF that you dropped into the top corner of the page may be very distracting to the viewer. Only use it if it is *directly* relevant to your page.)
- What is the USP of this site? In other words, what is unique enough about this site to make it sticky?

Layout and design

- Is the text easy to read? Are the graphics easy to understand? Your site may reach an audience for whom English is not their first language. Make sure the language and structure are accessible.
- Think about the fonts you use – sans serif fonts such as Arial, Verdana or Comic Sans are much more appropriate than serif fonts (such as Times New Roman), which are hard to read on the screen. Web designers are normally taught to restrict themselves to only two fonts on a page – one for the body text and another for the titles.
- Be careful about the fonts you choose to use. It is all very well using the 'perfect' font for something, but if that font is not installed on the viewer's computer, their machine will just guess a font, destroying all your hard work and intentions. Designers usually create these 'fancy' fonts by actually making the word or phrase as a picture and importing it into the page as an image. That way the formatting of the font is not affected.

- Do the graphics support the site by establishing an appropriate theme to reflect the intentions of the site? It is good design practice to think about the size and position of each graphic and keep a similarity. Restrict your colour palette – using too many colours can make your site hard to read.
- Does the product look professional? It can be worth learning how to make rollovers or downloading some good quality buttons to make your site look more professional. In the world of web design, where the 'catch' for customers is measured in seconds, looks really do matter.

Poor design elements – what to avoid

Backgrounds

Grey default background colour.

Text and background colour combinations that make the text hard to read (no lime green backgrounds with yellow text!).

Busy, distracting backgrounds that make the text hard to read – for example, a busy graphic with large dark areas such as shadows behind black text.

Text

No margins.

Centred paragraph text.

Paragraphs of type in all caps.

Paragraphs of type in bold.

Paragraphs of type in italic.

Links

Links that do not show clearly where they will take you.

Links in body copy that distract readers and lead them off to remote, useless pages (although links to remote sites, such as a reference to support a point being made, may be very valuable).

Text links that are not underlined, so it is not clear that they are links.

Dead links – always check!

Graphics

Large graphic files that take forever to download.

Graphics with 'halos' around them because they have been poorly manipulated.

Missing graphics (because the creator did not copy the files from their hard drive!).

Anything that blinks, especially text.

Animations that never stop.

Navigation

Having to scroll sideways.

Unclear navigation; overly complex navigation.

General design

Entry page or homepage that does not fit within a standard window (640 X 460 pixels).

No focal point on the page or too many focal points on a page.

Navigation buttons as the only visual interest, especially when they're large.

Lack of contrast, for example, the use of two fonts from the same family.

Non-contrast background and text.

Good design elements

Text

Background does not interrupt the text.

Text is big enough to read but not too big.

The hierarchy of information is perfectly clear.

Columns of text are narrower than in a book to make reading easier on the screen.

Navigation

Navigation buttons and bars are easy to understand and use.

A large product has a clear map page.

Links

Link colours coordinate with page colours.

Links are underlined so they are instantly clear to the visitor.

Links give the visitor a clue as to where they are.

Graphics

Buttons are not big and overpowering.

Every graphic link has a matching text link.

Graphics and backgrounds use browser-safe colours.

Animated graphics turn off by themselves.

General design

Good use of graphic elements (photos, subheads, pull-quotes) to break up large areas of text, and the style of the page reflects the content.

Every page in the site looks as if it belongs to the same site: there are repetitive elements that carry throughout the pages (this is 'consistency of design' and usually means that the same background, layout, colour scheme and navigation structure appear on each page).

Using images

JPEG

Photographs, as well as other images that are similar to photographs, should usually be saved in JPEG format.

Save as:

- 72ppi (pixels per inch) – used when referring to the resolution on the screen.
- Lowest quality level (although you may need to use higher levels to achieve a reasonable image) – experiment with the slider.
- Formal options – choose Baseline optimised for the best colour quality or choose Progressive to enable the file to load progressively from low resolution to high resolution as the page downloads.
- RGB colour mode (changed via Image>Mode>RGB colour from the top menu bar). However, you should find you are working in RGB colour most of the time anyway.

NOTE: JPEG compression throws away information in order to reduce file sizes. If you resave a JPEG file, it will throw away even more information as it compresses the file again. The amount of information lost will depend on the image so always keep your original, uncompressed file in case you need to start again with your JPEG!

GIF

Diagrams, cartoons and simple drawings are best saved in the GIF format. GIFs are 8-bit, not 24-bit, so you don't need to worry so much about the colour depth.

Save as:

- 72ppi.
- Indexed colour mode (changed via Image>Mode>Indexed Colour from the top menu bar).
- Reduce the colour palette to the minimum necessary to maintain the image.
- To save a GIF in a graphics program you need to complete your work on the graphic and then choose File>Export>GIF89a Export from the top menu bar.
- Choose the 'adaptive palette' in the export dialog box and set colours to the smallest number available. Click the Preview button to see what the file will look like. If it doesn't look good enough, close the Preview window and try a higher number of colours. Keep adding colours until your image becomes acceptable and then click OK.
- Click the 'interlace' checkbox and click OK to interlace your image.

Technical skills to develop

Use images, text, sound and video for the task set

Web-based material depends on a combination of text and image to create meaning. In some cases sound and video are also vital. For example, a site to promote a new film would be a poorer site if it did not include at least one trailer for the movie. However, video and sound need to be used sparingly on a website as there can be difficulties with downloading sound and video material because it takes so long.

Use appropriate software for developing your site

While it is perfectly possible and indeed common for web programmers to create websites by hard coding HTML, it is unlikely that media students will want to spend the time and effort required to learn this skill. There is a wide range of software available to do the work for you and allow you to concentrate on the design aspects of your site. These range from free software through to professional products. If you have access to excellent software such as Macromedia Dreamweaver, all well and good, but there are plenty of free products which will do the job, such as Netscape Composer (part of the Netscape Navigator® Internet browser). The most important thing is to ensure that you can use the program.

Key design pointers

Think about using a background colour. Do not use a background image unless for a very good reason, as this makes it very hard to read a page. As with print documents, use contrasting font sizes and styles in your formatting, for example, bold and headings. Do not use serif fonts on a webpage – they are very hard to read. It is best to use a sans-serif font and to use a standard one such as Arial or Courier. If you use a complicated font and the viewer does not have a copy of it on their system, their computer will substitute a different font and all your formatting will come to nothing. Many web editing packages will let you use only the common sans-serif fonts, for this reason.

If you do want to use a particular font for a particular effect, the best way to do so is to create an image of the text on a suitable background by using an illustration package or your photo-editing package and putting it into your page as an image. That way the formatting cannot be altered, whatever fonts are installed on the viewer's computer.

Identify your target audience

Identify the target audience for your site quickly as this will define your approach. A site aimed at four- to six-year-olds will probably use different fonts, colours, images, layout and content to one targeting 25–30-year-olds. A site appealing to high income earners will be very different to a website presence for a magazine such as *Loaded*. You will probably need to carry out some research, once you have started to plan your site and defined your target audience, to identify how best to appeal to this audience on the web. This research can prove a valuable part of your evaluation.

Appeal to your audience

It is important to ensure that your website is easy to navigate and interesting, and that the images set an appropriate context for the site, just as with print-based work. In other words, you need to make sure that

as the site comes up it is communicating with the viewer. Just as a magazine front cover or the opening sequence of a television programme sets the context of what follows, so a site's opening page should establish its position quickly – background colour, layout, use of images etc. should all add to the effect.

Following on from this, the opposite is also true. It is easy to get carried away with a website and include too many effects. Endless animations, over-clever menus, too many flashing lights, a background sound to every page and text scrolling across the page can detract from the site itself and can even put people off. If you regularly visit high quality websites, you will notice that there are clear thematic links between pages, navigation is 'transparent' (that is, easy to grasp), the pages are uncluttered and straightforward and they load quickly.

Link your pages effectively

This means that you have to create hyperlinks to the different pages in your site, possibly within the pages themselves if they are too big to fit in a browser window, and probably to other sites. We would expect to see a menu bar or some navigation system somewhere on every page. Link text is normally identified in some way, often by being in a different colour and underlined. If your pages are so long that the viewer would need to scroll down the page, it is better to create a 'table of contents' at the top of the page with links to the different sections on the page and 'back to the top' links at the end of each section, to make it easier for the viewer to move around the page.

It is also a good idea to use images as links when you can, either by creating little icons such as a picture of a house to represent the homepage of your site, or by using larger images or parts of images. For example, if you were creating a site with information about various stars from a particular film, you might want to use a still from the film showing all the characters but with a link for each star from their face to 'their' page.

Using the conventions of web publishing appropriately

You should now be aware that you cannot produce an appropriate webpage without some degree of research to see what conventions are used in similar types of site. Nor can you make an appropriate webpage without some investment in learning about the software and what it can do. Some effects, such as rollover buttons and drop down menus, can really add to the effect of your page; others merely detract and should be avoided.

An example of a typical web page layout is shown opposite.

Obviously there are many other ways of laying out a web page – look at examples for similar sites to get an idea. Look in particular at sites that are deliberately 'divergent' to create impact or where the production values are very high, such as film release sites. Try the *Atom Films* site or the *Little Ninja* site to get ideas about how the production values of a film can override conventional design principles to create something powerful and effective which creates a clear branding and concept in the user's mind.

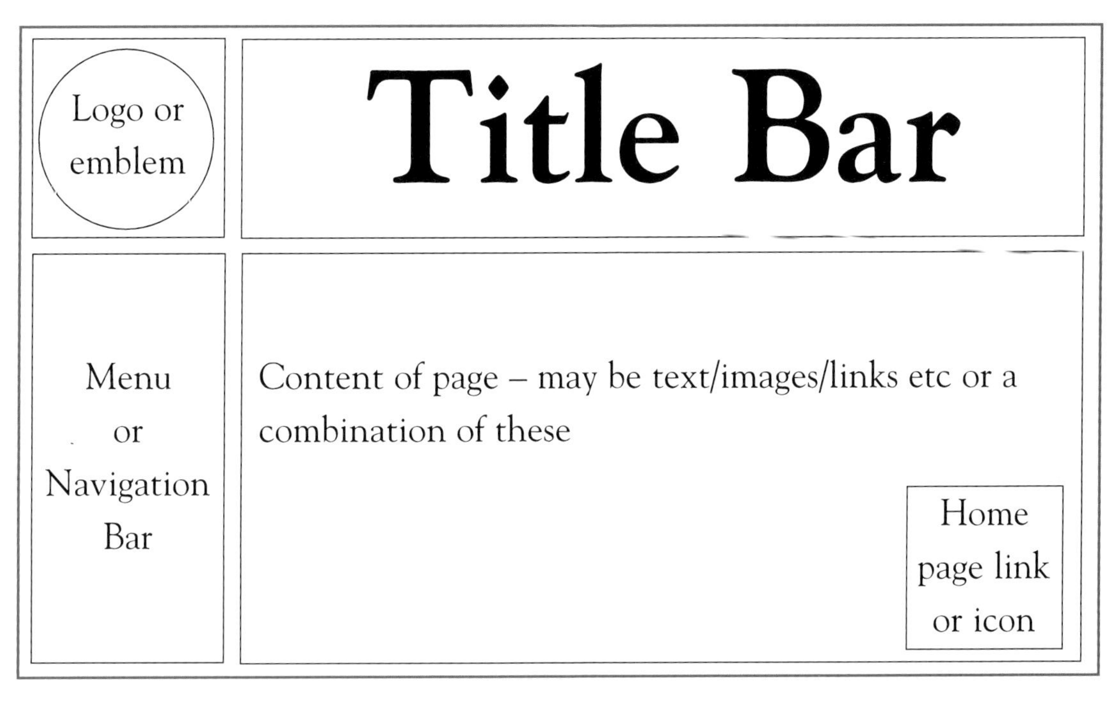

A typical web page layout

Part Five

Production report

There are four sections to the Production Report and they are all important. There is also a maximum length of 2000 words for the whole report, so editing skills are important. The report is not a description or diary but a reflective and analytical review of your work, to be developed alongside the product, to ensure that the theoretical aspects of practical production are to the fore during the production process as well as the practical points.

Section 1 – Introduction and research

The report needs to start by clearly identifying the chosen brief. You then need to explain what research you have undertaken into contemporary products and services. Specific reference must be made to research into similar media texts and target audience.

Section 2 – Planning

It is essential that you plan your work properly using appropriate documentation, such as the planning sheets that have been suggested earlier in this section, to give evidence of the planning process.

Storyboards, scripts and original photographs before cropping or manipulation should be essential working documents during the planning and construction process, so immaculate records are not expected. A perfectly drawn storyboard for an advert that does not deviate in any way from the final product has usually been created after the advert was finished, as an artificial exercise to conform to

exam regulations. Not only is it usually fairly easy to spot 'post-production planning' in this way, but using this approach will not enable you to score as highly. Battered sheets with evidence of redrafting are sometimes more credible as genuine working documents and if the production report indicates that they were indeed essential planning tools, you will probably score well despite their poor condition.

You are also required to show evidence that you have carried out audience research (which might be quantitative or qualitative or a mixture of both), but it must be relevant and the conclusions clearly taken on board while creating your media text.

Section 3 – Construction

The next section of the report is the evaluation of the construction process. You need to give an analysis of how you approached the production process, the decision making which was undertaken, working practices, successful and unsuccessful ideas and approaches and analysis of how the media text was formed. This is perhaps the most difficult section of the report, since it is very easy to allow this section to become a 'production diary' that will gain very little credit because it is simply a description of the production process and not, as it should be, a reflective analysis.

As a rule of thumb, when writing this section you should beware of writing sentences which begin 'Then' and be especially wary of falling into the recording habit, making statements such as 'we then needed to put the clips in order on the timeline' rather than the more reflexive 'when ordering the clips on the timeline we wanted a balance of length of shot as well as a thematic structure and development. We lost some clips due to clumsy lighting and so had to 'cover' these gaps with a cut-away to a close-up to ensure a smooth sequence.' The latter example has not only justified decisions made without simply documenting them, it has also shown an understanding of an appropriate technical vocabulary and the opportunities and difficulties inherent in the editing process.

Section 4 – Evaluation

The final section of the report is an evaluation of your production. You should deconstruct the product in some detail and give comparative analysis against a range of equivalent productions and within the context of the designated target audience. It is quite appropriate to reflect that the production is not fully successful at this point, as long as you can indicate how you might have made it more successful. The limiting factor here will be the word limit. You may use annotated pictures here. You must also ensure that the analysis does not become a repetition of the production process but remains a deconstruction of the final production.

It is not easy to get all that into 2000 words. However, remember that this limit was set intentionally to require you to think carefully about what you include in the report. If there were no word limit, there would be a danger of rewarding length of analysis more than quality of analysis and this would be unfair. The quality of thought and intention in your production and the technical ability and creative skills that you have employed in creating this production will be rewarded, not endless notes.

Effective use of an appendix

The specifications state clearly that '*pre/post production paperwork should be provided in an appendix to the Log, as evidence of planning.*'

You should include details of research you have undertaken into similar products. Photocopying an A4 advert onto a piece of A3 paper, deconstructing it in terms of form, style and function as well as content, to provide evidence for your design approach, can give far more information than a mundane essay-type approach about a series of advertisements.

As suggested above, planning sheets such as storyboards, scripts, original art work and layout plans may also be included in the appendix. If you have used questionnaires as part of audience research, then a chart showing the results might be included together with a copy of the original questionnaire.

All of this is regarded as evidence of research and is not included in the formal word count of 2000 words.

Important note

Note there is a difference between teacher assessment and moderation. Your work will initially be assessed by your teacher and then (depending upon the number of candidates in your centre) the candidates' work will be sent to be externally moderated.

It is essential that your teacher sees all the documentation that offers evidence of research and planning. It is on this that your mark for planning and research will be assessed. However, when it comes to submitting your work for moderation to an external moderator, you do not have to include every single item. Moderators do not expect to receive every response to your questionnaire, or every annotated analysis of half a dozen colour supplement front covers. At most, select the items that you and your teacher think best represent your research and planning work, and present these as your appendix.

Preparing for moderation

Although the assessment procedures are primarily the responsibility of your teacher or lecturer, there are some very important things that you can do to help yourself and your work.

First, you should ensure that your work is neatly presented. If you have produced work on videotape, finding the time to put it into a case with a title inlay will help. You may not have time for a proper video front cover but the tape box *and* the tape itself must be labelled with your name, candidate number and centre number as well as the name of your film.

If you are presenting a print media text, try to get a laminated colour copy to send off if you can. (If your school or college does not have laminating facilities you should be able to get a local print shop to do this.) Again, do not forget to put a sticky label on the back stating your name, centre name and number. The same advice goes for all the media you produce – make sure you have labelled your work carefully and taken time to present it as well as possible. Every loose item must be separately labelled.

Whenever possible, evaluations should be word-processed. Include a header or footer showing your name, candidate number and the page number on every page of your analysis so that pages do not go missing.

Finally, make sure you retain a copy of your project before your centre sends it off for moderation. You will then have a backup copy if anything should happen to go missing.

SECTION 3
TEXTUAL ANALYSIS

Part One

Moving image

Introduction

As part of your study of media texts, OCR's AS Unit 2731 (Textual Analysis) gives you the opportunity to develop your analytical skills and assists you in learning how media texts are constructed. The genre for Section A (Technical Aspects of Moving Image Language and Conventions) is currently action/adventure films.

Section A of the Textual Analysis paper focuses on technical analysis. This means that you need to study the techniques used to construct the given texts, rather than simply studying the text in depth. This is intentionally a detailed focus, to ensure that you can research the forms and conventions of the specified genre in detail.

Remember that the examination is 'unseen'. This means that you will not know in advance what the text is that you will watch in the examination. This is so that you can study a range of texts in the specified genre and look at how the forms and conventions are used, rather than simply studying a single text and then being tested on how well you can remember your notes about that text. The questions you will have to answer will assume that you have never seen the text before, and thus will ask about the technical codes used in the text without any assumption of knowledge of the text outside this extract.

It is *not* a unit where you need to study the history of the genre in depth or know details or facts about a particular programme. This is because we want you to learn about how texts are constructed and to learn to use technical vocabulary and approaches while analysing texts. These are essential skills for both understanding how media texts are constructed and for constructing your own texts for practical production units. Your understanding of media debates and ideologies is tested in other units.

Form of the assessment

The extract given will be between three and five minutes long and there will be 30 minutes allowed for four viewings in total, with time allowed to take notes after the first viewing. However, you will be able to read the questions before any viewings so that you know what you need to be watching for. We assume that it will take you 45 minutes to plan and write your response to these questions. The text may or may not be familiar to you. You will be thinking about the technical codes employed in the text, not the content (of the text), so you won't need to know any background about it.

Genre

You will need to show evidence that you have studied the conventions of the relevant genre. The codes employed in a text are defined by the genre and thus these conventions are associated with that genre. For instance, it is a generic convention of news programmes to provide a summary of that day's stories at the beginning of the edition. It would make for a less effective game show, however, if the host announced the winner and the final score as part of the opener to the programme.

Equally, there are technical codes associated with a genre. If you are watching an action/adventure movie, you would expect to see some spectacular special effects and to see the hero overcome the odds to defeat the villain, for example.

ACTIVITIES

Try one or more of these suggested activities:

In groups, make a list of ten conventions that you associate with the genre of action/adventure films. Do you need to make different lists for different types of action/adventure movie or is there an overall list of key conventions?

Identify at least four texts within your chosen genre and qualify their use for each of these conventions in terms of 'very strong', 'moderate' and 'does not really conform'. Be prepared to justify these choices in discussion.

Swap lists with another group and attempt to order their conventions from 1 to 10 in terms of their importance. What conventions have they used that you have not used? Can you combine the lists to make a better list?

Swap lists with a third group and create a short definition of the genre using the first three or four conventions on their list. Does this also match the conventions agreed between you and the second group? Feed back these definitions to the rest of the group and discuss how they might be improved. Are there any that might be interchangeable between genres? Can you adjust your definitions so they are exclusive to your chosen genre? Once you feel each one is fairly representative of a genre you might like to put them up on the wall to keep you focused.

Prepare a presentation about each of the three films you looked at in terms of genre conventions, justifying to the rest of the class why that film does/does not conform or sometimes conforms to the genre conventions. Use detailed analysis of sections of the film to justify your argument.

Prepare a presentation about the heroes of each of your films. In what ways are they representative of typical heroes of action/adventure films and in what ways do they not conform to the conventions? Are they typical of films of their era?

Compare two action adventure films from different eras (such as *Captain Blood* and *Pirates of the Caribbean*). In what ways does each film conform to or subvert the genre conventions?

Take a short section of an action/adventure film you are studying, storyboard it and give a presentation to the rest of the class about how the technical codes have been used in each shot to create meaning for an audience. You might want to think about framing, angle, *mise-en-scène*, setting, costume, props, editing, soundtrack and representations for each shot.

Technical codes

Technical codes, such as the camera, the lighting, the editing or the use of sound and music, create expectations, control the audience's perceptions and signify the genre of a film. These codes are different for different genres, such as comedies or teen movies. They are intended to engage the audience with the text. It is the use of technical codes to create tension during the last fight or battle in an action/adventure movie, for example, which helps us to respond emotionally. One key code can be the lighting of characters, for example, whether a character's face is lit from top or below, giving him/her a soft or a harsh expression. Another example would be the camera angle: while a high-angle shot makes the character seem small and vulnerable, a low-angle shot can make them seem powerful and strong. This is one reason why actors who are short may need to stand on a box in certain shots, to ensure the right effect.

Character codes

Character codes include the costume, make-up, gestures and language of a character. These codes signify much about the character to the viewer, such as their social grouping, job or personality. Stereotypes are often used because they build on the viewer's previous experience in terms of their own world as well as television/film observation. They are, therefore, predictable and can be either maintained and used almost as a 'shorthand', or broken for dramatic effect. In many films it is important that the audience can identify 'goodies' and 'baddies' immediately. For example, in film noir (where colour and lack of colour are often very symbolic) the *femme fatale* is usually portrayed wearing red or black to convey her siren status, whereas the heroine is usually dressed in white to symbolise her innocence.

ACTIVITIES

Collect video clips of four examples of action/adventure movies and show them to an audience outside your Media class (for example, other students). Can they identify the genre of the film and guess at the narrative even if they don't understand what is happening?

What genre elements do they observe? Why do you think this is?

Are these the same genre elements that you observed? Why is this?

Specific analysis

Now that you have explored the genre conventions and basic codes, you need to study specific texts in detail to look at how the technical codes are employed to establish the genre. In the unseen examination you will be given a short extract of a text to watch and you must comment upon how the text communicates with/manipulates/engages the audience through the use of the technical codes. As a conclusion for each question about the technical codes, you will be asked to comment upon the rationale behind this approach and reflect on its success. This is intended to ensure that you do not simply describe the technical codes employed without considering their function. You must go beyond describing *what* you see and hear and explain *why* and *how* the texts are constructed in the way that they are.

We will look at how you might approach an answer to a particular text later, but first we need to clarify the form of the technical codes you need to be able to analyse and consider their likely function in the text.

It will not be relevant or feasible to discuss all of these codes for every text in 45 minutes, but you cannot make an informed decision about which are the most significant codes unless you can select from a wide range of possible codes upon which to reflect.

The list of codes that follows, although quite comprehensive, is not in any way intended as a definitive list. Some of these codes may be irrelevant to the text you are given; there may be other codes, which are not mentioned here, but are useful for considering the unseen text. By researching a range of relevant texts and considering as many of the possible codes as possible, you should gain an understanding of the likely codes and conventions to be employed in the unseen text and be confident that you can deconstruct it appropriately.

Camera work/cinematography

The camera is subjective when the audience is engaged as a participant (e.g. when the camera is addressed directly or when it imitates the viewpoint or movement of a character). The point-of-view (POV) shot in a horror movie can put the audience in the position of the victim seeking to escape the killer, or the killer looking for the victim, for example. Quentin Tarantino uses POV shots throughout his films and one of the most iconographic shots in all his films is the 'trunk shot', a POV from a character in the boot of a car. This is used in *Kill Bill*, when Beatrice opens the boot (trunk) to question Sophie Fatale.

The objective view involves positioning the audience as an observer. For example, the 'privileged point of view' involves watching from omniscient vantage points such as being able to see characters behind the hero when he/she is confronting the villain. Keeping the camera still whilst the subject moves towards or away from it is an objective camera effect, since the camera seems of higher status as it does not move.

The person looking and talking direct to camera establishes their authority or 'expert' status with the audience. Only certain people are normally allowed to do this, such as announcers, presenters, newsreaders, weather forecasters and interviewers. This is not such a common technique in action/adventure films. However, it can be used to good effect by directors who like to use different techniques, such as the way 'The Bride' talks to the camera during the opening sequence of *Kill Bill 2* to establish the narrative and tone for the film.

Stills from *Kill Bill*

Still from *Alfie*

Camera techniques

Framing and camera angle

Long shot (LS) – a shot that shows all of a fairly large subject (such as a person) and usually much of the surroundings. This is useful to give a perspective and context for a scene. For example, a long shot of a robot framed in a laboratory would give a different interpretation of events from a shot of the same robot framed in an old people's home.

Extreme long shot (ELS) – sometimes used as an establishing shot. In this type of shot the camera is at its furthest distance from the subject, emphasising the background and reducing the importance of the subject. For example, the use of an ELS at the beginning of a chase sequence in an action/adventure movie will start the build-up of tension to the chase or fight, while also giving important visual clues to the location and the likely sequence of events.

Establishing shot (ES) – an ES is commonly used to open a film or a stage in a film, showing the location in which the action will take place and establishing the *mise-en-scène*, tone and atmosphere of the action to come.

Master shot (MS) – used at the beginning of a sequence as a reference point for the rest of the sequence to follow. It shows the composition and the key relationships between the subjects and enables the audience to contextualise the action before it happens.

Medium long shot (MLS) – in the case of a standing actor, the lower frame line cuts off his feet and ankles.

Mid-shot (MS) – in such a shot the subject and its setting occupy roughly equal areas in the frame. In the case of the standing actor, the lower frame passes through the waist. More body language can be seen as the face, chest and hands are in frame.

Close-up (CU) – a picture that shows a fairly small part of the scene, such as a character's face and neck, in great detail so that it fills the screen. It abstracts the subject from the context. Other types of close-up include MCU (medium close-up) – head and shoulders, BCU (big close-up), sometimes referred to as ECU (extreme close-up) – forehead to chin.

Close-ups focus on emotions or reactions and are sometimes used to show a character's reaction to something or to help the audience understand what a character is thinking during a particular sequence. A CU can be very effective in revealing a character's emotions. For example in *Open Water*, CUs are often used to show the characters' tension as they look around in the water and try to work out where the sharks are.

Angle of shot – in a high angle the camera looks down, making the viewer feel more powerful than those on screen, or suggesting an air of detachment. A low-angle shot places the camera below the subject, exaggerating his or her importance. The hero is usually shot from below, to give a sense of power and status.

Point-of-view shot (POV) – a shot made from a camera position close to the line of sight of a character, to imply that the camera is 'looking with their eyes'. A common use of this shot in an action/adventure movie is when the hero is hiding from villains and the audience sees a POV from the hero's hiding place while he is watching his pursuers.

Movement

Zoom – when zooming in the camera does not move; the lens is focused down from a long shot to a close-up whilst recording. The subject grows in the frame and attention is concentrated on details previously invisible as the shot tightens. It may be used to surprise the viewer. Reverse zoom reveals more of the scene (perhaps showing where a character is, or a person to whom he or she is speaking) as the shot widens. Zooming is unusual in Hollywood films because of the possible disorientating effects; jump cuts are used instead.

Tracking (dollying) – when tracking, the camera itself moves (smoothly) towards or away from the subject while the focus remains constant. Tracking in (like zooming) draws the audience into a closer relationship with the subject; moving away tends to create emotional distance. Tracking back tends to divert attention to the edges of the screen. The speed of tracking may affect the viewer's mood. Fast tracking (especially when tracking in) is exciting; tracking back eases tension. Tracking in can force the audience to focus on something such as the expression of a contestant. During chase sequences the camera will often 'track' with the action to emphasise the sense of speed.

Pan – the camera moves from right to left or left to right to follow a moving subject. A space is left in front of the subject to ensure that the pan 'leads' rather than 'trails'. A pan usually begins and ends with a few seconds of still picture to give greater impact. The speed of a pan across a subject creates a particular mood as well as establishing the viewer's relationship with the subject.

Hand-held camera – a hand-held camera can produce a jerky, bouncy, unsteady image, which may create a sense of immediacy or chaos. This is perhaps most familiar from *The Blair Witch Project*, which used hand-held camera shots to add to the atmosphere and tension being created in the film.

Steadicam – the steadicam is a hand-held camera worn as a kind of harness by the (highly skilled) cameraman. It uses a gyroscope system to ensure the camera remains perfectly level and smooth as the cameraman moves. For example, a steadicam was used to film a lot of the fight scenes in *Pirates of the Caribbean*. This enabled the camera to be within the action to engage the audience more directly and allowed for more humour in the action as well, by using reaction shots.

Editing techniques

Cut – a change of shot from one viewpoint or location to another. The most common type of cut is a jump cut where the action 'jumps' from one shot to another. This may be done to change the scene, vary the point of view, elide time or lead the audience's thoughts. For example, at the opening of *Open Water*, the long shot of Daniel bringing bags out to the car cuts to a CU of the suitcase handle as he picks it up. The audience immediately makes the assumption that the hand and the character are connected. There is usually a link between the shots which might be a match on action (moving from one character holding the telephone and talking to another character on the other end of the telephone, as at the beginning of *Open Water*), an elliptical cut, where the audience supplies the logical association between the two cuts (e.g. showing a man leaving his house and getting in his car to go to work and then jumping to when he pulls into the car park) or a spatial cut (showing a LS of the car park and then a CU of the piece of glass on the ground which will slice up his tyre).

There is always a justification for a cut, even if it is as obvious as switching between two characters in an argument. Where the transition itself is important it can be highlighted, for example, by using a fade to black to suggest a passing of time or a change of scene.

Reaction shot – any shot (often also a cutaway) in which a subject reacts to a previous shot.

Invisible editing – the vast majority of narrative films are now edited in this way. The cuts are intended to be unobtrusive except for special dramatic shots. Invisible editing supports rather than dominates the narrative: the plot and the characters are the focus. The technique gives the impression that the edits are motivated by the events in the 'reality' on screen.

Mise-en-scène

Meaning is communicated through the relationship of things visible within a single shot. Composition is therefore extremely important. All features of the background, costume, proxemics, lighting, style of production and framing are significant. For example, it is the *mise-en-scène* of *The Day After Tomorrow* that establishes the aggressive, dark, serious tone of the piece and creates tension. The use of the harsh neon lights, urban landscape and blue and orange lighting adds to the atmosphere and establishes expectations for the audience about the narrative they can expect.

Setting – can be location or studio, realistic or stylised. Aspects of the setting or props in the text may take on symbolic meanings, such as the red and blue pill in *The Matrix*.

Costume and make-up – these follow on from and develop these concepts. At the beginning of *Pirates of the Caribbean*, Elizabeth is tied tightly into a new corset before attending a formal naval ceremony. There are frequent shots showing how uncomfortable it makes her and how difficult she is finding it to breathe and this reflects her feelings about being trapped in this formal and oppressive world. When Captain Jack Sparrow rescues her, he immediately sees that the corset needs to be ripped off, to allow her the freedom to breathe.

Costumes in *The Matrix Reloaded* are futuristic and aggressive, with frequent use of sunglasses for effect and impact. This heightens the atmosphere of the film and imparts depth to the characters.

Sound

Music or sound that belongs 'within the frame' or can be considered to be a natural part of the narrative, is called **diegetic** music. The source of the sound is often, but not always, visible on screen. When the sound (usually music) is used without being part of the action (such as the use of a music track behind the action to add tension to climax sequences in *Open Water* or the music played whenever Neo is pushed between the matrix and reality in *The Matrix*), it is defined as **non-diegetic**.

Music is a key sound code. The type of music used in a text can convey a great deal of information about the mood and tone of the text. Tension can be established, emotions communicated and the music can be used as a comment on the action, to set the context for the next sequence or to provide closure, such as at the beginning and end of a round in a quiz show or the entry of a new guest on a chat show. The music can be very powerful in shaping the form of the text. The rhythm of music can dictate the rhythm of the cuts, such as the way the drum controls the cuts in the fight sequences in *Crouching Tiger, Hidden Dragon*, or can be used to establish tension such as in *Troy*. The music can be an important association for an audience and serve rapidly to establish an atmosphere – such as the familiar music accompanying the hordes of Storm Troopers in *Star Wars Episode III – Revenge of the Sith*.

Silence can also be used to create tension in the audience. It is unusual in action/adventure movies but when used can be very effective. It is silence broken only by the sound of lapping water which adds tension through much of *Open Water*.

Voice-over/narration, where used, is important. Although this was a common technique in film noir and has been used in neo-noir films such as *Blade Runner*, it is obviously less common in action/adventure films, as it takes the audience 'out of the action' and breaks the sense of realism.

Sound can be used as a bridge, to maintain continuity in a sequence by running a soundtrack under a series of images to link them. This can be useful in chase sequences, for example, both to create tension and link the parallel stories of chaser and victim. The music in *The Matrix* acts as an underscore in this way on several occasions.

Special effects and graphics

Titles are central to the opening of a text and may be interspersed at different points during the text. They can be used to provide information (such as an overlay giving information about time and place) or to act as markers to define the action (the context information at the beginning of a film – such as at the beginning of *I, Robot* where the robot laws are stated at the beginning of the nightmare sequence) or to give essential information such as the use of subtitles to the Japanese speech in *Kill Bill*.

The style of text on screen can be deconstructed just as with a print text and the choice of font, colour, size and so forth will all be directly related to the text.

Graphics can be used in many ways. Where used, they can be analysed as part of the *mise-en-scène* of a piece and should not detract from the text. Still images can be superimposed on each other on screen to create an effect – superimposed images are merged to some degree as opposed to overlaid images, which hide whatever is behind them on the screen. Insets are a particular type of overlay, used to show a second part of the action simultaneously.

CGI (computer-generated imagery) is becoming increasingly common in film and television and yet increasingly hard to identify. Whereas with older texts it is easy to identify that two characters in a car apparently driving down a motorway are in fact in a static car in front of a back projection of a road, it is not so straightforward with more sophisticated techniques and equipment.

Most action/adventure movies make great use of special effects in this way now. Many Hollywood blockbusters, such as *I, Robot*, *The Day After Tomorrow* and *Troy*, depend on the special effects to create the spectacle which is the film.

Action is frequently shot against a 'blue screen' or a 'green screen' so that the appropriate background can be constructed using CGI and the two merged to make the scene. The use of the blue screen or green screen means that this simple colour is easy to identify and 'key out' of the scene using a computer. It is, however, important that actors or presenters do not wear clothes of the same or similar colours, or they can seem to disappear off screen.

Stunts, models and pyrotechnics – these traditional special effects are still used today, for example, making and filming models of vehicles, buildings or other objects and inserting them into the scene so that they blend seamlessly with live action. Stunt people are always in demand to double for well-known actors or to perform minor stunts that require a trained professional. Explosions of all descriptions are still a staple element of action sequences.

Action/adventure films are usually exciting stories, often set in exotic locations. The plot will be action-driven with danger and excitement throughout. The audience may experience conquests, explorations, battles, discovery, creation of empires and situations that threaten to destroy the main characters. There are likely to be several spectacular chase sequences and extensive use of CGI.

Adventure films historically were intended to appeal mainly to men, creating major heroic stars through the years, such as Arnold Schwarzenegger and Will Smith. These courageous, patriotic or altruistic heroes often fought for their beliefs, struggled for freedom or overcame injustice. More modern films have become more balanced with female stars as well. Tarantino has extended the genre considerably with *Kill Bill* and very bloodthirsty female characters as well. The genre can be very broad and may encompass the mythic fantasies of *Lord of the Rings*, comic book superheroes such as *Spider-Man* and sci-fi epics like *Attack of the Clones* as well as the cop action of *Die Hard*.

ACTIVITIES

You are the casting director for a new action/adventure movie that will be similar to *The Terminator*. Draw up a character description for your lead character, assuming he will be a conventional hero. Decide who you feel should play this role. Now draw up a character description for the villain and decide who should play this role. Present your decisions to the rest of the group.

Define at least five conventions for this role, such as 'tall, dark and handsome, wearing sunglasses'.

Justify your choice of conventions to the rest of the group.

Now describe and cast a non-conventional hero and villain for this movie.

What are the implications of these changes?

Is this an easy task?

Why do you think this is?

The first full-length adventure films were the early swashbucklers from the Hollywood studio machines. These included many 'stock elements' such as lavish sets, costumes and weapons of the past. They were often built upon action scenes of sea battles, castle duels, sword and cutlass fighting and the rescue of the female lead. One of Hollywood's most famous 'swashbucklers' was Errol Flynn, who appeared in such films as *Captain Blood* (1935), *The Adventures of Robin Hood* (1938) and *Sea Hawk* (1940). Burt Lancaster, who had been a circus performer, established his reputation by alternating his serious and sensitive dramas with high-action acrobatic roles in films such as *The Crimson Pirate* (1952). *Pirates of the Caribbean* has built upon the swashbuckler in the comic action/adventure form, using our expectations of swashbucklers both to help audience expectations of the text and to subvert these expectations simultaneously. Johnny Depp's portrayal of the camp, esoteric Captain Jack Sparrow both pays tribute to these early heroic portrayals while also mocking them for a modern audience. Disney ensures the success of the film equally by portraying Orlando Bloom as the Errol Flynn swashbuckler with a deliberate masculine performance against Depp's mincing pirate.

Action/adventure films have tremendous impact, continuous high energy, lots of stunts, possibly extended chase scenes, rescues, battles, fights, escapes, non-stop motion, spectacular rhythm and pacing and adventurous heroes – all designed for pure audience escapism with the action/adventure sequences at the centre of the film. The cinematography and sound are directly structured to sustain this level of activity throughout. Within the genre these days, there can be said to be many genre-hybrids: sci-fi, thrillers, crime-drama, kung-fu, westerns and war. Always, however, they have a resourceful hero/heroine, struggling against incredible odds or an evil villain, and/or trapped in various modes of transportation (bus, ship, train, plane etc.), with resolution

Still from *Pirates of the Caribbean: The Curse of the Black Pearl*

achieved at the end of the movie, after two crisis points along the way. Action/adventure films have traditionally been aimed at male audiences, aged 13 to mid-30s, although modern action/adventure films have featured strong female characters to attract a wider audience, such as the enigmatic heroine of *The Interpreter*, who is both victim and not victim, played by Nicole Kidman.

One of the most well-known and well-defined modern day action/adventure-heroes is James Bond. Beginning in the 1960s, the slick Bond 'formula' appealed to large audiences with its exotic locations, tongue-in-cheek dialogue, high-tech gadgets, fast-action suspense, impossible stunts and stunning women. The action hero battled unlikely and incredible criminals, usually without even staining his dinner suit.

The action/adventure-film genre has been among the most successful genres in recent years. Raw, indestructible, powerful and muscular heroes of modern, ultra-violent action/adventure films are often very unlike the swashbuckling heroes of the past. Each decade has tended to define its own heroes for the genre and this has defined the style of action/adventure film.

Arnold Schwarzenegger made a career out of starring in action films in the 1980s and 1990s, most notably in the action/adventure films *Conan the Barbarian* (1982), *Commando* (1986), *Raw Deal*

ACTIVITIES

You have been asked to create a new fantasy style action/adventure film, to be made by Fox. You are required to:

- investigate the target audience for this type of film
- write the synopsis, identifying who would play each role and why
- storyboard the pre-credit sequence for the film
- present your ideas to the rest of the group and justify your choices.

(1986), *Predator* (1987), *Red Heat* (1988) and *True Lies* (1994), as well as in hybrid sci-fi/action/adventure films. Bruce Willis defined the action/adventure hero for the 1980s in the *Die Hard* trilogy, while recent heroes have included Will Smith in *Independence Day* (1996), *Men in Black* (1997 and 2002) and *I, Robot* (2004), and Orlando Bloom in the *Pirates of the Caribbean* series (*The Curse of the Black Pearl* (2003), *Dead Man's Chest* (2006) and *Pirates of the Caribbean 3* (2007)), as well as the *Lord of the Rings* trilogy (2001, 2002 and 2003) and *Troy* (2004).

By studying the careers of these actors you will be able to see how the persona of the hero has changed over the decades – from the stiff-upper-lipped swashbucklers and heroes of early Hollywood stars, through the macho men portrayed by Schwarzenegger and Willis, to the more rounded, often more comic and sensitive portrayals from Smith and Bloom, for example. A pivotal actor in this transformation was of course Harrison Ford, whose injections of humour into *Star Wars* and *Raiders of the Lost Ark* redefined the role of hero for many critics.

To analyse the technical codes for the action/adventure genre is essentially the same as to analyse the technical codes for most mainstream Hollywood output. There are stock conventions used in action/adventure films but these should be familiar to you from many films that you have seen. The process of analysing will be more straightforward since you will have a more secure frame of reference than if you were researching a less populist genre.

ACTIVITIES

Try one or more of these suggested activities:

Research what are the top 10 action/adventure films in the charts at the moment. Which companies distribute each film? Are they typical action/adventure films? Survey among your peer group to find out which of these films they have seen and/or which ones they would like to see. What criteria make them want to see a film? How important is genre to them?

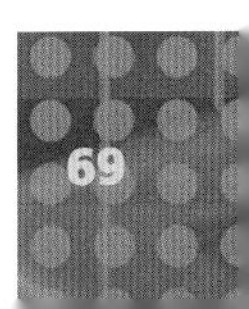

Research and explore how a film is promoted in different countries. For example, compare international and US-oriented trailers for *Troy*. How differently do they promote the film? What does this suggest about different cultural and genre expectations?

Analyse this poster for *Star Wars Episode III – Revenge of the Sith*. In what ways does it set up expectations for the audience about the narrative of the film?

Choose one actor who commonly plays the hero in action/adventure films. Compare and contrast the way he/she is presented visually in at least three films. Analyse using stills from each film if you can. How do framing, editing, costume, gesture and *mise-en-scène* contribute to or emphasize their heroic status? For example, look at these three pictures of Orlando Bloom from different films and suggest how these technical codes portray him as a hero – even though he is not the star of any of these films.

Still of Orlando Bloom as Legolas in the *Lord of the Rings* trilogy

Orlando Bloom in *Troy*

Orlando Bloom in *Pirates of the Caribbean*

DISCUSSION

Given such a wide variety of Hollywood films which might be considered as action/adventure films, discuss the following questions:

Why is there such a demand for this type of entertainment?

Is it the audience's natural desire for excitement and release?

Is it merely a route of escapism? Does an audience feel rewarded at the end when the hero wins?

Do audience members automatically identify with the hero/heroine and aspire to be like them?

ACTIVITIES

Watch approximately the first 10-15 minutes of *I, Robot* (until the end of the conversation with Lawrence Robertson).

Identify at least five key moments when Will Smith is clearly shown as a misfit who is 'outside the system', although still a hero. Try to analyse how and why you are manipulated by the text at these points to have sympathy for him, yet be aware of his isolation.

You have been asked to prepare a proposal for a new action/adventure film, which will be a combination of *I, Robot* and *Die Another Day*.

List the factors from each text which you would borrow. Be prepared to justify your choices.

Choose a title for this new film, which will reflect its genre and expectations.

Cast the hero/heroine and villain for the film and be prepared to justify your choices.

Storyboard a trailer for the new film and be prepared to justify your choices.

CASE STUDY 1

The Day After Tomorrow (2004)

The Day After Tomorrow is a typical disaster movie, using every special effects trick in the book to establish its narrative about the dangers of global warming. Professor Jack Hall (Dennis Quaid) is a climatologist who ends up having to save the world (and his cute son) from a catastrophic storm which engulfs New York at the beginning of a new Ice Age. It's a very contemporary disaster movie with its theme of the dangers of global warming, and makes extensive use of CGI to show the effects of storms, blizzards and so forth on New York. It features New York as the primary location, being a conventional Hollywood movie promoting American values and expectations globally. The narrative is very typical, starting with a sense of normality and equilibrium featuring the individual against the system, as Hall attempts to warn the US government of the dangers of global warming – which they regard as unimportant. A series of natural events leads Hall to realise that disaster is going to come more quickly than expected, rapidly shifting to disequilibrium as the weather starts to erupt, and finally back to a new, cautious re-equilibrium at the end of the movie with the conventional theme of 'we will survive'.

The Day After Tomorrow is pretty representative of disaster movies of this type, from *Towering Inferno* onwards, and it is generally assumed that audiences will be familiar with blockbuster disaster movies as a sub-genre of action/adventure movies. The environmental warnings in the film make it pretty contemporary and it is also easy to see that this was made by the same director as *Independence Day* (Roland Emmerich), when you watch the set-piece disaster sequences such as the blizzards in New York.

There are generally three typical elements to a disaster movie of this kind. The first is the CGI spectacular, which frames the action of the film with several enormous set-piece disasters. The second is the human interest – we must identify with the key protagonists and want them to survive (hence why Hall must return to New York to rescue his son). Finally there is the moral dimension – as we said above, the film has a moral warning for us and for those in authority that this 'might' happen if we do not take global warming seriously.

Not surprisingly, most of the disaster sequences in the film are shot with a lot of blue and grey, to reflect the appalling weather conditions featured in the film, and there is a tremendous number of ELSs to show the scale of the devastation. Frequently these are intercut with CUs shot in much warmer light to emphasise the human nature of the tragedy. Emmerich does so to intertwine the spectacular and the human themes and also makes frequent use of sound beds to link the sequences.

CASE STUDY 2

I, Robot (2004)

As a futuristic action/adventure movie, set in Chicago in 2035, this obviously draws heavily on *Blade Runner* in terms of *mise-en-scène* and construction. Will Smith plays Detective Del Spooner, a misfit in the police department, just as Harrison Ford was a misfit in the LAPD in *Blade Runner*. He is suspicious of robots, just as Ford was suspicious of the 'augments', and,

in the nature of the genre, he is proved correct. The early *mise-en-scène* establishes the futuristic nature of Chicago with monorails and endless advertising boards but it is a far friendlier place than *Blade Runner*'s Los Angeles. As in *Blade Runner*, much use is made of blue and orange light but here it is often explicitly contrasted, with blue lighting and composition for 'robot' or action scenes and warm lighting with lots of orange for human or emotional action.

Typically for a modern action/adventure film, humour is an important aspect of the film, such as Spooner's delight at the arrival of a new pair of trainers early on in the film – 'vintage circa 2004'. An early chase scene sees him assuming that a running robot carrying a handbag must be a thief and he quickly gives chase ... only to discover that the robot was running back to his mistress because her inhaler was in the bag which she had left at home and she was suffering an asthma attack.

Once Spooner starts to investigate the death of a top scientist at the corporation that makes the robots, he is quickly accompanied by the glamorous robot psychologist, Dr Susan Calvin (Bridget Moynahan). This is a classic generic relationship between hero and heroine/helper. Again, this is a stereotypical relationship – commonly the 'brawn' of the cop and the 'brain' of the psychologist.

Once in the corporation, good use is made of framing and camera angle to create a sense of spectacle and awe at the immensity of the buildings and thus, implicitly, of the corporation. Careful use of lighting, colour and composition ensures that Spooner does not 'fit' in the location, reminding us that he is the outsider.

Not surprisingly, Spooner soon uncovers a dangerous plot and discovers that the robots are not as harmless as they had seemed, and there is extensive use of CGI during the ensuing chase and battle scenes leading to the resolution.

Case study exemplar

For the written examination, you will be shown a sequence from an action/adventure film which will be approximately four minutes long. You need to write about this sequence in detail, focusing on the five technical areas (see below) to structure your answer. You must write something about all five technical areas, but you don't need to write equally about each one.

1. **Camera angle, shot, movement and position**
2. **Editing**
3. **Sound**
4. **Special effects**
5. ***Mise-en-scène***

You will now look at how you might write about the two case study films mentioned above, using a sequence from each film for analysis. You will need the DVD copy of each film in order to locate the sequence fairly easily, so that you can write in detail. Here, we are only using a few stills from the sequence to show you a little of what it is like, but obviously a series of still pictures can't show you very much about editing or movement and certainly can't tell you much about the sound in the sequence!

The Day After Tomorrow

The sequence we have used here is from Chapter 14 on the DVD ('Wall of water'). It starts with the wall of water drowning the Statue of Liberty as it sweeps toward New York and ends with the overhead shot of the water surrounding the building the characters have taken refuge in, before changing to another scene.

We have included some suggestions for points you might make about this extract for the five technical areas. Remember, these are only suggestions, not a definitive list of things to say – we've left plenty more for you to add to the list. It's also important to remember that the quality of your analysis is more important than how many points you manage to make. You must remember to justify and explain why a technical feature has been used, not simply describe what is happening; for example, you need to explain how the use of an ELS adds a sense of heightened drama and tension and gives a sense of the magnitude of the disaster, not simply identify where an ELS is used.

Camera angle, shot, movement and position

Establishing shot; master shot; close-up (and variations); long shot; wide shot; two-shot; high angle; low angle; aerial shot; point of view; pan; crane; tilt; track; dolly; zoom/reverse zoom; framing; composition; hand-held; steadicam.

Examples

- **Contrast between long shots to show approaching wall of water and MS. CUs to show individuals caught up in drama.**
- **Framing of people rushing into library to try and escape water.**
- **Use of mirror shot when bus driver looks in side mirror to see wall of water coming up street behind him.**

- **Overhead shots to show how water surrounds library as it continues to advance. 'Over the shoulder' shot as water cascades down street toward library.**

Editing

Sound and vision editing – cut; fade; wipe; edit; FX; dissolve; long take; superimpose; slow motion; synchronous/asynchronous sound.

Examples:

- **Contrast between shots of wall of water advancing and small-scale human drama – mother and child trapped in taxi; girl returning to taxi to rescue the mother's handbag.**
- **Frequent jump cuts between water and people to establish tension.**
- **Linking of sections – Ellis Island being submerged and Statue of Liberty seeming to struggle to remain above water as prelude to human drama to follow.**
- **Use of reaction shots to show impact of sight of wall of water.**
- **Linking shots with street bum and his dog to add extra emotional impact.**

Sound

Soundtrack; theme; tune; incidental music; sound effects; ambient sound; dialogue; voiceover; mode of address/direct address.

Examples:

- **Orchestral music backdrop to scene to add drama and tension – mood-controlling – majestic, imperial and dominant. Sound of rain and crashing waves heard above this.**
- **Characters shouting – dimly heard above water/music – adding to tension.**
- **Use of theme music to signify climactic moments.**
- **Sam's words being whipped away by wind as he attempts to warn girl of dangers of water coming toward her, to emphasise the danger and tension.**
- **Contrast between relatively calm voices at beginning of extract as people complain about rain, with increasing volume as danger gets closer – and increasingly hard for audience to make out their words, to intensify this sense of tension.**

Special effects

Graphics; captions; computer-generated images (CGI); animation; pyrotechnics; stunts; models; back projection.

Examples:

- **CGI to show water wall sweeping over Statue of Liberty and crashing into New York.**
- **Views of wall of water as it sweeps through city toward library and then surrounds the library where our individuals have taken refuge.**
- **Stunts to add tension, such as people climbing over cabs to try and escape from water and being flung into air as wall of water reaches them.**
- **Stunts including girl reaching into car in flood as wall of water rising; girl being rescued by Sam – just making it past revolving doors before water hits.**

Mise-en-scène

Location, set, studio/set design; costume; properties; ambient lighting; artificial lighting; production design period/era; colour design.

Examples:

- **Use of colour – cold blues and greys for water and storms against warmer colours for human interest sections.**
- **Location firmly established as New York – yellow cabs, street bum, people escaping from flooded subway, manhole covers, uniformed security guards for library, bus driver etc.**
- **Costume used to help focus on main characters – most others in shades of black/brown whereas main characters wear more colours – dog is mostly white to stand out.**
- **Use of yellow carrier bag on head of street bum to help identify him quickly in crowd as well as establish his credentials.**
- **Statue of Liberty just managing to keep Flame of Hope above water, suggesting hope in the end.**
- **Light decreasing at beginning of sequence as water and storm hit – contrast between lighter shots of characters before wall arrives and later as the disaster hits.**
- **Limited colour palette to heighten awareness of particular elements; for example, yellow of taxicab as swept through bottom windows of library.**

I, Robot

The sequence we have chosen here is from just before the opening of Chapter 10 on the DVD. It starts with Spooner and Calvin entering the US Robotics Corporation warehouse to question the robots and lasts until the point when the renegade robot is caught in the net and Spooner and Calvin are looking down at it on the floor (towards the end of Chapter 10). In this sequence there is a good range of shots, dramatic editing, good use of sound and careful *mise-en-scène* to establish the conflicting cultures.

Establishing shot; master shot; close-up (and variations); long shot; wide shot; two-shot; high angle; low angle; aerial shot; point of view; pan; crane; tilt; track; dolly; zoom/reverse zoom; framing; composition; hand-held; steadicam.

Examples:

- **Contrast in robot lab between LS of ranks of robots and Spooner in MS (also *mise-en-scène* here with use of colour).**
- **ECU of trigger of gun just before first robot is shot.**
- **Use of CUs to show interaction between powerful robot (low angle) and**

defenceless Spooner (high angle), before robot attempts to escape. Contrasts with high angle on robot in net once caught and low angle MS of Spooner looking down at it.

- **Framing of Spooner and Calvin as they enter the robot lab creates a sense of power and also a sense of entering alien territory because of the huge horizontal doors with the US Robotics logos.**
- **Tracking shots of escaping robot, mimicking other action/adventure films (e.g. *Spider-Man*) as he seeks to escape.**
- **Framing of robot as pulls wall of lab apart and breaks through – then caught in the spotlight.**

Editing

Sound and vision editing – cut; fade; wipe; edit; FX; dissolve; long take; superimpose; slow motion; synchronous/asynchronous sound.

Examples:

- **Use of 'bullet time' as robot seeks to escape from lab.**
- **Quick jump cuts during chase sequence before robot escapes from lab to create tension. Contrast slow editing as Spooner follows robot out of wall of lab once robot is caught.**
- **Use of panning shots at beginning to emphasise the vast ranks of robots Spooner and Calvin are talking to – interspersed with MS of the two humans, edited to set them apart from the ranks of robots.**
- **Use of cutaways as they are talking to show reaction/lack of reaction from ranks of robots.**

Sound

Soundtrack; theme tune; incidental music; sound effects; ambient sound; dialogue; voice-over; mode of address/direct address.

Examples:

- **Overlapping voices of Spooner and Calvin to show oppositional attitudes to the robots.**
- **Use of high-tension score as robot tries to escape, to create tension and drama.**
- **When Spooner starts to shoot robots there is over-amplification of gunshots reverberating around lab to add to atmosphere.**
- **Conflict between quietness of bullet time sequence and '*Spider-Man*' sequence, as robot tries to escape against cacophony of noise from police ranged against it.**

- **Use of additional sound effects such as echoing footsteps when Spooner searches ranks of robots for the renegade.**

Special Effects

Graphics; captions; computer-generated images (CGI); animation; pyrotechnics; stunts; models; back projection.

Examples:

- **Creation of ranks of robots for Spooner and Calvin to address.**
- **Use of time effects and CGI to give effect of robot trying to escape.**
- **CGI used to enable robot renegade to interact with Spooner and also to look slightly more 'human' than others (until in net at end).**
- **Pyrotechnics to create sense of arsenal of guns unleashed by police when robot leaves lab.**

Mise-en-scène

Location, set, studio/set design; costume; properties; ambient lighting; artificial lighting; production design period/era; colour design.

Examples:

- **Obvious contrasts in colour palettes between Spooner and Calvin as human characters (darker palette) with robots – light palette.**
- **Calvin wears clothes that blend into the US Robotics lab, suggesting her role there, although her dark hair contrasts and matches Spooner's colour palette.**
- **Harsh spotlight when robot gets out of lab creates a sense of a criminal having been caught. Similar lighting used when Spooner goes through gap in laboratory wall but not so harsh – he has power and control.**
- ***Mise-en-scène* of police marksmen confronting escaping robot is very threatening – they're clearly a professional unit and very intimidating.**
- ***Mise-en-scène* of lab is very futuristic with robot armies, technology etc. (hints of *Star Wars* and the Storm Troopers?)**
- **Typical of genre – harsh blue light is used for the robots/technology whereas warmer orange lights are used for human interactions.**
- **Colour, light, framing, costume and non-verbal language all serve to isolate Spooner among the ranks of robots when he is first seeking the renegade.**
- **When Spooner holds a gun to the head of a robot, his stance is threatening. Editing back and forth to Calvin's reaction adds tension.**
- **Spooner and Calvin are given great status against robots at beginning (almost on a platform) by use of *mise-en-scène*, framing, colour, lighting and set design, so we are aware of the overarching relationship between robots and humans.**

Getting started with comparative textual analysis

Aim

The aim of this section is to understand the concept of **representation** using two texts for comparison and in response to one of five set topics. You will be assessed in the form of a written essay. The specification states that '*Candidates need to be prepared to analyse the representation of social groups (including self-representation as appropriate) and messages and be able to describe the relevant kinds of social significance for the chosen topic.*'

By now you will have studied the various technical terms and techniques that determine the languages and conventions of action/adventure films.

In this section, the topics you will study are those set for examination:

- Consumerism and lifestyle magazines
- Celebrity and the tabloid press
- Music culture and radio
- Conflict/competition and video/computer games
- Gender and television situation comedy.

Example questions

Examples of typical questions that will be set for each topic are shown below. Remember that you will not have a choice of questions for each topic in the examination. There will only be **one** question for each topic.

Consumerism and lifestyle magazines

- Compare the ways in which consumerism is represented as attractive and appealing to the target audience of your two chosen magazines.

Celebrity and the tabloid press

- Compare how the representation of celebrities in your two chosen tabloid newspapers demonstrates a mutual dependence between the press and celebrities.

Music culture and radio

- Compare how the music culture represented in your two chosen radio programmes targets its audience.

Conflict/competition and video/computer games

- Compare how conflict/competition is represented by visual elements in your two chosen video/computer games.

Gender and television situation comedy

- Compare how the representation of characters in your two chosen television programmes reveals issues of gender.

Messages and values

How do we interpret the meaning, messages and values of texts: for example, film images and sounds?

Meaning

We can do this by first analysing our own responses, thoughts and emotions prompted by the material in the texts.

- Do we feel sad, angry, exalted, indifferent, excited or happy? Do we want to watch the texts again?
- How far do we feel convinced that the texts are 'truthful', relevant to us or meaningful? Are there elements to celebrate and enjoy?
- Do we think that these texts were made for another person or social group and their interests and values? Do we have a need to reject these texts and disagree with the way they have represented certain elements? Is there a problem with the wrong subject matter or is it more the treatment, the tone or the style of representation?

Messages and values

Second, we may look at the texts' *intended* meanings and analyse how they are constructed to produce explicit and implicit meanings.

Explicit message

We may not know what the author actually thought about the meaning of their texts, although we can often find out from interviews. The point is we can usually tell if we are *meant* to be shocked or amused. For example, in the film *Bruce Almighty* (2003) the main character criticises God, and this conflicts with our expectations. We know that we should laugh at the main character when he first discovers he has omnipotent powers, by the representation of the action on screen. We can tell that we are meant to laugh or cry at certain points of a film by the treatment of elements of the screenplay such as the dialogue, the actors' mannerisms and the music.

Explicitly, a film such as *Bruce Almighty* is a moral story about a character who has to learn to become a better person. Disillusioned newsman Bruce Nolan is highly critical of God, blaming Him for his disastrous life. God decides to give Bruce His powers and Bruce, who at first enjoys his omnipotent power, rapidly learns that with power comes responsibility for others. Eventually he learns that he also has to earn respect and love from his girlfriend and begins to take responsibility for his own life and actions as well.

Implicit message

The implicit message in the film is that we all have free will and we are free to choose to act in a positive or a negative way. The film teaches us that living positively will bring satisfaction whereas living negatively and blaming others for our problems will get us nowhere. As Bruce realises that being omnipotent is not as wonderful as it might appear to be, partly due to allowing others to have free will, he learns how his actions can affect others and learns about social responsibility.

Subtext

Does the text have a message about life, morality, society or social groups? Is there any attempt to smuggle in ideas that might be considered taboo or provocative in another culture or period of history? Does the film have anything to say about the attitudes, messages and values of contemporary society?

Consider, for instance, the film *Shrek 2* in which Shrek and Fiona go to visit her parents after the wedding. Much of the film is centred around the potion which transforms both Shrek and Fiona into typical hero and heroine. At the end they realise that beauty is only skin deep and they love their ogre realities more. Fiona cannot be won over by the handsome but shallow and greedy Prince Charming – despite the machinations of the Fairy Godmother. This message is the subtext. The viewer reads this but the characters in the film cannot.

Summary

While we have so far used the example of film as a way of talking about messages and values, the idea of the social context is true for the press, magazines, radio and sitcoms. In analysing the texts you should consider social themes in terms of:

- Gender
- Sexuality
- Race
- Age
- Class
- Disability
- Belief system.

Preparation

It is likely that your teacher will select the topic you are going to study, but you may be able to choose one or both of your specific texts to compare in terms of similarity and/or difference. This entails you having a full and detailed knowledge of these texts, and being able to provide a close detailed analysis of key elements and contexts, audiences and production.

Consumer and lifestyle magazines

Aims

The number of consumer and lifestyle magazines available to read increases every year as new magazines attempt to find a niche in this popular genre. For this unit, you need to study two of these magazines in detail and consider:

- how they are constructed (textual analysis)
- their content and how they target their audience
- how they reflect their audience's lifestyles and aspirations (contextual analysis).

As part of this, you need to be aware of the mechanisms by which such magazines identify, quantify and qualify their audience and the organisations which help them with this.

Objectives

As with the other topics in 2372, the main objective is **to develop the textual analysis skills to compare two texts in terms of what they represent**. It is advisable, therefore, to select two texts that offer the richest areas of **contrast** and **difference** for comparison.

A comment that is often made about answers to this question in the exam is that students have not always chosen the best magazines to compare. You need to choose two magazines which have some similarities but – more importantly – also have some differences. It's hard to write in much detail about differences between *Woman's Own* and *Bella*, for example. A better comparison would be *Woman's Own* and *Vogue*, because although they are both women's magazines, they target very different audiences and therefore offer different aspirations and make use of very different representations.

A good starting point when analysing a lifestyle magazine is to begin by thinking about the lifestyle it offers to its readers.

- What does it assume about the reader's tastes?
- What sort of products does it assume the reader buys?
- What aspirational lifestyle does it offer the reader?
- What does it assume about the reader's lifestyle in terms of material wealth, lifestyle, friends and relationships?

By beginning your analysis with a clear identification of the target audience and the lifestyle the magazine offers them, you are far better able to analyse the form of the magazine in terms of how it does this. This in turn will make your textual analysis, exploration of representations, and analysis of how the magazine is shaped by the marketplace and by cultural and social expectations much clearer. You may wish to select two titles from different niches (e.g. a women's magazine and a men's magazine) or you may wish to take two magazines that are separated, for instance, by class, as

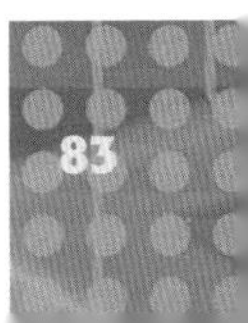

mentioned above. For example, you could compare *Vogue* with GQ magazine, both of which target an upmarket audience but different genders. Both magazines are owned by the Condé Nast publishing group.

ACTIVITIES

Research the layout of the magazine racks and the position of magazines in a large newsagent like WH Smith or a supermarket.

How many different types of magazine are available for teenagers?

How do these magazines break down between male and female?

Are any magazines unisex? (N.B. Are the music magazines unisex?)

Observe the layout and display of the shop's magazines and identify which type of magazines take up most space. Draw a plan to explain where the different groupings of magazine are placed; for example, are all the in-house WH Smith titles nearest the queue for the tills? Which magazines are the most prominent and accessible? How does the shop identify the different segments? Which magazines are on the middle shelf, which are on the top shelf, and which are tucked away on the bottom shelf?

Lifestyle magazines

Mode of address

The mode of address is the way the magazine 'speaks' to the reader. Depending on the vocabulary used, the style of writing and the use of punctuation such as exclamation marks, different magazines will have a different tone and manner – directly targeted at the primary audience. For example, a magazine aimed at teenage rap fans will have a very different mode of address to that of *Vogue*.

The mode of address goes beyond simply the words used, however, as it also puts the reader into a particular role. The mode of address in an upmarket, serious magazine is different to that in a comic, for example, and therefore the reader responds differently to the text. This can be due to the language used but also to the role expected of the reader. *Country Homes* creates its aspirational mode of address through pictures of glamorous upmarket houses and carefully posed owners. Its audience yearns to 'be like them', but is also very aware that they are not part of this world and can only admire from afar. This is another reason why the Society Report is so important in magazines such as *Tatler*, because it creates a sense of a glamorous world that the reader is expressly not part of, since they were not invited to the parties shown and do not know the people who attended. The Society Report generates the implicit message for the audience that by reading this magazine they will be brought a little closer to this world.

Baby glossies

An interesting comparison with the adult glossy magazines can come from the 'baby glossies': *ELLEgirl* (Emap) and *CosmoGIRL!* (National Magazines) are aimed at teenage girls. The National Magazines

Company's research shows that 94 per cent of teenagers buy a magazine every month. According to Datamonitor, they have increasing amounts of money to spend because of three trends: the average age of parenthood has gone up; there are more dual-income families; and parents have less time on their hands – and therefore more guilt. If you look at the front covers of these magazines, you will see that they promote a very consumerist lifestyle and the front cover image is clearly very aspirational, just as with mainstream women's magazines.

The strapline for *CosmoGIRL!* is 'for fun, fearless teens' and the brand promise and core buyer are very carefully defined by the publisher, National Magazines, primarily for the advertisers. Advertisers need to be able to identify quickly the core buyer of a magazine so they can target their products successfully. Equally, it is the products that appear in a magazine which construct much of the brand image of that magazine. Consumerism controls the content of the magazine as well as controlling which products are advertised – which in turn controls the content; and so it goes on.

CASE STUDY

CosmoGIRL!

Mission statement

To celebrate fun, glamour and a passion for life, and inspire teen girls to be the best they can possibly be.

Brand positioning

CosmoGIRL! addresses the issues that all teenage girls face today. Confident, sexy and inspiring, it reflects all that is exciting and challenging about being a teen girl, encouraging *CosmoGIRL!*s to achieve what they really want from life.

Brand proposition

The only brand that truly celebrates and inspires teenage girls' lives.

Brand promise

Glamorous, gorgeous and gutsy as well as frank and intimate, *CosmoGIRL!* celebrates being a teenage girl by recognising that teen girls today are stronger, braver and more exceptional than ever! *CosmoGIRL!* supports, encourages, congratulates, entertains, amuses, inspires and uplifts – helping *CosmoGIRL!*s to be the very best they can.

Brand values

Passion for life
Sexy
Glamorous

Intimate
Fearless
Empowering
Trusted
Fun
Vibrant
Supportive
One-stop
Interactive.

Core buyer

Aged between 12–17, *CosmoGIRL!*s are defined by attitude rather than demographic. Intelligent and inquisitive, the *CosmoGIRL!* is determined to succeed: at home, at school and in her relationships with her friends, family and boys. She wants to take full advantage of the many choices and opportunities open to her but understands that self-fulfilment comes from having fun, treating yourself and feeling good, as much as from working hard at school and material things. Boys, friends, family, music and shopping are an essential part of her life. She is part of the post-feminist generation who assume they have equal rights. She is growing up in a world that is getting progressively smaller and more accessible, so she is far less constrained by society's rules, physical boundaries or tradition than her predecessors. She will judge her success on her own terms.

(Source: http://www.natmags.co.uk/magazines/magazine.asp?id=20, March 2004)

Advertising

Magazine production costs are significantly higher than newspapers and production values are high – especially for monthly glossy magazines. Magazines therefore rely heavily on advertising revenue and this makes it even more important for a magazine to identify and target its core reader accurately, so advertisers will want to use the magazine as a way of reaching this specific audience. Display adverts can be 78 per cent of revenue for a magazine, so they are an important influence on its shape and content. This is also why magazine publishers take such care to define key brand values and core readership on their websites and in their advertisers' packs, along with their rate cards, to attract the right advertisers to their publication.

T3 magazine from Future Publishing promotes itself as:

> 'the world's leading technology magazine. It uses stunning photography and a powerful blend of news, reviews and features to bring its readers bang up-to-date with everything that's happening in the fast-paced world of consumer technology.
>
> Aimed at the style-conscious, technologically aware, early adopter, *T3* covers all that is practical, weird and astonishing in the arena of cutting-edge technology.
>
> A typical issue will contain hardware reviews, competitions, design and photographic features plus other regulars.' (Future Publishing, March 2005).

A key component of the magazine is therefore the reviews and the related adverts, all of which are targeted at selling a lifestyle associated with these sophisticated gadgets, rather than the functionality of the gadgets themselves.

Audience profiles

Before a magazine can be successfully launched into this busy marketplace, market research companies carefully research their audience, using a variety of qualitative and quantitative research methods to define the target audience very carefully. Remember, this is not only to make sure the content can be very closely defined but also to ensure the right advertisers are attracted and therefore the appropriate consumer values are defined.

For example, *Company* magazine, published by National Magazines, has identified that its core readership is aged 18-28 and ABC1. It positions itself:

> 'Fashionable and fresh, *Company* magazine is for young women who are going all-out to enjoy their freedom years: the exciting stage in a young woman's life when she's breaking free from the restrictions of her teens but isn't yet burdened by financial or family responsibilities – a time characterised by self-discovery, growing independence, experimentation, optimism and fun with a capital 'F'. *Company* magazine is honest, trusted and always takes her side; it champions every aspect of her life in a real and positive way ... *Company* magazine is the best friend you wish you had.'

It defines the values of the magazine (and therefore, by implication, those of the target reader) as 'Cheeky and sexy but never smutty; direct but never aggressive'. As with other magazines from the same institution, the website also defines the core buyer very clearly:

> 'She has a sense of real freedom. Although she is aware of the future and wants to be successful, she is determined to get the most out of life right now! She is seeking to be in control and wants to appear confident and assertive. She likes to be 'in the know' on personal, sexual and social issues and loves anything that is new, stylish, fun and fast-paced. Subconsciously, she is still searching for her own identify and trying to establish her own style – this is the time of her life when she really has the chance to experiment and grow. She needs guidance, but wants to be presented with choices rather than dictated to.'

Audiences and the appeal of lifestyle magazines

As you can see, this core buyer is defined in terms of her lifestyle. The consumer approach of the magazine is grounded in giving the reader the perception that she is a sexy, confident, stylish, fun and assertive reader who leads an exciting and independent lifestyle – the magazine sells the aspiration to this lifestyle to the average reader. In the same way, the front cover of a magazine such as *Vogue* presents an aspirational and glamorous model for the average reader to aspire to by buying the magazine. If the reader buys the magazine, reads the articles, buys the clothes and make-up featured in the magazine and goes to the places recommended in the magazine, then the reader will become more like this figure. Again, by buying the magazine the reader can buy the lifestyle to which she aspires.

ACTIVITIES

You are creating adverts for a new range of packet soups. How would you advertise the soup differently for carers reading *Woman's Own* and aspirers reading *Country Living*?

Now see if you can track a range of similar products across different niches of magazines and see how similar products are sold differently, to appeal to different lifestyle segmentations. Discuss your ideas with your partner and share them with the rest of the class.

Create a group wall chart showing what sort of products are advertised in different genres of magazines and how they are promoted in terms of lifestyle.

ACTIVITIES

Select two different magazines from within one category, preferably examples that you have never looked at before, in order to analyse their content. For example, you might consider looking at male/female magazines from the same publisher, or magazines for the same hobby from different publishers. Alternatively, choose two magazines where the audience is differentiated by age. Try to make sure different teams in your group cover most of the primary genres, so you can make comparisons across the different genres, as well as within them.

How many advertisements are there in each of the publications?

- Make notes on each advertisement and specify the fraction of page used
  - ¼ page, ½ page or full page.
- How many pages does the product advertising take up? What percentage of the total is this? Does this vary for different genres of magazine?
- How many pages do features take up?
- How many pages do the listings inserts for TV and radio etc. take up?
- How many pages do the smaller ads at the back of the magazine take up?

What types of advertisements are there; for example, perfume, charity appeal, computer game, furniture? How many of each type are there?

Create a block or pie chart to illustrate proportions of advertisements to other content.

How much space (pages) is devoted to:

- the editorial
- letters pages
- full-page articles?

Aspirations

An aspiration is a desire for something better. In our affluent American-influenced culture, this is very much focused on material goods – better clothes, food, entertainment, houses, cars etc. In other cultures, where the quality of a person's spiritual life is more important than their possessions, the aspirations of an audience are obviously different. In a capitalist culture like the UK's, it is an assumed part of society's shared values to produce and to consume more material goods and wealth, and this is obviously encouraged by government as well as industry, to ensure increased consumer spending.

One example of this is the number of property programmes that we can see on our televisions. Previously, the trend was for DIY programmes, which taught the audience to aspire to improve their home and live a more aspirational lifestyle. Now the emphasis is on bigger and better houses, and the latest property programmes are aimed at people who wish to buy two houses (*Relocation, Relocation, Relocation*) – a key aspirational goal for many – or those who are encouraged to buy a run-down house and do it up, to make a substantial profit (*Property Ladder*).

Another trend in TV programmes has been the documentaries featuring people giving up mundane reality and escaping to new lifestyles abroad (*Get a New Life*); rethinking their lives and eating habits to discover a thinner, more energetic inner person (*You Are What You Eat*); and the many programmes featuring plastic surgery and other means of looking younger (*10 Years Younger*).

Aspirational television and magazines are a fundamental aspect of our society now. This is also evidenced in the growing popularity of shopping channels such as QVC on cable and satellite, which offer a vast range of material possessions, all sold on lifestyle rather than practicality. With all of these programmes and magazines, the basic message being promoted is that happiness can be achieved by 'buying into' the lifestyle being offered. Even the 'escape' programmes focus on consumer values, because they feature families who wish to have a better standard of living by escaping, not those who reject capitalist society and material goods.

Consumerism

Critics of this focus on aspirational lifestyles point out that there are still many people in our society living below the breadline, for whom basic needs such as health, food, warmth and education are aspirational goals. If we compare the aspirational images which feature so predominately in glossy magazines with the appearance of starving children and adults in our newspapers and news bulletins, what does this reveal about the values of our society? Or can we combine this aspirational lifestyle with social awareness and a means of helping those who need it?

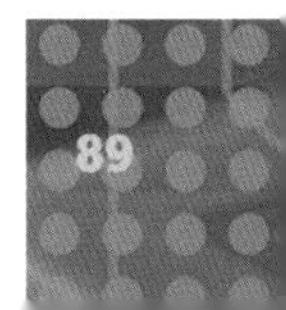

Consumerism might be viewed as excessive when it moves beyond practicality towards greed. After all, how many pairs of shoes does one person need? Logically, we can all make do with a single pair of shoes, yet the average *Vogue* reader will be continually receiving information to suggest that she should have many pairs of shoes, to match her mood, her outfit, the weather and the occasion. These values are continually promoted through lifestyle magazines.

Audience definitions

It may seem an obvious statement to make, but a definition of an audience depends on who is defining it. These might be:

- the publishing institution, who judge audience as circulation and readership figures – a constructed audience
- research bodies who analyse audience demographics, and those who look at audience values and audience identity
- advertisers, who segment audiences in terms of lifestyle and aspirations in order to sell products to them more successfully (adverts aim to sell the benefit of a product, not the features).

Market researchers continually try to define new ways for an audience to be segmented, because each time a new audience group is identified it opens up a new raft of opportunities for consumer and lifestyle advertising, magazines and promotions.

For example, a market research company might start to think about males, aged over 50, with no partner and with reasonable amounts of disposable income (money which they can spend on hobbies, interests and luxuries). If the market research company can identity particular ways in which this new audience group like to spend their money, such as frequent holidays, a niche begins to appear for a new magazine for the globetrotting 50-year-old single traveller, and advertisers have another specific lifestyle to promote to consumers.

Segmentation

Advertisers use their own categories of people to define audience groupings, in addition to standard demographic groupings of age, gender, race and location. One of the most common is to divide or segment an audience in terms of their attitudes and psychological character:

1. Succeeders
2. Aspirers
3. Carers
4. Achievers
5. Radicals
6. Traditionalists
7. Underachievers.

Given that advertisers try to sell lifestyles rather than products, they can therefore create different adverts for these different segments. Which of these lifestyle groups do you think advertisers are most likely to target for luxury consumer products? Which group are they least likely to target for most luxury consumer products? Why? What products might they advertise to this group?

Social values

Another way in which advertisers seek to segment audiences, in order to be able to sell to them more successfully, is to define them in terms of their attitudes to work and play. These groupings are specifically all about lifestyle and therefore attitudes to consumer products.

These segments are:

1. Traditionalists, who like to keep things the way they are.
2. Materialists, who like to own products now and are happy to pay later.
3. Hedonists, who play and spend hard now with no thought to later.
4. Post-materialists, who are prepared to wait and work hard to succeed later on.
5. Post-modernists, who want to play, own things now and be successful and secure later.

Forms and conventions: typical elements

All magazines have some elements in common, even if they are a listings magazine or a simple advertising vehicle. Common elements are:

- Advertising
- Advice columns
- Book adaptations
- Campaigns
- Competitions
- Contents page
- Covers
- Diaries
- Do-it-yourself features
- Fiction
- Horoscopes
- In our next issue
- Letters page
- Make-overs
- Merchandising
- Opinion columns
- Quizzes
- Reviews
- Strips (comic)
- Supplements
- Surveys.

ACTIVITIES

Choose two magazines and check how many of the typical elements shown above each magazine contains. Are there any different elements? What reasons do you think there are for these differences? How far do the magazines reflect/identify the season/month in which they are published? (You may well notice that women's magazines and decorating magazines are directly related to the month/season.) Why do you think this is?

Most brand name magazine titles are owned by a small number of companies. Indeed, sometimes the same publisher will own competing titles and use them to increase market share by forcing them to compete with each other. In the consumer sector, IPC Magazines remains the largest publisher, publishing *Essentials*, *Now*, *Country Life*, *Mizz*, *Woman's Own*, *NME*, *Rugby World* and many others. Reed Business Information is the leading business publisher. Other major companies include BBC Magazines, Future Publishing, Condé Nast, DC Thompson, Emap, G&J of the UK, H. Bauer, The National Magazine Company and Reader's Digest. HarperCollins is owned by News Corporation, which also owns the film company 20th Century Fox, as well as the newspapers *The Times* and *The Sun*.

A typical cover of a glossy mainstream leisure/lifestyle magazine shows what is inside and doesn't tend to put content on the front. However, some features it might have are:

- Plugs
- Issue number
- Cover price
- Main cover line
- Straplines
- Feature article photographs
- Main cover lines – 'sell-lines'
- Puffs
- Masthead
- Typeface
- Point sizes
- Bar code.

ACTIVITIES

Consider the unique selling point of the magazines you have selected. Analyse the:

- images and words on the cover
- editorial
- letters page.

Make sure you cover the following concepts:

- messages and values
- forms and conventions
- layout and design.

ACTIVITIES

Analyse these two front covers in terms of the images and words on the page, the layout and branding.

Consider how these elements contribute to the messages and values being communicated to the reader, the conventions being employed and the ideologies and expectations being constructed for the readers by these two front covers.

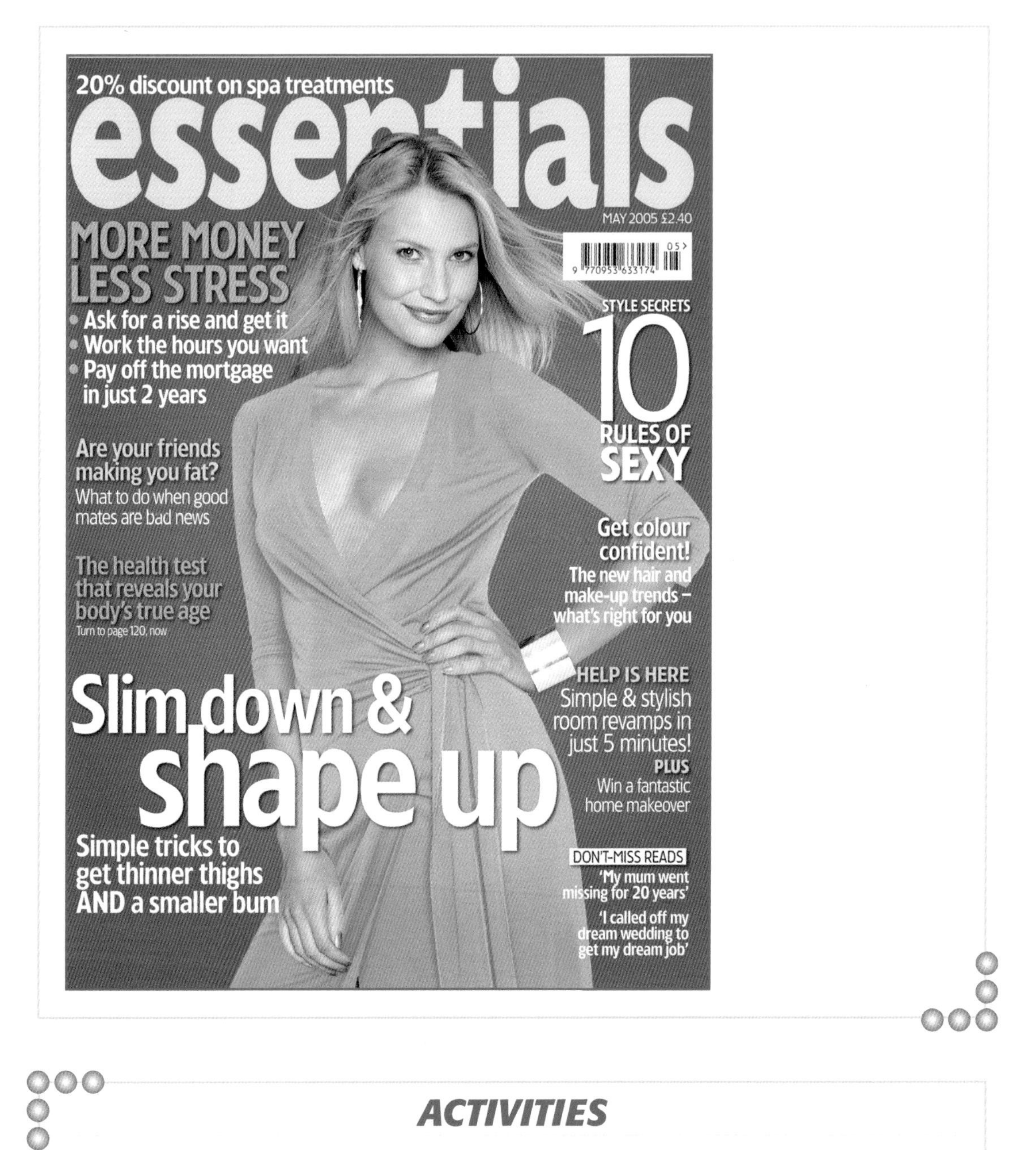

ACTIVITIES

Compare the covers and content list of two different consumer or lifestyle magazines.

What are the main elements of the cover lines?

How do they define the age of their audience?

Denotate and connotate the images and printed text on the front cover.

What is the difference between the two magazines?

DISCUSSION

Which magazines do you or your family purchase?

Are there any magazines that everybody reads? Are there magazines which only one person reads? What magazines do other family members read secretly? Why do you think this is?

Construct a survey of ten people in a particular group, for example, girls or boys aged 11–14 or girls or boys aged 14–19. Find out what magazines they like and why. Is there a common response? Are there any big differences in response? Can you segment this audience in any other ways to account for differences?

ACTIVITIES

Study a range of magazines targeted at teenagers aged 11–19 and young adults aged 15–24.

Discuss the range and variety of interest in the content of these magazines for the audience of each magazine. Consider the:

front cover (images, headings, puffs, straplines and price)

contents page

advertisements.

CASE STUDY

Compare the ways in which consumerism is represented as attractive and appealing to the target audience of your two chosen magazines.

If you were writing in response to this question in the exam, you would obviously refer to the whole edition you had studied of each magazine and the research you had undertaken about the magazines. We are just going to refer to the front covers of the two magazines here, because you cannot see their inside pages.

Obviously, your analysis needs to stem from a good understanding of what the target audience for your magazines is and how the institution constructs the core reader. This will help you to analyse the audience in terms of their aspirations and lifestyle and hence consider how the magazines either lead these aspirations or fulfil demands from the audience.

It is important that you choose two appropriate publications for this question – here we have used *Harpers & Queen* and *Esquire* for comparison. Both are considered 'upmarket' titles but target different markets in terms of gender. If we compare how National Magazines (the company which produces both magazines) defines this market, we can see the core values they assume in this market.

Harpers & Queen

Core buyer

Smart, upmarket, sophisticated women AB(C1), 30+, who are affluent, well-travelled, cultured, image-conscious and socially active. Set apart by their breadth of vision, seeking inspiration and information, they read *Harpers & Queen* to keep in touch with the very latest international trends, issues and personalities. Acquisitive but highly selective, with the money to match their aspirations, *Harpers & Queen* buyers insist upon quality, style and value in the brands they choose to buy.

Brand universe

The *Harpers & Queen* brand universe includes all stylish, sophisticated individuals who want to keep in touch with the very latest international trends, issues and personalities. Acquisitive but highly selective, with the money to match their aspirations, they insist upon quality, style and value in the brands they choose to buy.

(Source: National Magazines website, April 2004)

1. **So the magazine defines the target audience not only as individuals but also in terms of their universe or lifestyle. What does this suggest about how the magazine might seek to make consumerism appealing to this audience?**
2. **What do these two descriptions reveal about values and attitudes espoused by the magazine?**
3. **What sort of adjectives are used in these descriptions? Why?**
4. **How do these make consumerism attractive and appealing?**

These descriptions are primarily written to attract advertisers to advertise in the publication. What sort of advertisers would this description appeal to? What does this suggest about consumerism in relation to this audience and these advertisers?

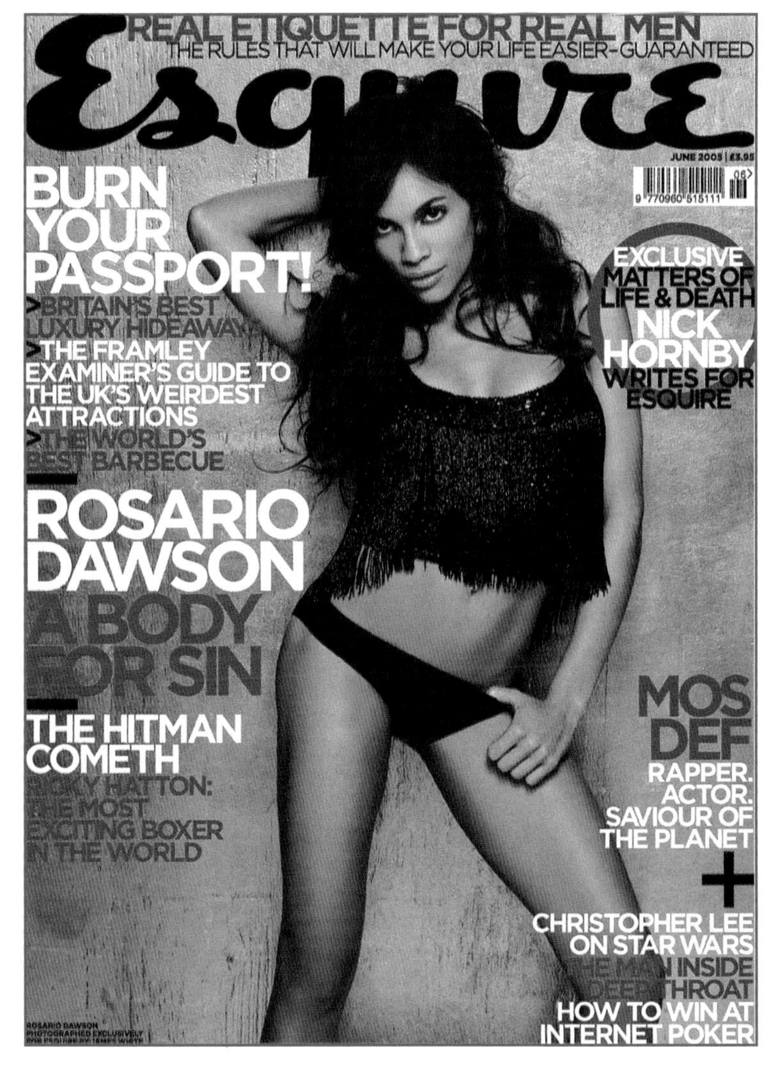

Esquire

Core buyer

Likely to be 28-40, he has commitments to his job, partner and home. He's well educated, career-minded and successful, and has reached a stage in his life where he is confident about who he is, what he wants and where he is going.

He buys *Esquire* to be entertained by sport, films, music, fashion, women, gadgets and personalities. He believes quality and style that reflect his individual tastes are more important to him than the latest trends.

Likely to be bored with the tone and content of the more laddish and immature titles, he feels *Esquire* offers a better balance which is more relevant to his current values, lifestyle and interests.

(Source: National Magazines website, April 2004)

1. **In what different ways is this audience described?**
2. **What does this description suggest about values and attitudes in the magazine?**
3. **How do the descriptions make consumerism attractive and appealing? Does this seem typical for this market?**

4. **In what ways is this magazine aspirational?**
5. **Why do you think that National Magazines takes care to define the *Harpers & Queen* core universe so carefully, in addition to the core buyer, whereas it only defines the core buyer for *Esquire*? (Hint – which one competes in a more congested advertising marketplace?)**

Once you have considered the question in relation to the target audience, you can consider other aspects of the publications:

Advertisers

It is a good idea to make a detailed list of the advertisers and advertisements in each magazine in order to compare them.

1. **What sorts of product are advertised in each publication? How are they presented and described?**
2. **Are there any products that are advertised in both magazines? How can you account for this in terms of consumerism and lifestyle?**
3. **How do these adverts make consumerism attractive and appealing?**

Content

Look closely at the content of the magazines and see if you can categorise the articles in them.

1. **How many articles are about objects to buy or own (e.g. product testing, reviews of new products, or articles about products to make your lifestyle better). What does this reveal about consumerist attitudes in the magazine? How do the two magazines compare? What does this reveal?**
2. **What about the adverts on the back covers of each magazine? How do they relate to brand profile, target audience and consumerist values? Are they typical of the magazine? Why do advertisers pay extra for advertising on the back cover of the magazine?**
3. **Study the editorial of each magazine carefully. How do the language and style of each reflect the consumerist lifestyle being promoted in the magazine? How do they encourage the aspirational values in the audience?**
4. **In what ways do these various aspects of the content make consumerism attractive and appealing?**

Front covers

Look closely at the front cover of each magazine.

1. **How does the central image used both encourage the aspirational values of the core buyer, make these seem attainable, and fit the brand image of the magazine?**

2. How many of the cover lines are product-related? Why is this?

3. How many create a sense of aspiring to a lifestyle? Why is this?

4. What other signs on the covers suggest this consumerist, aspirational lifestyle?

5. How do these covers make consumerism seem attractive and appealing?

Once you have thought about all these aspects of the magazines, you can construct your answer to the question at the beginning of this case study. You will be able to write in detail about the particular editions you have studied. You will be able to demonstrate that you know something about the target audience and aspirational goals of each magazine, and in particular you will be able to write in depth about the consumer values promoted by each magazine and how they relate to the target audience.

Remember that for this question the key was to identify ways in which the magazines make consumerism seem attractive and appealing, so that should be central to your answer. When you are in the exam, it is very important to read the question carefully and ensure you structure your answer to fit that particular question. Every year, examiners comment about the number of candidates who write very good answers but who write them as if a different question had been set – often the one from the previous session which they have studied together in class. So, although such candidates write very well, their answer does not obtain such good marks because it is not focused on the question that has been asked.

Part Four

Celebrity and the tabloid press

Aims

This section is about the relationship between celebrities and the tabloid press. The concept of 'celebrity' is becoming increasingly important in our society, as more and more people are turned into celebrities. This has been partly encouraged by the growth of 'reality TV' from *Big Brother* onwards, which takes ordinary people and subjects them to intense scrutiny as part of a game show for a period of time. Once people have appeared in these programmes for a length of time, they gain celebrity status simply because the audience feels they 'know' the person through having watched them on the television so often. Whereas celebrity status was once rare, and most of those who were considered celebrities had worked very hard to attain that position, now even brief television exposure results in celebrity status, and the number of people claiming celebrity status is increasing.

It is not just reality game show contestants that become celebrities, but also the many presenters of programmes on various cable and satellite channels, as well as those celebrities who are famous simply for being famous, such as Tara Palmer Tomkinson. Television may produce these celebrities, but it is often the newspapers that play an integral part in maintaining or destroying that status. In this topic we consider the nature of the relationship between the tabloids and these celebrities, and the representations that are maintained or manipulated by that relationship.

While you are studying this section, you should select two tabloids which you can study in detail. In particular, you should make a habit of reading each of these tabloids every day (some are easily

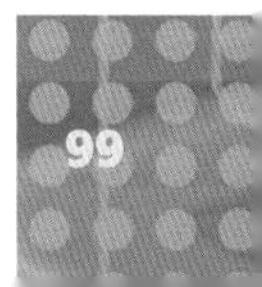

available on the Internet so you don't need to buy a copy every day). Keep a copy of relevant articles and images which will help you with primary source material for your study. Use these articles and images as reference material when you are working through these activities. It is a good idea to get into the habit of skimming the front pages of the tabloids in newsagents every day. This is the best way to see what stories are breaking and also to see where a story pans across different papers – possibly with a different spin on the story in different newspapers, depending on their allegiances.

As with the other topics for this unit, your research and writing will need to be grounded in detailed analysis of the representations of particular celebrities. You will also need to demonstrate an understanding of the tabloid press and how these celebrities are represented within the papers.

Definitions of celebrity

A celebrity is generally considered to be someone who is well known beyond their normal circle of friends and acquaintances, and in today's media age is defined as being someone whose life and activities are reported in the news.

Previously, celebrities were considered to be very famous people such as royalty and very successful music stars but, as mentioned above, contemporary society bestows celebrity status on a far wider range of people. Celebrity status now extends across many types of people. Well-known politicians are now celebrities and it is often said that modern elections are fought on the basis of celebrity and the personality of the party leaders, rather than the policies of the parties. If you think back to the election in 2005, you may remember that Charles Kennedy, the leader of the Liberal Democrat party, had his first child while campaigning for the election. He used his celebrity status and the media attention this generated to try and get maximum media 'exposure' as a happy dad, in the hope that this would gain him votes due to audience familiarity. Tony Blair took great care to be photographed with his family as often as possible, to demonstrate his family values and down-to-earth nature – again, communicating an image through the media rather than campaigning on policies.

The rise of celebrity culture

Celebrity culture is predominant in the media, both in the US and the UK. The tabloids have 'celebrity news' sections and search out celebrity news daily. As our culture has become more visual, so celebrity news has become increasingly important, because it allows for more images in the news and fewer stories. An important starting point for this topic is to consider what started this rise.

When celebrity status was less common, newspapers tended to regard themselves as above reporting scandal. Instead, they considered that their role was to report news and have political influence over their readers, who generally agreed with the political stance of the newspaper they chose to read.

The *Sun* was the first of the tabloids to realise that the future of newspapers was in less serious news and more celebrity gossip etc., and its formula of 'sex, sensation and sport' was very successful. Of course, as the other tabloids began to focus on similar stories, the demand for content went up and celebrity culture started to grow.

However, we cannot simply assume that this alone caused the growth in celebrity culture. PR consultants such as Max Clifford were beginning to promote their clients hard in the news, based on the belief that any kind of media exposure was better than none. Celebrities (and especially 'wannabe celebrities') were only too happy to be snapped leaving nightclubs or dating other celebrities.

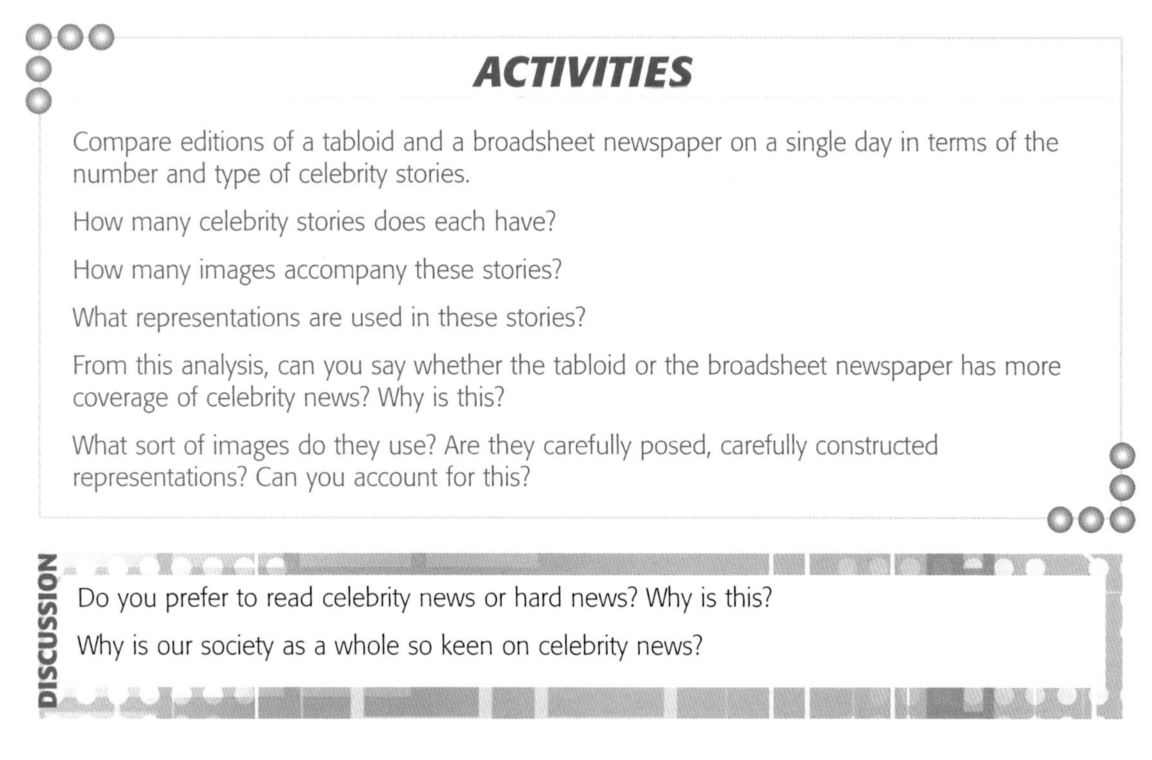

ACTIVITIES

Compare editions of a tabloid and a broadsheet newspaper on a single day in terms of the number and type of celebrity stories.

How many celebrity stories does each have?

How many images accompany these stories?

What representations are used in these stories?

From this analysis, can you say whether the tabloid or the broadsheet newspaper has more coverage of celebrity news? Why is this?

What sort of images do they use? Are they carefully posed, carefully constructed representations? Can you account for this?

DISCUSSION

Do you prefer to read celebrity news or hard news? Why is this?

Why is our society as a whole so keen on celebrity news?

The role of the paparazzi

Along with the increasing number of celebrities and PR agencies seeking exposure for their clients came the opportunities for 'unposed' photos and scandal stories featuring these celebrities. The tabloids quickly realised that these stories appealed to their readers far more, and celebrity news increased in volume and (arguably) decreased in quality. For example, 'kiss and tell' stories such as 'My night of passion with a premier league football team' soon became popular. With these stories came the paparazzi photographers – freelance photographers who earned their living by taking the photos which celebrities did not want taken, such as the pictures of Princess Diana and her lover James Hewitt, or the pictures of Michael Jackson dangling his baby son over a hotel balcony.

A list and Z list celebrities

As we said at the beginning, in recent years, celebrity status has become easier to achieve. Monica Lewinsky became famous because of a scandal (her 'non-affair' with Bill Clinton), while Jade Goody became famous for being an unsuccessful contestant on *Big Brother*. Both became big name celebrities very easily and such celebrities are usually very keen to maintain or increase their celebrity status, knowing that this will be profitable for them.

Following on from the success of *Big Brother* in making celebrities out of ordinary people with no claim to fame, fading or obscure celebrities quickly realised that this kind of reality exposure was a good way to become really well known to an audience and therefore raise their celebrity profile. While the primary aim of *Celebrity Big Brother* was to raise money for charity, a bonus for those celebrities that took part was that their celebrity status increased after the programme.

More recent programmes have clearly been used by less well-known celebrities (often those on the fringes of celebrity culture, sometimes called 'Z list' celebrities) to bolster their careers. Well known examples include Peter Andre in *I'm a Celebrity, Get Me Out of Here!*, who not only managed to kick-start his celebrity status again by being in the programme and getting together with Jordan (Katie Price), but also managed to relaunch his pop career by writing a song in the jungle which he recorded once he came out, called 'Insania'.

Celebrity status

The behaviour of celebrities is an important question to consider within this topic. Historically, celebrities were high-status figures such as royalty. With celebrity status was deemed to come expectations about behaviour and so forth. Members of the royal family, for example, were expected to have high moral standards and to behave with decorum.

Some people have put the change in this status down to particular events, such as the infamous *It's a Royal Knockout* in the 1980s, where the younger royals were seen on television behaving in a very 'unroyal' way. Others have suggested that the decline came with the collapse of the marriage of Prince Charles and Princess Diana, with the intense media coverage of their marriage – made more intense by Diana's manipulation of the press and the way she used the newspapers to fight Prince Charles.

Others have suggested it is down to the work of PR consultants such as Max Clifford, who work so hard to get maximum exposure for their clients at all times. Another school of thought suggests that it is the rise of reality television that created this new type of celebrity, resulting in increased interest and hence increased exposure.

DISCUSSION

How far is each element responsible for the creation of this new celebrity culture?

The relationship between celebrities and the tabloid press

Clearly, the relationship between celebrities and the tabloid press is very different in contemporary society from how it was in the past, and a lot less sympathetic. What you need to think about in this topic is the extent to which either side has control of the relationship. Do the newspapers have control because they can print anything and the celebrities must just accept this exposure? Or do various celebrities seek to use and control the media, in order to get the exposure they wish?

ACTIVITIES

Compare the sorts of stories to be found in *Hello!* magazine with the newspapers you analysed earlier.

Are there any stories about the same celebrities?

Are they represented in the same ways?

Would you say the stories in *Hello!* or those in the newspapers are more positive? Why is this?

Where celebrities are represented negatively in the newspapers, is this because the newspaper is operating an implicit moral code about their behaviour? Account for your answer here.

Contextual analysis

Newspaper circulation

Newspapers have been selling progressively fewer copies every day since the 1970s. As new forms of media provide instant, visual news-gathering, so the daily newspaper has gone into decline. To find out about a 'breaking news story' people now expect to tune in to a 24-hour television news channel, instantly find the story on the Internet or receive the news broadcast on their PDA or SmartPhone. By the time the news reaches the newspaper the following day, it is 'old' news and therefore less interesting.

Given this, the tabloids realised that they would have to reinvent themselves to maintain and attract more readers. And so, rather than concentrating on giving accurate hard news every day, they began to branch out. We have already mentioned the successful *Sun* formula of sex, sensation and sport, and this strategy of celebrity news, gossip, wider interests and in-depth features has helped maintain sales for the tabloids.

Tabloid newspapers

These include the *Sun*, the *Star*, the *News Of the World* and the *Mirror*. A tabloid newspaper is usually A3 in size, with a large masthead at the top of the page. The popular tabloids gained the nickname 'red tops' because this masthead is usually red.

Most of the tabloids use more images than writing on the majority of their pages. The front page in particular will usually have a single lead article which will have a very large picture and a couple of paragraphs of a story to lead into the rest of the paper. There is usually at least one celebrity story on the front cover to attract an audience.

The content of a tabloid newspaper might include:

- Special offers
- In-depth features
- Celebrity news

- Letters page and editor's comments
- Gossip columns
- Sports coverage
- Television and radio listings
- Crosswords, horoscopes and cartoons.

ACTIVITIES

Make a table identifying the content of both the tabloids you have been researching.

What conclusions can you draw about the type of content of most tabloids?

How important is celebrity news to this mixture?

Would the celebrity news be as attractive to audiences without pictures? Can you account for this?

How much coverage is fair?

The tension in the relationship between the newspapers and the celebrities comes from the debate around how much and what sort of coverage is deemed appropriate. Celebrities argue that they have the right to be photographed and reported only when they choose to be public and that they have the right to remain private the rest of the time. The newspapers argue that since celebrities know the price of fame, they must accept that privacy is not possible for those who are famous and they can be photographed or watched at any time. They argue that the celebrities are only too happy to use the media to build their careers and get exposure when they want it, and that they must therefore accept media coverage the rest of the time as well.

A useful case in point occurred recently when the former nanny to David and Victoria Beckham sold her story to the *News Of the World* about what life was really like at 'Beckingham Palace' and the relationship between David and Victoria. Furious with her revelations, the Beckhams fought to get a court order banning the story, arguing that it was an invasion of their privacy and not true. The judge rejected their case, telling them that because they were such arch media manipulators when it suited them, they must expect this kind of coverage as well and they did not have the right to control all media coverage of their lives.

The following case study contains an article from *The Observer* newspaper which appeared the following week. It contains some important points about the relationship between celebrities and the tabloid press, which you may like to consider for this topic.

CASE STUDY

Putting the boot into Posh and Becks Inc

(Source: Peter Preston, *The Observer*, 1 May 2005)

So, that old chestnut pops yet again into the fire. What is the 'public interest'? Where does it lie when (say) an ex-nanny slops a bilious bibful about the supposedly screaming, straying Beckhams and nets £250,000 or more from the News of the Screws (less Max Clifford's commission)?

For once, the privacy lawyers can be put to one side for a moment. For once, because our courts said 'publish and be damned' rather than 'injunct and be silenced', you, the reader, also have a chance to play juror in the celebrity court of public opinion.

Let's take our core definition from the Press Complaints Commission's own code, the one that all papers (including the Screws) pledge allegiance to. Were Posh and Becks involved in a 'crime' or 'threat to public health'? No way. The clause that matters here is the one about 'preventing the public from being misled by an action or statement of an individual or organisation'.

That obviously covers Whitehall whistleblowers incensed about government figures they think are phoney. It also covers whistle-tooting private employees distressed by bad or hypocritical behaviour – the supposedly beneficent company paying slave wages, the celebrity chef on a secret Atkins diet and so on. But where does the job of preventing you from being misled run out?

Our courts, so far as they have a settled view on privacy and confidentiality (which they don't), broadly think that insider-generated stuff about Mary Archer's facelift or Naomi Campbell's temper does not rip aside a veil of any importance. You can't be seriously misled by nips, tucks and tantrums. But is that quite the case with Brand Beckham?

Call morality correspondent-in-chief, Melanie Phillips from the *Daily Mail*: 'What Mr Justice Langley was effectively saying is that people can't have their cake and eat it – especially when the cake happens to be a vastly lucrative one . . . for if you look at the titillating details of Ms Gibson's allegations, the essence of what she's saying is that the Beckhams have made a mint out of an enormous public lie they have assiduously created'.

In short, we're dealing with Posh Promotions Inc. here, not human beings in need of a little peace. And, by chance, the cover story in last week's *OK!* seems to make her point precisely – 'David and Victoria, World Exclusive. She is My Life'. Featuring the pair in Paris celebrating Posh's birthday, a £3,000 a night Coco Chanel suite at the Ritz, a 'sumptuous dinner at L'Arpege' and enough Dolce & Gabbana to fill three pages.

Is this a romantic or a commercial break? It's certainly overloaded with conspicuous adoration: 'I love my wife very much.' And are the couple's three children off-limits in full Tony Blair mode? No, Victoria prattles away about Brooklyn, Romeo and Cruz without pausing to draw breath. Brooklyn loves hip-hop apparently, just like his mum, whose newly designed collection of clothes for Adidas 'was inspired by the hip-hop world'. Coincidences don't come more gallumphing than that.

Of course there are countervailing arguments. Philip Hensher in *The Independent* reckons that 'simply because someone has said "yes" to *Hello!* in the past doesn't imply that they have no subsequent right to say "no" to complete invasion'. *The Guardian* worries about a moment when nannies are replaced by planted newspaper snitches.

As usual Clifford wins both ways: 'The biggest part of my job is stopping stories. I've had so many phone calls in the last few days from major stars and former clients who are genuinely worried now. Suddenly, their confidentiality is open to question.'

And the final decision – as I have said – comes right back to you, the reader. Eighty-five thousand extra punters, many of them ABC1s full of education and curiosity, bought the *News Of the World* last Sunday – while the *Mail* and the *Express* both dropped 100,000 plus. Nanny Gibson pocketed enough loot to keep her in Adidas or Dolce & Gabbana for a decade (and began hawking second rights). Meanwhile, in a tat-for-tit retaliatory strike, her 'ex-pal Fiona' tells *Mirror* readers that she's a 'greedy, sex-mad schemer'.

Becks is still chatting away to Real Madrid press conferences and Richard Desmond's finest, revealing that: 'I've had offers from Hollywood to make a film about my life. At the moment I don't think so, but who knows? I do see myself in a film such as *Gladiator* or *Braveheart*.'

You couldn't quite make it up – and you can, perhaps, see why Mr Justice Langley and then Mr Justice Eady declined to stop the Screws printing (or re-printing). What was there left to defend in the public domain? The familiar dividing line in these matters distinguishes between public interest and what interests the public. It could just be that the Beckhams, making and spending their millions, have finally wiped away that line – and turned two distinct interests into one monster marketing mash beyond the reach of any of my or their learned friends.

ACTIVITIES

Do you agree with this judgement? Why?

How much right to privacy do you think the Beckhams should have?

Are there any areas of people's lives that should not be reported in the newspapers?

Textual analysis exemplar

Compare how the representation of celebrities in your two chosen tabloid newspapers demonstrates a mutual dependence between the press and celebrities.

Obviously, when you are writing in response to the exam question you will write in detail about the two tabloid newspapers you have been studying. You may find it helpful to use two complete editions of the newspapers and analyse these in detail, or you may wish to track certain stories across several days to see how the coverage changes and how different tabloids treat the same story. Either way, the most important thing is that you have enough detailed evidence to give specific examples to support your argument in your answer.

We cannot reproduce a whole series of articles or even whole editions, so comments are limited to the pages shown here. Remember that you will need a broader range of material for the examination.

Design

- Masthead to signify newspaper institution.
- Red to stand out.
- Main headline with few words, sub-headline and a couple of paragraphs of story to lead inside.
- Sans serif font to attract attention.
- Large letters to stand out – especially with red in the headline and articles to link with masthead.

DAILY Mirror

Saturday April 30 2005

MAKEPOVERTYHISTORY 50p

A date with Two Jags..

SEE PAGES 14 & 15

FREE 50 Summer bulbs for EVERY reader

SEE PAGE 22

JESSIE JILTS LOVER

.. by fax from her lawyers

By FIONA CUMMINS

EXCLUSIVE

EASTENDER Jessie Wallace yesterday dumped her fiancé fireman Dave Morgan by fax.

Jessie, 33, sent the message from her lawyers' office after Dave, dad of her baby girl, secretly tried to sell their story. Dave, 29, who has always won her back before, is "devastated". Jessie told friends: "This time it's final."

FULL STORY: PAGES 4&5

WALK OUT: Jessie leaves her home yesterday

Layout

- Use of WOB (white on black) for main story headline – with red in *Mirror* story for emphasis.
- Main story always on bottom half of page – usually text on one side and image on the other.
- Generally one main story and two other items on front page, such as other stories, free gifts or competitions.
- Balance of large image, smaller images and limited text on page to attract audience.

Content

- Language shocking and aggressive.
- Use of bracketed phrase on *Sun* front page to heighten the impact of the headline.

- Both stories start with 'Jessie' because that's the primary interest for the audience.
- Celebrity news used as a hook for audience for both papers – no hard news or serious stories.
- *Sun* also uses sport on the front page to attract audience.

THE Sun 30p

Monday, May 9, 2005 30p www.thesun.co.uk

WHY I HAD TO HAVE GAV

by Charlotte Church

INTERVIEW & AMAZING PICTURES: PAGES 4 & 5

WIGAN IN THE PREMIERSHIP!

SUPER goals BLUE

PLUS all the other ups and downs in 39 pages of Sport

Jessie Wallace blasts lover

YOU EVIL LOWLIFE PARASITE

(And they're the words we CAN print)

EXCLUSIVE

By VICTORIA NEWTON and SARA NATHAN

FURIOUS EastEnders star Jessie Wallace last night branded her ex-fiancé an evil, lowlife parasite.

Jessie, 33, laid into Dave Morgan for selling secrets about her.

She blurted out her feelings to pals in a rant worthy of TV character Kat, and said: "He is a parasite who sponged off me. It's sick, evil and lowlife and I hate him for it."

Morgan, 29, claimed Jessie was a boozer who craved kinky sex.

A friend of the star said: "She is devastated by his betrayal."

Full story – Page Nine

Images

- *Sun* shows publicity picture of glamorous Jessie whereas *Mirror* uses 'snapshot' – both suggest power and determination
- Charlotte Church snapped getting out of a swimming pool in an action shot which is less than flattering – sense of media intruding on her life?

Representations

- Jessie Wallace shown as aggressive in both stories – gives a sense that she won't be mucked around (has she released this story to the papers?)
- Powerful image in *Sun* – looking down in challenge.
- Representation of Charlotte Church less flattering and sexual innuendoes to story to attract readers.
- Language very firm – 'Jessie jilts lover' (typical alliteration for headline) and a sense that she has given this story to the papers because she is feeling vindictive (NB. the following week, articles by her ex-lover were published, accusing her of being a drunk and violent toward him). Both parties are using the press to fight their battles over their daughter while they are separating.

ACTIVITIES

This is not the first time that a celebrity couple have separated and used the media to fight in public – Kerry and Brian MacFadden are another recent example.

What other examples can you think of?

Do you agree that celebrity couples should use the media in this way in their battles?

Do you agree that the media should find out what is happening in their relationships and report this?

What (if any) right to privacy do you feel celebrities should have at these times?

Do you like to read the celebrity news? Why? Do your answers here conflict with your answers to the last few questions?

Part Five

Music culture and radio

Aims

For this case study area the key word to focus on is 'culture' and as a term it may seem obvious. We are all familiar with 'mainstream' radio such as Radio 1 or Capital Radio – but have you stopped to think about whether all audiences are catered for by these stations, or indeed have you looked at the range of stations that broadcast purely one particular music type, now that the legislation has been relaxed?

Case study question

An example of the type of question you might have to answer in the exam is shown below. As you work through the activities that follow, you will be making notes that will help you answer this question.

- Compare how the music culture represented in your two chosen radio stations/programmes targets its audience.

Later in the section we will look at a case study which compares a programme on a minority music station with the approach taken on a national BBC station: Energy Mix (an Internet-only dance radio station broadcasting from London) and BBC – 1Xtra (the digital BBC radio station dedicated to black music).

Representation of music culture

In dealing with the key issues of representation, messages and values, discussion on this topic can be divided into three areas:

- Cultural appeal
- Broadcasting strategy
- Radio as institution.

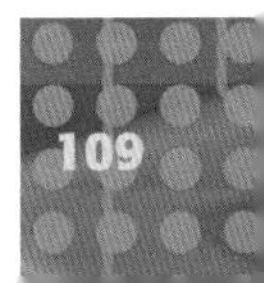

These discussion areas would include consideration of presenters, music type, accessibility (radio, DAB, Internet), format, scheduling, finance, audiences, jingles, advertising, discourse, key moments (textual analysis) and audience responses.

Identifying the audience

Radio is what is known as an 'intimate' medium because it addresses each listener as an individual. Radio is often used as 'background noise' while we are doing other things. We might be in the car, at work or school, studying or getting ready to go out, but the key factor is that we are doing something else and our attention is not on the radio. In the case of music stations, we usually identify a station by music type first and then decide if we like the content and delivery.

When we are searching for a station to listen to, we may not immediately be able to identify the name of the station we find, yet we will quickly be able to establish the genre of the station/programme and assess whether we are likely to be in the target audience. For a music programme especially, we will quickly identify whether we are in the target audience for the music itself. Indeed, when we find a station we are familiar with 'by accident', we can almost always tell which station it is without needing to wait for the 'ident'. An ident is a jingle or phrase used as a 'signifier' to identify the programme or station.

We quickly learn to interpret the use of codes and conventions to identify the type of radio station and hence the type of music we can expect, if not the actual station.

A significant advantage of radio advertising for potential advertisers is, therefore, that the audience can be seen as 'narrowcast'. Advertisers can be sure of maximum exposure to the target audience, unlike most 'blanket' advertising which has a lower hit rate since it cannot be so explicitly targeted. A commercial radio station needs to ensure it is broadcasting to a niche audience which is interested in the products advertised, as well as ensuring it appeals to advertisers. It also needs to be sure there is a market for its particular type of music culture in the area in which it broadcasts.

The four main codes of radio

In *Understanding Radio* (London; Methuen 1986) Andrew Crisell defines the main codes of radio as:

- Words
- Music
- Sounds
- Silence.

He argues that all the signs in radio are sound-based and thus the combination of these four signs and the manipulation/use of time is the way to deconstruct a radio programme. He suggests that each of these four codes can be treated as a sign and deconstructed, just as we do with visual signs. By listening to the combination of the use of these four codes over time during a programme, we can deconstruct the programme effectively and draw conclusions not only about the style and format of what we are listening to, but also its form and function. This means we can also draw conclusions about the target audience and the institutional factors which influence the chosen broadcast.

ACTIVITIES

Listen to the 'breakfast show' on at least three different radio stations. Try to ensure that one of the stations is national, one local and that at least one of the programmes is one which you are not familiar with.

Using the factors and codes given above, try to deconstruct each of these programmes. Look at the way the programme establishes its identity, how it defines and categorises the target audience, and how it defines and conforms to the identity of the station which presents the programme.

How different are each of these breakfast shows?

Do you feel that the form and style of the programme match the music played (if appropriate)?

Does this surprise you?

Why is this?

Is this significant in how audiences are represented on radio?

Messages and values

As you will have read in Section 2, the concept of **representation** refers to the meanings in the media text that convey messages and values about people, places, events and ideas. All media texts contain ideas about society's values and belief systems. For example, media texts represent and reproduce ideas about a society's morals, cultures, religions, laws and social attitudes. Target audiences are the primary audience for a particular text. A target audience may be wide or narrow but every media text is targeted at a particular audience. A niche audience is a small audience – which is an audience identifiable through one particular interest or cultural context rather than the 'mass' audiences at which many mainstream texts are targeted. Many music radio stations can be considered as niche stations because their audiences are small, but these audiences are often very committed, listening a large proportion of the time.

ACTIVITIES

Select a programme on Radio 6 to listen to. Record it and answer these questions.

How would you define the target audience of this programme?

Is this a wide audience? Why is this?

Now choose a programme from your local independent radio station (ideally one broadcast at a similar time of day) and do the same.

What differences do you notice in the target audiences?

Account for these differences.

When you have done this, see if you can identify the ways in which each programme targets its audience – you might want to consider scheduling, use of music, presenters, vocabulary, use of background sound/other people, structure, content and presentation.

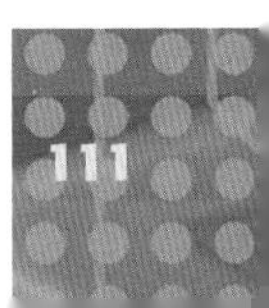

Radio and target audiences

Key criteria define niche groups and can be explicitly identified and exploited by radio institutions. How do we know into what groups the audience are placed? In other words, what techniques are used to establish, define and represent the audience on air? What techniques are used to establish, define and represent the music? What links are there between the music and the audience? Can you account for this?

The main issues in representation of music culture across various radio stations are reflected in the themes of shared cultural values, community and identity.

ACTIVITIES

Study any music-based radio programme. Identify the language used in the programme:

How much of the language implies that the audience are already members of a community?

How much of the language is specific?

Who uses this language – single presenters, joint presenters, audience members ringing in? What does this tell us about the programme?

How can this identity be sustained? What methods are used to 'hook' the audience into returning?

Textual analysis and representation

In order to attract an audience, a music programme must establish the type of music and therefore the cultural expectations for that programme or station in a variety of ways for an audience. This can be done through listening to the type of music being played but also by listening to the presenter(s). Other factors help construct this cultural identity as well – for example, the website for a station or programme or adverts for the programme will also seek to reflect this culture visually. You should try to collect any examples of visual representations for your chosen programmes/stations that you can, as well as recording programmes or sections to help you analyse the cultural context in detail.

ACTIVITIES

With reference to your two programmes/stations, identify, where relevant, the different types of:

Scheduling

Presenters

'Branding' music (e.g. theme tunes, jingles)

Discourse (i.e. the language used on the programme and the style of speaking)

Programmes

Content

Opinions stated/revealed/suggested by presenters

Advertising placement.

How are the presenters represented?

How is the music represented?

Is the audience actively engaged (e.g. with phone-ins and competitions) or is the audience assumed to be passive? Why is this?

How do these elements contribute to the cultural expectations about the music in this programme that the audience receives? With reference to one of your chosen stations/programmes, use the headings above to make a list of how it is represented. (It is probably better to choose a specific programme to analyse here – trying to address the whole of Radio 6 in an exam answer would probably be impossible.) Repeat this exercise for your second chosen station or programme.

Carefully consider in your analysis how the two are similar or different.

DISCUSSION

Which comes first? Does the music sub-culture generate a following and then a radio station to feed the audience's enthusiasm or can a new sub-genre of music develop through bands and radio and therefore create an audience?

ACTIVITIES

Describe a short sequence – maybe five minutes – of your chosen programme and analyse it in terms of the codes of radio discussed above.

What does this reveal about the station/programme?

How far does your analysis show how the station/programme creates and sustains a target audience?

How far does it allow you to define this target audience? Why is this?

How many features of this segment serve to identify and emphasise the musical culture of the programme?

ACTIVITIES

Write an analysis of the connotations of the following elements within your chosen programme. How do they establish the representations being used in the programme?

Music	Layering of sound
Voice	Structure and timing of these elements
Silence	Discourse
Non-diegetic sound	Audience hooks.

CASE STUDY

BBC – 1Xtra

One of the new BBC digital stations, BBC – 1Xtra is a 'black music' station. It is available on DAB, over the Internet and from cable/satellite TV receivers, but is not available as an ordinary FM or MW station. The BBC was granted a licence to expand its minority programming a few years ago, in order to support more minority audiences, but it can only broadcast these stations digitally.

BBC – 1Xtra covers a wide range of musical sub-cultures within the overall tag of black music and the listings on the website are searchable by music sub-culture as well as by scheduling. As this is a digital station, there is also the opportunity to listen again to any programme broadcast in the last seven days, so audiences are quickly able to catch up, join in and feel part of the group.

The website also reflects other aspects of the representations used on the station to attract and construct a target audience. The images used reflect the target audience very closely and the language is far closer to 'street talk' than conventional BBC language, again both to represent and to construct the audience. There is a balance between trying to be a contemporary urban 'street culture' station and the requirement to be a national broadcaster, under the banner of the BBC.

CASE STUDY

Sweet FM 89.4

Sweet FM tags itself as 'London's Number 1 Station for urban flavours' and describes its market position as:

'driven by a passion for playing you the sweetest beats, rhythms and melodies from the underground to mainstream, as well as catering for the music connoisseurs who want to hear timeless classics, mixed with the soulful sounds of today's future stars.'

(Source: Sweet FM 89.4 website April 2005)

Sweet FM offers live radio feed from their website (www.sweet894fm.co.uk) as well as on the radio, but they operate as an independent radio station as well. The programmes are created by individual DJs and each has a particular sub-genre of music and therefore a different audience within the general grouping which defines the audience for the station as a whole.

Sweet FM is an interesting comparison with BBC – 1Xtra because seemingly they both target the same audience and employ the same representations. However, by comparing the two, it becomes easy to see the difference between the more straightforward street culture of Sweet FM which is far more centred on the DJs and their representations, and the far bigger construction of the BBC behind BBC – 1Xtra. Sweet FM is far more immediate – you can text or call the studio direct using the number on the website and a large part of the homepage on the website is taken up with adverts for upcoming club events. This station is far more 'grass roots' in its representations of musical culture. The profiles of the DJs on the website are far more personal and straightforward and there is even a photo gallery where listeners are encouraged to add their own pictures. Very much a sense of this station and therefore the representations it employs stem from the group of people who started the station. In other words, the representations of the target audience have defined how the station represents itself and those who work there – and therefore logically the music which is played as part of this apparent daily party.

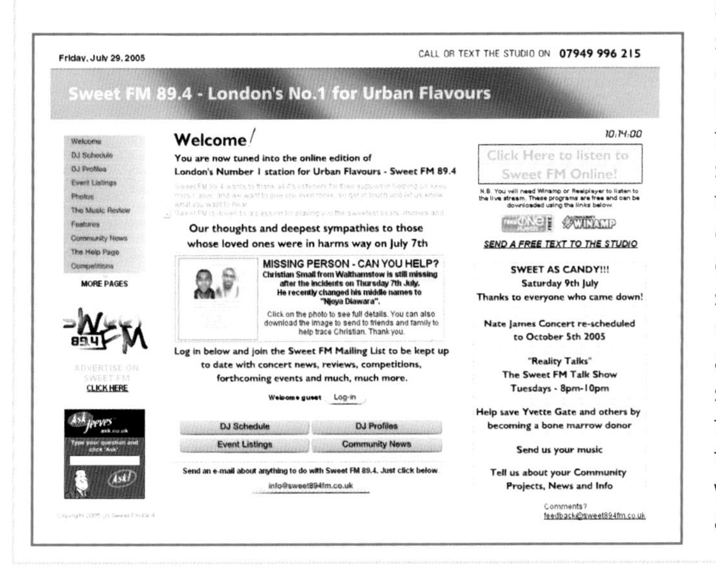

Case study question revisited

At the start of this section an example of the type of question that you might have to answer in the exam was given:

- Compare how the music culture represented in your two chosen radio programmes targets its audience.

By looking back at the notes you have made about your chosen stations and programmes and in particular about the representations of music, presenters, audience and context in the specific programmes you have studied, you should now be able to draw out some specific points in answer to this question. For example, you might want to write about how each programme uses hooks to keep the audience listening (free gifts or interviews with bands, for example). You could describe how audience members are represented when they participate in the show – not only in vox pops but also competition phone-ins or even simply how they are presented or described when they have written or texted in, maybe for a dedication.

Does the representation of the presenter or presenters match the assumed audience profile? Is it similar to performers within this musical genre? What does this tell us about the ways the culture is represented to target a particular audience.

When answering a question like this, it is important to consider how the relationship between music culture and audience is created and therefore how a target audience is created and indeed maintained. In what ways does the programme seek to connect music culture and audience? Does the programme control this relationship (as it might with a particular, less well known music culture and a small, local station) or does the relationship between audience and music culture create expectations and representations that the programme needs to employ to be successful?

Summary

You have been looking at case studies to analyse the concept of representation. To be able to compare both stations/programmes effectively you will need to consider that:

- radio broadcasting offers lots of ways to address minority groups
- stations and programmes have particular identities which can be easily defined and their representations explored
- as radio broadcasting has changed and progressed, so has the representation of different groups
- new media are changing both access to radio stations and the way that stations operate.

Video/computer games and conflict/competition

Aims

Video and computer games, played on computers and on a range of consoles, are an increasingly dominant part of the entertainment industry. Globally, the computer games industry is one of the fastest growing entertainment industries. For example, sales of *Grand Theft Auto: San Andreas* were over £60million in 2004 alone.

These games are an important part of our culture because not only do many people play on consoles and computers, they also play online and belong to online gaming communities. So why do many people criticise these games?

The opposition to the games seems to come from the amount of violence in them. If you are playing *Half-Life 2*, for example, the only way you can play the game is by battling with the 'Combine' (the enemy army) to escape and free Earth from oppression by this alien race. This is not done by debate and diplomacy but by fighting and killing.

Many of the computer games created and released each year are based on conflict in this way. The central narrative of *Grand Theft Auto: San Andreas* puts players in the role of Carl Johnson, who had run away from his hometown to escape a troubled background. When he returns, he is forced back into a life of crime and players need to fight for his survival.

There are, however, games where there is less emphasis on conflict – *FIFA Football 2005* is about managing a top football club, for example, and achieving success at the end of the season. *The Sims* is about building and maintaining a family and a neighbourhood. In these games there is substantially less conflict but there is plenty of competition.

So an important question to ask yourself when thinking about these games is 'Why do people play these games?' Is it the powerful narrative? Is it the high production values? Is it the chance to kill aliens? Is it the challenge and competition?

Obviously your answers to these questions will be different, depending on the games you are analysing, but it's worth making notes to see if there is a general pattern or any conclusions you can draw across a range of games.

DISCUSSION

Would you say that conflict or competition in a game is more likely to appeal to gamers? How would you define the difference between the two?

Do you think there is too much violence in computer games? Should there be more restrictions on the types of violence in computer games?

Video games and representations

For this unit, the key focus is 'representations' and so you will need to be able to write about the representation of different elements in your chosen games, explaining how these elements create conflict and/or competition for the gameplay or narrative of the game. These elements will obviously be examples using the key concept areas which you have studied already.

ACTIVITIES

Research the top 10 games for this week on Amazon.co.uk or Gamesworld.com. Would you say these games are based on conflict, competition or both?

How much of your knowledge of these games is based on previous experience? Is this because you have played the games or because others have talked about them? Why is it significant that so many people are familiar with the games?

What are the classifications of these games? Do you and your peers play games classified as 3+? Why?

Look at the packaging of each game in this list. What can you tell about the narrative of each game from the packaging?

What character representations are used on the packaging? What does this tell us?

Analysing video games

Genre

A good starting point for analysis of any game is to categorise the genre of the game. Many games will identify their genre on the back of the game as a selling point. Why is this?

ACTIVITIES

Imagine you are creating a new game called 'Alien Death', which will be a typical game of its genre.

Identify what this genre will be.

Write a list of 10 generic codes and conventions which you would expect to use in the game.

Draw/design the central hero figure.

Be prepared to explain to the rest of your group how you have constructed this character in terms of generic codes and conventions.

Look on Amazon.co.uk to see how current games are categorised by type. Identify five key features of each game genre from looking at some of the games in each genre.

How many genres are there?

Would you say these genres are conflict or competition based? Is there an equal number of each?

Which are the most popular genres? Why is this?

Structure

Different games are structured in different ways, but again there are some typical structures that you can explore. For example, most narrative-driven games start with some kind of back-story to get players into the game and help them understand and explore their character. This is a little like the pre-title sequence in a film, but it usually happens after the primary title sequence.

Most complex games are divided explicitly into levels – 'you have now killed enough aliens to proceed to level 4', or they may be more subtle – it is simply a question of reaching checkpoints in the narrative as the game play gets harder.

ACTIVITIES

Choose two games to study and analyse the structure of each.

Is each game divided into levels?

How do players move between levels?

Do the games progress between levels? (It may be a continuous narrative or there may be progressive levels of difficulty).

What preparation does the player get at the beginning of each game?

Narrative

The narrative of most contemporary games is very important. This may be a loosely scripted narrative, such as with *Grand Theft Auto*, where there are many sub-narratives to explore and many ways of engaging with the game, or it may be a fairly specific and structured narrative, which leads the game play on, such as in *Half-Life 2*.

DISCUSSION

Which sort of games do you prefer to play – those with a very linear narrative or non-linear narrative? Be prepared to justify your choice to the rest of the group. Does your preference change depending on the genre of game you are playing?

Action

The action of a game is obviously going to be dependent on the genre and the narrative. A game such as *FIFA Football 2005* will have a very different type of action to *Half-Life 2*, and operate in a different

genre and with a very different narrative. This is one area in which games are very different to a film, for example. Whereas both a film and a game will have a narrative, the action in a film is a very different concept. In a film, the term 'action' is used to refer to specific scenes where something is happening and is often used to describe spectacular action, such as a big disaster scene in an action/adventure movie.

However, in a computer game, action also refers to the interaction between the player and the game. A game must be played; it cannot be passively consumed and this makes it utterly different to almost all forms of contemporary media, which assume a more passive audience. This is also one reason why games seem to stir up so many worries about violence corrupting players: many theorists argue that while people can watch a horror film without being influenced by it, they are far more likely to be influenced by the action of a computer game they have been playing. This is because it is interactive and they have had to make conscious decisions to kill aliens during the game, for example. The game *Manhunt* was withdrawn from many shops because it was blamed for the murder of a teenager, allegedly because his friend was acting out part of the game for real and killed his friend.

DISCUSSION

Do you think video games are more likely to influence people in this way?

How do representations of heroes and villains shape our perceptions of action in the game? Is it easy stereotypically to say 'I am playing a hero, therefore I will behave very morally at all times'?

How realistic do you think game play should become in computer games as the technology improves? Do you think there should be differing levels of realism and plausibility for different game genres?

Textual analysis

When you are writing about how representations are created in your games, you will need to write in detail about the text itself. You may find it helpful to choose particular parts of the action from your chosen game and to watch these sections several times so you can make notes about what is happening in the sequence. In this way you will have detailed textual references to support points you may wish to make about representations and game play when you are writing in the exam.

Visuals

- Camera
- *Mise-en-scène*
- Editing
- Special effects

A good starting point, just as with the first part of this unit, is to start by thinking about the visuals of the game. Using the sequence you have selected, you can make notes about the *mise-en-scène* of the game, the editing, how special effects are used and how the camera is used. For example, when playing the opening levels of *Halo: Combat Evolved*, once you have landed on the planet the *mise-en-scène* makes it very clear that this is an alien world, with an unusual planetary configuration and a landscape and location featuring slightly different colours. It is also obvious that in some ways this is a civilized area, with features such as the rock bridge connecting parts of the ground. As the game starts, the smoking and damaged shuttle behind you quickly establishes the narrative and the editing moves the action on quickly so that you must react and attempt to destroy the Covenant forces. The special effects are dramatic – the sweeping gun ships, highly mobile Covenant forces and the use of overlays etc. in your protective armour to provide information on the location of enemy forces – and all help to symbolically engage you in the game. This is important because you are engaged in the game in a slightly distanced way – almost as if you *were* in a protective suit – and are to some extent separated from the action.

Sound

- Music
- Speech
- Sound effects
- Interactive sound

Sound is a vital component of almost all computer games, from the very repetitive but catchy tunes repeated endlessly in early *Tetris*-style games onwards. In contemporary games, the sound adds to the atmosphere, as in a film, but is also significantly more interactive than in a film. Characters speak to you and you must respond to them in some way, and there are frequently layers of sound action happening, to emphasise activity and fighting in different places, for example, or to structure the game play. If you are playing a football game such as *FIFA Football 2005*, for example, the use of music around and during the game adds atmosphere. The game would be far less successful without the sound effects of running feet, kicking footballs, responses from the crowd to the action, and commentary from the box.

ACTIVITIES

Select a sequence of one of your chosen games to study and play it several times without the sound turned up.

How much more difficult is it to play the game without the sound cues?

What does this tell you about the use of sound to control game play and therefore create representations and expectations in the player?

Messages and values

- Catharsis
- Conflict/competition
- Heroes and villains
- Cultural context

There are inevitably messages and values (i.e. ideologies) inherent in any game that you play. It may be a desire to win the competition that engages the player, or the sense of catharsis that can come from engaging in a killing spree in *Halo: Combat Evolved*.

Catharsis is described as a kind of emotional cleansing, first defined by the ancient Greeks. It describes the ways in which violent game play or watching a horror movie, for example, allows us to express deep emotions which we cannot adequately express in daily life and yet are an important part of our psyche. So, for example, although we might not want to kill anyone in real life, being able to rampage around an alien world and kill as many aliens as possible can be a form of catharsis, allowing us to explore those violent emotions which we would otherwise always suppress. Some would argue that by releasing such emotions though game play, we become better people, as our emotions are not buried.

Following on from this, it is important to remember that all the games tend to assume **heroes and villains** and, by definition, the player is usually cast in the role of hero at the beginning of the game (although they may not always choose to act heroically). *Grand Theft Auto: San Andreas* bucks this trend, by requiring you to play a small-time villain but there are opportunities all the way through the game for you to play as a 'good guy', promoting the stereotype that you had only gone off the rails to begin with because of social pressures.

It is always seen as important to win the games or to succeed in all the conflicts, and a key part of this message is the rewards and praise you receive each time you manage to achieve part of this objective. (Is it possible to design a computer game where there would be no winning?)

Games tend to operate in particular **cultural** contexts as well, which inform and shape the values they communicate. For example, if you were playing *America's Army* (available free from www.americasarmy.com), it is important to remember that the game was first designed as a training tool for new recruits to the US army and then released as a recruitment tool once they realised how many soldiers enjoyed playing the game. The cultural values of the American military are very explicit in the game, therefore, and this informs the *mise-en-scène*, the audio, the visuals, the game play and the values you must espouse to be successful in the game. Indeed, when you undertake your training and when you are later able to engage in online games with other players, you soon realise that many of the locations look very like Baghdad and the representations of many of the villains are obviously Arabic in appearance. The ideology of the game is therefore very clear in the game play and also in the content, such as the visuals, audio and character representations. Interestingly, in this game you are only ever 'soldier' without a specific identity (unlike most games) (perhaps again reflecting US military ideologies?).

Characters

- Player
- Helpers
- Enemies
- Representations

Perhaps more so than with linear media forms, characters are often 'types' in computer games, and indeed many of those types can be identified with Propp's character types, based on his theories of narrative (see www.egglescliffe.org.uk/media/narrative/propp.htm). There is usually the hero (you), the

enemy (whether that is aliens or another football team), helpers along the way and often key characters such as a princess who needs saving. Careful use of stereotypes is made in most games because when the game play is active you need to be able to sum up characters very quickly so that you can decide how to react – stereotypes make this process a lot quicker. Inevitably this means that many representations in the games are very stereotypical. In particular, you may notice that female characters are frequently represented in a very glamorous way, with a particular body shape and mode of dress, for example.

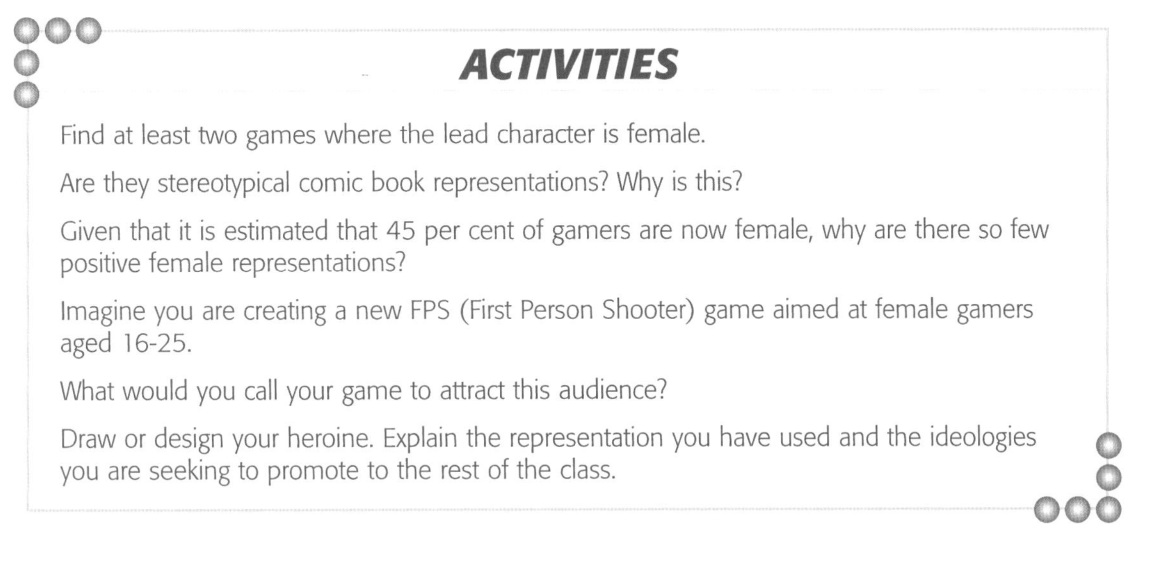

ACTIVITIES

Find at least two games where the lead character is female.

Are they stereotypical comic book representations? Why is this?

Given that it is estimated that 45 per cent of gamers are now female, why are there so few positive female representations?

Imagine you are creating a new FPS (First Person Shooter) game aimed at female gamers aged 16-25.

What would you call your game to attract this audience?

Draw or design your heroine. Explain the representation you have used and the ideologies you are seeking to promote to the rest of the class.

Player experience

- Game play
- Excitement/tension
- Interactivity
- Pre-knowledge
- Online/offline play

Ultimately, the deciding factor in the success or failure of any one game will be the player experience. This is based on all the factors discussed above but also, above all else, on player experience. If the narrative and game play are sufficiently engaging, the player will accept poorer graphics. If there is enough excitement and tension in the activities they must undertake, they are going to be less concerned about the use of stereotypes.

We have already discussed the importance of tension to engage a player and the importance of interactivity. Pre-knowledge can also be important – not only the establishing information offered in print form with a game (which allows a player to start with some knowledge and understanding of the enemy, for example) but also pre-knowledge based on experience from other games. Competent gamers are very familiar with the actions needed to survive in a particular environment and easily able to transfer skills from one game to another, meaning that they are also quicker to spot assistance or ways of handling a situation.

Finally, it is important to remember that for most games there is a substantial difference between online and offline play. Online play, by definition, assumes that there will be other 'live' players in a game and therefore substantially more unpredictability. This is because the narrative will not be pre-resolved for a situation, unlike a single-player offline version of the game. This can have a dramatic effect on game play, with different representations if players have been able to construct their own characters in the scenario, for example, and also different expectations. In this situation it is usually essential for characters to learn to work as a team in their game personae as well and this requires a level of skill and negotiation, and good communication skills – making this type of game play even further removed from conventional linear narrative texts.

ACTIVITIES

Select two games that have the conventional offline player mode but which also offer an online play mode (be careful which games you choose, as some require subscriptions for online play) and play both modes. Write a list of 10 differences and 10 similarities between the two modes of play. Which did you prefer? Why?

DISCUSSION

Online gaming is set to take over from single person offline gaming. Do you think this will be a good thing for consumers and/or the gaming industry?

Representations and audience

As already stated, when writing about your chosen games you need to focus on the representations used in those games. These representations can be visual, aural, action, narrative, character representations and so forth. As you are analysing your chosen games in terms of the concepts used above, remember to ask yourself why something has been represented in this way. What expectations does this set up in the audience? How does this help shape our responses to the game?

There are particular representations that you need to think about and make notes on too. Obviously, in this context the most important representation to think about is the representation of conflict or competition in your chosen games. Is it represented in a positive or negative way? Is it represented as something to be avoided at all costs or something to be encouraged? You can explore this in relation to our cultural values as well. In particular, our culture generally encourages competition (think of the extensive competition-related vocabulary we use every day), yet discourages conflict. Do your games reflect this or is conflict represented more positively? Why is this? How is this representation constructed? Is it through the narrative or the characters, the action or player expectations? For example, when you play *Halo: Combat Evolved*, the box not only holds the DVD with the game on it but also a booklet which details all types of Covenant forces and their weapons and all the weapons which might be available to the player at various points in the game. What sort of expectations does this set up?

The conflict or competition can also be represented by the characters and actions. If the narrative constructs a scenario where a player in *FIFA Football 2005* must choose between fouling a player on

the other side and losing the ball to an opposing player who could score a winning goal, how is this represented in the action? Does this representation allow the gamer to choose either path or has the representation forced them to make a particular decision? Is there any danger that the referee will not notice this bad behaviour and therefore the gamer will get away with it? How does this shape the representations and expectations of the game?

We have already thought about how the opposing elements are constructed and represented in the game, both as character types and as functionaries in the game. Remember that you need to explore in detail how this is done. Look at how these characters are represented visually and consider how far these representations are stereotypical. What about the relationships between characters? How are these interactions represented? How do the opposing elements interact with the gamer? Are these representations typical of the character functions or is the game more complex than this? Can you account for these representations?

In a competitive game such as a sports game, how are winning or losing represented? It may be that there are fewer characters in a sports game but actions such as penalties or goals can be represented in particular ways to make them seem positive or negative. How are they represented in the games you have been studying? If you have been studying conflict-based games, remember that winning and losing a battle are still represented in particular ways – how is this done in your games? A further point to think about here might also be how the game play is restarted if the gamer 'dies' or loses. Is this a quick action and the gamer is straight back into the action where they left off, or is it more complex than this? What does this suggest about representations of effective game play?

Finally, it can be worth visiting the website of the institution that produces a game, as you'll often get a far clearer sense of the visual representations of the game, though perhaps little about narrative and game play. However, it is also important to notice whether the representations on the website match the game or whether there is a difference, which might suggest that the game is actually targeting a different audience to the specified audience (as with 18 certificate games which are often played by younger gamers). There may also be forums, FAQs and even 'official' cheat pages – which also tell you a lot about the representations of a game and the audience expectations and engagement with the game.

ACTIVITIES

Find the websites for two conflict-based computer games and two competitive games with which you are not yet familiar.

What visual representation is used to suggest the context of each game?

Are there generic similiarities which you can spot?

How are the characters of the game represented?

How can you identify whether this is a conflict or competitive game?

What assumptions can you make about the target audience for each game?

What cultural representations are evident? Why is this?

What generic codes and conventions are being employed on the webpages? How do these match the representations in the game play?

CASE STUDY

Compare how conflict/competition are represented by visual elements in your two chosen video/computer games.

Half-Life 2

Half-Life 2 was released in 2004 as the sequel to *Half-Life*, both made by Sierra Games, which is part of Vivendi Universal. Sierra markets the game by setting out the context very clearly:

'By taking the suspense, challenge and visceral charge of the original, and adding startling new realism and responsiveness, *Half-Life 2* opens the door to a world where the player's presence affects everything around him, from the physical environment to the behaviors – even the emotions – of both friends and enemies.

The player again picks up the crowbar of research scientist Gordon Freeman, who finds himself on an alien-infested Earth being picked to the bone, its resources depleted, its populace dwindling. Freeman is thrust into the unenviable role of rescuing the world from the wrong he unleashed back at Black Mesa. And a lot of people – people he cares about – are counting on him.

(Source: www.sierra.com April 2004)

Half-Life was one of the first of the FPS (First Person Shooter) titles to give such emphasis to the narrative and the cinema quality graphics and the more sophisticated technology for *Half-Life 2* has taken this even further.

As a player you again play the part of Gordon Freeman, the theoretical physicist who saved the world from invasion at the end of the previous game. However, at the start of *Half-Life 2* you are in a train entering 'City 17' somewhere on Earth. This ghetto holds the remaining humans on Earth now that the Combine has conquered the planet, running it with a puppet human government. Your task will be to liberate Earth from the Combine. Interestingly, you always remain in character as Freeman (offering no opportunity for objective perspectives on the action such as you would get in a film or in some other games), so you have a first-person viewpoint throughout the game.

Camera angle, shot, movement and position

Establishing shot; master shot; close-up (and variations); long shot; wide shot; two-shot; high angle; low angle; aerial shot; point of view; pan; crane; tilt; track; dolly; zoom/reverse zoom; framing; composition; hand-held; steadicam.

Examples:

- **POV shots throughout so you are clearly playing as one character.**
- **Zoom function available via keyboard so you can get in closer.**
- **Tracking and panning controlled by mouse – as if player is looking around scene.**
- **Often weapon appears in bottom right corner of screen – partly for targeting but also because this helps locate player in action by providing sense of perspective; also adds to tension.**

Shots from *Half Life 2*

- **Use of close-ups when talking to Combine troops, for example, creates threatening atmosphere because of fierce appearance of soldiers with lack of facial features behind masks.**

Editing

Sound and vision editing – cut; fade; wipe; edit; FX; dissolve; long take; superimpose; slow motion; synchronous/asynchronous sound.

Examples:

- **Action moves with character, so little use of editing – except in establishing narrative (called a 'cut scene') such as at the beginning of the game which is fully cinematic and uses conventional jump cuts to move between screens.**
- **High-speed action, especially in battle scenes.**
- **All scenes made in 360 degrees and with detail at any zoom level – fully immersive.**
- **Frequent splattering of blood during battles to add to sense of conflict and drama, and many scenes bear scars of previous battles, with dead bodies and pools of blood.**

Special effects

Graphics; captions; computer-generated images (CGI); animation; pyrotechnics; stunts; models; back projection.

Examples:

- **Overlay used to show status of Freeman's body armour and availability of weapons/ammunition – can be turned off by player.**
- **Flashlight available to player to turn on light so can see in darker places.**
- **All weapons produce recoil and spit fire etc. to suggest realism but also exaggerated to heighten tension and hence game play.**
- **Layering of graphical effects: for example, frequent use of projection screens in the street promoting Combine propaganda – reminiscent of *1984* and other similar dystopian fiction.**
- **Tension added by need to watch out for helpful items (such as energy rechargers which are hidden on walls) to enable player to recharge suit and continue playing.**
- **Burning fires in many scenes add to sense of dereliction and hence conflict and danger.**

Mise-en-scène

Location, set, studio/set design; costume; properties; ambient lighting; artificial lighting; production design period/era; colour design.

Examples:

- **Environment is run-down and clearly urban – strong sense of ghetto New York in colour of buildings, style of buildings, tenement buildings and sidewalks.**
- **Environment very similar to contemporary US to help player identify with this world – until player gets outside City 17, when it becomes a little more barren and fantasy-driven.**
- **Outside City 17, environment is very dystopian, barren and run-down, to suggest a world very similar to our own which has been destroyed. Many of these locations feel very desert-like.**
- **Wide range of monsters (described as 'bestiary' in accompanying literature) – some are mechanical, some organic – all are typically 'fantasy' monsters with echoes of other contemporary films and games in their construction.**
- **Costumes are all similar to contemporary US urban trends but with an emphasis on military-style clothing and Kevlar (equivalent) body armour to add to atmosphere and tension.**
- **Lighting is very harsh in the City to reinforce the sense of surveillance – darker in underground areas but lit by flashlight as required, adding tension and suspense.**
- **Much of landscape is wasteland, again demonstrating the previous battles and serving as battlefield for this battle.**
- **All characters seem to carry weapons of some kind at some point, again emphasising that this is a war-driven environment.**

Character representations

Goodies and baddies; costume; facial expressions; actions; location; values implied; level of interaction; gender; weaponry.

Examples:

- **Combine forces fully covered with armour, so no sense of an organic being behind the armour – especially intimidating with non-human mouthpiece and blank eyepieces. Standard soldier headset not dissimilar to nuclear, biological and chemical suits worn by US troops in Iraq. Combat Elite soldiers have more sophisticated-looking armour which is less bulky and more threatening due to reflective materials used etc. All carry imposing weaponry. All this adds to sense of danger from them and has connotations of Storm Troopers and other sci-fi enemy armies, which increases the tension and conflict in the game.**

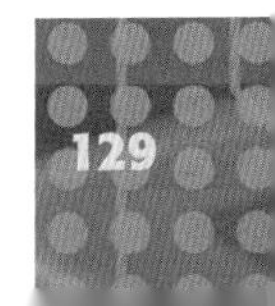

- **Human associates are dressed in shabby street clothes, suggesting a 'resistance' to the Combine. Again, they are usually armed with large guns to suggest conflict and tension.**
- **Various ugly insect-like beasts (lots of leg and very little head for maximum terror impact) move in ugly, scuttling ways around the wastelands, maximising their horror connotations and again heightening tension and conflict.**

Grand Theft Auto: San Andreas

Grand Theft Auto: San Andreas was released in 2004. It is produced by Rockstar Games and follows on from *Grand Theft Auto: Vice* City and the other *Grand Theft* titles now available. The games are notorious for many complaints about the level of 'mindless' violence that is possible in the games, and for the ways the games appear to promote and encourage violent street culture.

Shots from *Grand Theft Auto: San Andreas*

Like many other conflict-based computer games, *GTA: San Andreas* is a First Person Shooter game and the action happens from your perspective most of the time. It is linked by cut-scenes, just as with other narrative-driven FPS games. The main difference between the *GTA* games and other FPS games is the many sub-narratives that are built in and the

opportunities almost to create your own narrative aligned with the primary narrative. Unlike many other games, you can decide not to be violent in many situations and you can even decide to avoid the primary narrative a lot of the time and simply enjoy spending time in the game, interacting with the other characters and enjoying the 'life'. Equally, you can decide to be excessively violent, killing everyone you come into contact with and driving forward the primary narrative quickly. Even when walking along the street, you can choose whether you walk past other people or attack them for the sake of it. This involves a very different level of conflict to *Half-Life 2*, where there is more of a sense of inevitable conflict to continue the game. Here the violence is chosen by the gamer and there are far more moral complexities to engage with, such as the complexities of Johnson's family troubles typified by the arguments between his brother and sister.

The narrative context for the game is clearly established in the Rockstar promotion for it:

'Five years ago Carl Johnson escaped from the pressures of life in Los Santos, San Andreas ... a city tearing itself apart with gang trouble, drugs and corruption. Where film stars and millionaires do their best to avoid the dealers and gang bangers.

Now, it's the early 90s. Carl's got to go home. His mother has been murdered, his family has fallen apart and his childhood friends are all heading towards disaster.

On his return to the neighborhood, a couple of corrupt cops frame him for homicide. CJ is forced on a journey that takes him across the entire state of San Andreas, to save his family and to take control of the streets.'

(Source: www.rockstargames.com April 2005)

Camera angle, shot, movement and position

Establishing shot; master shot; close-up (and variations); long shot; wide shot; two-shot; high angle; low angle; aerial shot; point of view; pan; crane; tilt; track; dolly; zoom/reverse zoom; framing; composition; hand-held; steadicam.

Examples:

- **Camera POV much of the time – cut-scenes shown more cinematically.**
- **Action tracks mouse and camera shake to respond to being hit, to create sense of fighting.**
- **Lots of long shots as Johnson moves down roads of city – zooming in as he gets closer to buildings for the sake of realism.**

Editing

Sound and vision editing – cut; fade; wipe; edit; FX; dissolve; long take; superimpose; slow motion; synchronous/asynchronous sound.

Examples:

- **Cut-scenes to add narrative structure – cinematic narrative segments to link action sections.**
- **Frequent use of transitions to mark progression in narrative when entering buildings: for example, as a way of masking change in location.**
- **Combination of camera effects, cuts and sound effects to create sense of realism during fights.**
- **When targeting a weapon at an opponent, the camera moves to just above CJ's right shoulder, so you can aim better – encouraging you to take part in conflict.**

Special effects

Graphics; captions; computer-generated images (CGI); animation; pyrotechnics; stunts; models; back projection.

Examples:

- **Overlays and health meters are used to show information during the game, such as the state of your car after a fight so you can evaluate what to do – adding decision making to the fighting process.**
- **All weapons produce some form of output to intensify effects.**
- **Larger weapons, used close up against opponents, destroy limbs for more tension and dramatic conflict.**
- **All cars, vehicles and weapons are from 1990s to maintain the associations with the stereotypes of that time.**

Mise-en-scène

Location, set, studio/set design; costume; properties; ambient lighting; artificial lighting; production design period/era; colour design.

Examples:

- **Set in 1990s California (recognisable locations from Los Angeles and 'Vinewood' sign, for example), which has connotations of ghettoes, constant low-level conflict, urban fighting and gang battles.**
- **Colour used to establish gang identities and hence gang battles: for example, one family group wears green and another purple – this causes instant conflict when they meet or when they go looking for conflict, such as in drive-by attacks.**
- **Harsh gritty lighting to add to the sense of tension and conflict and irritability throughout.**
- **Humour in *mise-en-scène* at times, such as shots of burly fighter with guns in front of a picture of the Virgin Mary – captures absurdity of the gang warfare which was common in the 1990s in California, where gangs would fight all Saturday night and then go to church with their families on Sunday morning. Also provides a reminder of the senselessness of much of the game's violence.**
- **Aggression and conflict throughout, as well as many elements that identify this is 1990s USA, such as the number of cops and the portrayal of them wearing sunglasses to make them seem more intimidating.**

Character representations

Goodies and baddies; costume; facial expressions; actions; location; values implied, level of interaction, gender, weaponry

Examples:

- **Frequent verbal and physical conflict between family members (e.g. CJ's brother and sister), offering different forms of conflict to a normal FPS game where the conflict is simply against the enemy.**
- **Realistic fight action, especially in fist fights, to emphasise street nature of conflict – damage caused as well as actions is seen on screen.**
- **Many stereotypical characters throughout game, such as the slimy lawyer and tough-guy hood.**
- **CJ must eat or he will grow thin and too weak to fight properly, meaning he is likely to become a victim. Equally, if he eats too much, he becomes too fat and therefore cannot defend himself. If he eats appropriately and makes the effort to keep fit, he will be more successful in his fights – what is the moral message being given to gamers here? Is it simply that eating properly and staying fit will keep you alive longer or is there more of a sense of the importance of being fit and healthy to 'win' here?**
- **Competition throughout and conflict in narrative – CJ must fight to clear his name and sort his family out. Creates a complex character and allows events to shape responses and other events to some extent. Conflict is always offered as a solution – even if players decide not to choose that option.**

Gender and situation comedy

What is situation comedy?

Situation comedies are based upon a single context, or 'situation', usually connected with work or the home, or in some cases both. The comedy grows out of the tensions or conflicts between the characters, usually a narrow group of friends or a family. Whereas soap operas demand a large number of characters, this is clearly not the case with sitcoms. Where there are characters outside the central group they are usually acquaintances or temporary inhabitants who provide particular comic storylines.

The narrative of a sitcom rarely continues from one episode into the next, although there are, of course, exceptions to this rule. This again contrasts with soaps where the on-going narrative is an essential ingredient.

DISCUSSION

Which sitcoms have on-going storylines? Why do you think their narratives are constructed in this way? Compare these with examples of sitcoms whose episodes are completely free-standing.

Even in sitcoms that have on-going storylines such as *Will and Grace*, with Will and Grace's ongoing friendship, each installment begins with a situation that is resolved by the end of the episode. Characters may be simple two-dimensional stereotypes or may be more complex and fully rounded, but they rarely change. Their basic 'situation' similarly remains the same from episode to episode. Although some of the running stories will resist closure until the end of a series, or, once again with *Will and Grace*, end a series with a cliffhanger, sitcoms are heavily reliant upon repetition.

What, or who, are we laughing at?

Sitcoms give us the opportunity to laugh at aspects of ourselves – sitcoms such as *Keeping Up Appearances* are successful because Hyacinth is almost plausible and we can all identify with characters like her. My *Family* defines a 'typical' family and then subverts their lives to create chaos – a gentle way for us to reaffirm our own roles in our own families and to feel more secure in our own worlds.

Other key characteristics of comedy are enigma (mystery) and comic suspense. Enigma can generate many sitcom plots – not just the obvious such as the 'secret' relationship between Chandler and Monica in *Friends*, but also the more subtle such as the sitcom *Goodnight Sweetheart* starring Nicholas Lyndhurst as someone living simultaneously in two timeframes. Other sitcoms border on farce, such as My *Parents are Aliens* or *Tracey Beaker*, where the comedy comes from watching the chain of events unfold and disaster building to a climax by the end of each episode.

Are we laughing *at* the characters or *with* them, when watching and sharing their fortunes and misfortunes? Does our laughter derive from our experience of disruptive surprise and its resolution? Is our laughter allowing us to sublimate or rehearse underlying or unconscious fears, anxieties or desires? Comedy and laughter allow us to stand outside our own ego and be taken over by events or circumstances outside our control. One example of this might be to consider how painful it can sometimes be to watch John Cleese in *Fawlty Towers*, endlessly thwarted in his neurotic attempts to control events, stay organised and organise others – in laughing at him are we also laughing at aspects of ourselves? Maybe this is why so many sitcoms remain grounded in the family or an extended family, to enable us to make these comparisons. *Absolutely Fabulous* offered extreme stereotypes but also reversed many typical relationships (such as mother/daughter). It explored typical situations, for example the mother introducing a new boyfriend to her daughter or the loneliness of an older single woman, but frequently subverted them to give a fresh perspective.

ACTIVITIES

Using the key features of sitcom referred to above, try to identify two sitcoms that conform to what you consider to be a conventional pattern. Now see if you can identify another sitcom that does not conform to the key features you have identified. Does this make it more or less successful? Why is this? How have they 'subverted' the format to create this comedy?

In terms of the formulaic element of sitcoms it has been suggested that sitcoms share a common ingredient, the comic trap, as Barry Took remarks:

> All successful comedies have some trap in which people must exist – like marriage. [The perfect situation for a situation comedy] is a little self-enclosed world where you have to live by the rules.

These rules may be those of the mini-community, such as that of the Home Guard in *Dad's Army*, or rules of family life as in *My Family*. In sitcoms characters often threaten the closely bound ties of the family or the social group but by the end of the episode any breakup of the family or community tends to be resolved in favour of the stability and importance of the group. Many of the plots of *Tracey Beaker*, for example, involve Tracey seeking to improve her circumstances, either directly or through self-betterment, but being unable to do so. Certain critics have suggested that this underlying thematic concern makes the form particularly suitable for the home-based television audience, going on to suggest that the sitcom, as a form, tends towards the reassertion of conservative values of the home and family (in terms of both setting and theme), and the stereotyping of racial, class, sexual and regional differences. Emphasis is also on the inside (of the home or social unit) against which the 'others' (neighbours or outsiders) are judged, rejected or simply viewed. In the case of a programme such as *Dad's Army* or *'Allo, 'Allo*, the question of who is the insider and who the outsider has all sorts of implications for wider questions of national identity and national self-identification.

Nearly all sitcom characters, be they American or British, are frustrated by being caught in a situation from which they cannot escape – hence the name. The situation may be physical, but it is more likely to be emotional. Rodney in *Only Fools and Horses* is trapped by his family, Geraldine in *The Vicar of Dibley* is trapped by her position as vicar. In *Absolutely Fabulous* Edina and Patsy are trapped in the fantasy of the mores of the sixties. This is not only built into the psychology of the sitcom but is fundamental to their structure as television products. A situation comedy is, by definition, a comedy with a set cast, and a set location that is repeated in each episode. In other words, the tendency not to change is external as well. Although characters may strive to change, they are in a sense doomed to return each time to somewhere very close to their starting point because that is the way the episodes are defined.

The first part of a typical sitcom episode is where the characters' expectations are elevated; the second part is the disequilibrium when their plans are dashed and they fall to a point below that from which they started; the third part is the return to equilibrium. Perhaps the most basic appeal of sitcoms (and most TV programmes) is the fact that predictably everything comes out all right. Nothing really changes.

At the end of the episode the cycle is complete, the situation restored and few, if any, lessons have been learnt. We are back where we started, ready to begin next week's episode. The point is that, unless an actor wants to leave the series or there is a major change of focus, the basic situation never changes. This is sometimes highlighted by the coda at the end of an episode, a brief comic moment after the closing credits. For example the short exchange as equilibrium and light-heartedness is re-established at the end of *Friends* or (more explicitly) the 'joke over a cup of coffee' at the end of *The Vicar of Dibley* where Geraldine and Alice share a joke that Alice never understands.

It is precisely this lack of change that gives a sitcom, for the audience, the sense of real life. The characters on the screen who play out their trapped lives every week are mirrors of the people who sit trapped in their own worlds, watching them every week. In the typical family sitcom, we see quick-witted but ultimately conservative teenagers running rings around their decent but rather dull parents. Kids enjoy these shows because that is how they often see their own parents. The parents also laugh because that is how they see themselves. But it doesn't matter. Sitcoms say to the audience, 'Look, it's like this for everybody. This is what life is like, so you're no different.' The message is that life is full of traps and most things you attempt are doomed to fail – but it doesn't matter. Laughter gives a release and reassurance to the audience.

Some of the better sitcoms allow for a strong sense of both the inside and the outside world. There are internal dynamics going on within the programme to create the humour: conflicts, comic devices and character squabbles in *My Hero*, relationships in *Fawlty Towers*. In some, the intrusion from the outside world motivates the plot – this is typical in *Fawlty Towers* where the situation of a hotel makes this logical as guests create comic narrative opportunities.

Mise-en-scène

Like all TV forms, sitcoms create their own special physical world. In *My Hero* there is the living room and the kitchen. In *Drop the Dead Donkey* it's the newsroom. In *Cheers*, it is the bar. Without their television and three-piece suite, the Royle family would be completely lost. In fact the sofa appears as an essential piece of furniture in innumerable sitcoms.

Sitcoms are set in particular locations – the shot of New York at the beginning of *Friends*, for example, established the location, and the action was then sited in the more intimate locations of the apartments or coffee shop to ensure focus on relationships. This is even more explicit in *Porridge*, where the title sequence establishes the distance from the outside world as we follow Fletcher into the prison and hear the story established. Once the episode begins, the audience accepts the simple sets quickly. The sitting rooms of most family-based sitcoms are very similar. Usually prosperous, they are carefully crowded with stuffed couches and comfortable chairs, coffee tables on which there are small objects, and walls on which conventional paintings are hung

Stereotypes

This is one reason why sitcoms depend on stereotypes and conventional settings to establish their environment quickly and to allow for more comic opportunities. The characters are central and establish the comedy and the action – sometimes generating comedy because of their character and sometimes through being exposed to situations that lead to comic action. Equally, we expect to see similar episodes every week and we do not expect to see the characters change, age, progress or develop. In *Men Behaving Badly*, for example, although the situations change superficially (for instance, due to impending marriage or children) these changes are explicitly external and do not affect the real dynamics of the relationships in any way, allowing the comedy to continue (an almost direct reversal of reality) where such events are pivotal and substantially change relationships and situations – perhaps a sign of what audiences seek from sitcoms? *Friends* is a good example of this artificiality – all the principal characters are attractive and appealing. All manage to live a prosperous life without working very hard (or in some cases not at all) and although there is talk of needing money, all seem to have sufficient income to enable them to live as overgrown, affluent students avoiding real responsibilities for a great many years.

ACTIVITIES

Watch an episode of *The Vicar of Dibley* and observe how frequently Geraldine uses comic one-liners. How often are these supportive of the other characters and how often do they put the other characters down in some way? How often are the jokes and shared moments gender-related? Why do you think this is so? Notice also that there are many confessional and sharing moments between Geraldine and Alice, David and the other characters. Why is this? How do they integrate into the story? Why are these moments used?

Like us, the central characters in sitcoms are surrounded by others, not merely by practical necessity or circumstance, but because their own goals and desires can only be achieved through other people. In their lives, as depicted on the screen, self-interest and social interaction are fused – the latter is a means to aid the former.

In their miniature societies, they scheme and deceive and give themselves away; they tell stories about each other; they misunderstand and reconcile; invent enemies; and make and break pacts and alliances. Most significantly, their interactions are based on various kinds of status and personal territory. As a result, things get out of balance until they are (usually) set right again, so the moral order embodied in the depicted relationships is restored.

But what makes sitcoms successful is the fact that the characters are more than this. What we respond to isn't merely the foolishness of their personal limitations. It is also, and most essentially, the fact that we can identify with the way they are trapped by their own limitations and have to struggle against those limitations to find happiness in their lives.

Representations

As already mentioned above, sitcoms generally depend on stereotypes to establish character. This sustains the security and dependability of the sitcom environment and offers the audience easy-to-grasp 'handles' on the characters and situations. Where this is not the case, it is usually because the sitcom is worked around an eccentric, such as Basil Fawlty.

British sitcoms tend to depend on characters who are socially, materially, emotionally and sexually repressed. They are terribly class conscious, with many earlier sitcoms being centred on social position, such as in *Keeping Up Appearances*, *Steptoe And Son* and *Till Death Us Do Part* – perhaps reflecting social and cultural values at the time. The upper classes are often presented as civilised, intelligent and slightly dotty. Their humour lies in their formality, their exaggerated correctness and their distaste for the lower classes. The lower classes are frequently represented as being loud, crass and shallow. Their humour lies in their bad taste, their bluntness and their distaste for the upper class.

The British comedy industry is highly differentiated but governed by the overall concept that we all have our little niche in society and somehow we all get by. Americans, on the other hand, are largely not concerned with class but with their own behaviour. Americans are desperately seeking the American Dream. They are always on the lookout for self-improvement, as shown in sitcoms such as *Seinfeld*, *Roseanne*, *Frasier* and *Cheers*. Their sitcoms are more personality-focused, using dysfunctional relationships and unsuccessful characters with whom the audience may compare themselves.

These national assumptions control much of the representation within each nation's sitcoms – American sitcoms are far less 'gentle' and plot driven than British ones – it is almost as if the British characters need to be represented as 'more sinned against than sinning' whereas the representation of characters in US sitcoms is dependent on audience neuroses and this generates a particular style of stereotype.

Gender

A key issue for representational studies in sitcom is gender and gender roles. In early sitcoms, roles and function were clearly outlined for male and female characters and these stereotypes were strictly maintained and many remain today. Hyacinth Bucket is totally 'female' and conforms to traditional stereotypes for middle-class women. Perhaps Margaret in *One Foot in the Grave* is a development – she shows independence and frequently needs to sort out Victor's chaos, but she still does so wearing an apron. Diana in *Waiting for God* was clearly an independent and forthright woman but she needed to work with Tom to organise the old people's home and eventually adopted a more gender conventional role despite her original protests that she would not do so.

Sitcoms such as *Absolutely Fabulous* and *The Vicar of Dibley* have begun to subvert some of the gender stereotypes, although it is worth noting that *The Vicar of Dibley* depends on audience knowledge of all those stereotypes to generate its comedy. Sitcoms now frequently play upon the fact that they will at one moment accept a stereotype and the next moment subvert it.

DISCUSSION

How far do you think that sitcoms either reinforce or subvert gender stereotypes?

CASE STUDY

Comparison

Absolutely Fabulous and *The Vicar of Dibley*

One comparison you might make between these two programmes is in terms of the gender portrayals – the female characters in *Absolutely Fabulous* are far more powerful and dominant than those in *The Vicar of Dibley*. Each sitcom, however, depends on a pivotal female character, so they are a useful comparison.

To what extent does each programme make use of caricature as well as stereotype? Some critics have suggested that Edina and Patsy are caricature not stereotype because of the way they are portrayed, yet Geraldine is both stereotype of a rural female vicar and a reversal of stereotypes throughout. (The show has received a lot of criticism for her sometimes flippant comments about religion and the church.) The male characters in *Absolutely Fabulous* are all very weak – is this part of the comedy of the show or would a strong male character be an interesting contrast? Equally, the male characters in *The Vicar of Dibley* are all strong in different ways – even Hugo cannot be dominated by his father, despite his lack of initiative or focus. Owen and Frank are strong in their own way – but are they also more caricature than stereotype?

Both programmes have been successful in the USA but *Absolutely Fabulous* was more successful – does this suggest that US women more easily identified with the brash Edina and Patsy than the more conventionally English Geraldine? Is part of the charm of Dibley the sense of 'English' culture and iconography which is so central to the text (think of the interior of Geraldine's typical English cottage – furniture, decoration, layout and ornaments) whereas the world Edina and Patsy occupy is considerably more metropolitan. Are these gender portrayals global?

ACTIVITIES

Study an episode from each of your chosen situation comedies and answer the following questions:

Identify who has the power in the programme:

1. in the domestic settings
2. in the workspace.

How can power be defined?

Is it through social status (i.e. position in the family or firm, police, army or government)?

Is it through emotional control (i.e. through seniority, maturity, manipulation, selflessness or greed)?

Textual analysis and gender

ACTIVITIES

With reference to your two situation comedies, identify where relevant the different types of:

Family – domestic unit	Family
Relations within the family	Talk
House	Possessions
Main characters' status, class or power, position in society	Aspirations, dreams and opportunities
Job	Clothes
Life events	Power

Use these headings to make a list of how the main characters and their family or domestic unit is represented. Analyse how your two situation comedies are similar or different in these respects.

Narrative

ACTIVITIES

Watch each of your chosen episodes of your situation comedies carefully and write a summary of the plot of each episode in no more than 500 words.

Make a numbered list of the key elements in your sitcoms' narratives, thinking about the stages in the narrative and how they relate to the segments of the comedy in relation to timing and breaks needed for adverts etc.

Then write a short list of the narrative moments in the comedy, breaking them down into the relevant segments. Now identify the key narrative moment for each of these segments and then one or two key frames that best illustrate these moments. Try to obtain freeze frame still shots of these moments and, if you can, print them off in colour so that you can annotate them in detail to help you.

Themes

ACTIVITIES

List the main themes in your sitcoms, e.g. trust, corruption.

Compare similarities and differences between the two situation comedies.

Key moments: cinematography

The following activities will enable you to analyse key elements in specific scenes to bring out the qualities and techniques of construction.

ACTIVITIES

Select one of your key narrative moments and describe four or five frames in one significant and dramatic sequence as though each was a still frame. For each of the frames, explain briefly:

- Camera shot types, angles of each character and the perspective contained within the shot: foreground, mid-ground and/or background
- Camera movement: tracking, zooming, static etc.
- Lighting: source (artificial or natural), direction and spread (dark or bright etc.)
- Clothing
- Body posture and position in relation to other people or space
- Diegetic and non-diegetic sound and music (identify genre of music and instruments/sound played).

ACTIVITIES

Write an analysis of the connotations of the following elements within your chosen situation comedies:

- Perspective (viewpoint of camera), lighting (effects), clothing (signifiers)
- Facial expression, body posture, gestures (meaning)
- Positioning and relationship of characters in the scene/melodrama, e.g. power relations/good and bad
- *Mise-en-scène*: background, setting, colour, furniture, props (signifiers)
- Diegetic and non-diegetic sound and music (associations with genre or music or mood/atmosphere conveyed)
- Themes and links with other parts of the situation comedy.

Summary

You have been studying the concept of representation through case studies. To be able to compare the two situation comedies effectively you will need to consider that:

- issues of gender and/or cultural values need to be explained by discussing social attitudes and the director's attitudes, e.g. sexism in '60s America is countered by the positive portrayal of the female characters

- characters convey attitudes which belong to a wider set of views and values held in society, i.e. power relations, gender roles
- key moments show the progression of a character's development within the narrative of the situation comedy
- ideas must be explored through the language of television.

The Vicar of Dibley and Absolutely Fabulous

In dealing with the key issues of representation, messages and values, discussion on this topic can be divided in three areas:

- Gender/status
- Social context
- Situation comedy.

The Vicar of Dibley was created by Richard Curtis and was first broadcast in November 1994. The most recent episodes were the two Christmas specials shown December 2004, for the 10-year anniversary of the soap. The sitcom started with the arrival of the new vicar to the small rural village of Dibley. "You were expecting a bloke with a beard, a Bible and bad breath," Geraldine says. "Instead, you got a babe with a bob cut and a magnificent bosom."

The stereotypical range of local residents were astounded to receive a female vicar and most of the early humour revolved around the adjustments they had to make to having a female vicar at the helm of the village. The show depended on the interplay between the vicar and these stereotypical (primarily male) residents, ranging from David Horton, the local 'squire' figure, living an affluent life in the Manor House and stereotypically a typical English gentleman; through Hugo, his dim-witted son; to the stereotypical simple villagers, such as Jim Trott and Owen Newett (the typical dishevelled sheep-farmer). To counterbalance Geraldine's liberalism, her verger was the dim-witted Alice, who was a stereotypical bimbo – comparable to Bubbles in *Absolutely Fabulous*. Much of the comedy of the programme stemmed from the gulf in experience and thought processes between the liberated and intelligent Geraldine and the naïve and simple Alice. The later wedding of Alice and Hugo and subsequent pregnancy and birth provided more opportunites for gender-based humour, revolving around Alice's attempts to look after Hugo and her baby.

Look at this publicity shot for the programme and analyse what costume, facial expression, proxemics and framing tell you about the gender roles and relationship between Geraldine and Alice.

Look at this still from the second series of the programme. What does it tell you about Alice, Hugo and their relationship?

So much of the humour in *The Vicar of Dibley* derives from very traditional, rural stereotypes, which have been used in sitcoms such as *To the Manor Born* for many years. To ensure the programme remained appealing to a contemporary audience, however, Geraldine was presented as a very liberated vicar – a photograph of a famous actor was always next to the picture of Jesus on her wall, for example, and in the episode 'Spring' during Series 3, for example, Geraldine was preparing to marry David Horton but dreams about the wedding being interrupted by Sean Bean, appearing at the back of the church and declaring his love for her, asking her to 'C'mon lass' and run away with him. A very unliberated and stereotypical dream for Geraldine, from which she awoke to call off her conventional marriage to David. Other cameo performances have also included the famous 'mirror' dance with Darcy Bussell in Series 2, where Geraldine appears on stage, dancing with Bussell – this time a deliberate send-up of the gender stereotype of a ballet primadonna, explictly contrasted with Bussell throughout the dance.

By comparison, *Absolutely Fabulous* was a very contemporary, urban representation with two explicitly non-conformist female leads in Jennifer Saunders's Edina and Joanna Lumley's Patsy. The traditional, stereotypical 'mother' was still there, played by June Whitfield (of *Terry and June* fame) but in a rather bizarre way. Seemingly conventional and stereotypical but not quite, suddenly making unexpected announcements or taking up new hobbies such as salsa dancing for example. Edina's daughter, Saffy, is the opposite of the conventional stereotype of a rebellious teenage daughter, being mature, sensible, committed to good causes and frequently having to sort out her mother. Perhaps the two best-known creations are, however, Edina and Patsy, both of whom are rumoured to be based on real people living in

London. They still regard themselves as young, vibrant and sexually attractive and they have achieved sufficient professional success that they are in control of their respective organisations – often to disastrous effect. This stereotyping of each of these gender exemplars can be easily identified visually by costume, gesture, make-up, hair, and framing.

Equally important in terms of analysis for *Absolutely Fabulous* of course are the secondary male stereotypes offered to the audience – John (Saffy's husband-to-be, who she met in Uganda); Justin, Edina's second husband (and Saffy's father), who is gay and runs an antique shop with his partner; Marshall, Edina's first husband and Serge's father, who left Edina for Hollywood and is now a Rabbi with a very loud and domineering girlfriend, Bo. Serge is Edina's son (only introduced in 2002) and, like Saffy, he has turned out surprisingly normal, when he finally appears after all the speculation.

For example, you can view Series 5 Episode 5, when Saffy's play is premiering at the local fringe theatre. Both Marshall and Justin are there to support her as well as John and the contrast between the principal female characters (trying to get the play cancelled) and the support Saffy receives from the far less powerful male characters is a significant reversal of normal gender expectations in a sitcom.

Case study comparison questions

- Compare how the representation of characters in your two chosen television programmes reveals issues of gender.
- When answering this question, it is important to note first that the representations of character are the focus here – not representations of place or time – and that by analysing representations of character, you will be writing about specific, individual representations, not representations of groups (although of course those individuals may be representing groups or be stereotypes, for example).
- Here, representations of gender are an ideal choice because there is such a range of gender types and sterotypes presented in each programme.
- To start with, therefore, you might define the primary female representations in each programme and their role in the narrative:

The Vicar of Dibley

- Geraldine – female vicar – a complex figure, stereotype but also individual
- Alice – the dim-witted verger – a stereotype of a dumb blonde but with more character than this stereotype might suggest

Absolutely Fabulous

- Edina – stereotypical caricature of non-conformist, career-orientated mother
- Patsy – stereotypical ageing lush
- Edina's mother – a sterotypical mother figure but also a little bizarre
- Saffy – explictly not the stereotypical rebellious teenager on the surface (although she is rebelling by being conventional!)

- In what ways do these characterisations subvert or maintain gender stereotypes?
- Why does each programme use a variety of female characters in this way?
- After analysing the female representations in this way you can do the same with the male representations (although, as we said, this is harder in *Absolutely Fabulous* because the men are so secondary to the women)
- In what ways do they represent or subvert gender expectations? Why is this?
- Why are the men in *Absolutely Fabulous* so secondary to the female characters?

Once you have analysed what the gender portrayals are in your programmes, you will be in a position to consider the question more fully. For example, asking questions about why the male representations in *Ab Fab* are so weak by comparison with the female representations leads to some interesting discussion about issues of gender in the programme. Is it enough to simply say that Jennifer Saunders deliberately set out to make a female sitcom or can you explore this relationship in more depth?

What about the issues of gender representation in *The Vicar of Dibley*, given that the pivot of the programme is a traditional male-orientated rural English village having to come to terms with a feisty female vicar for the first time?

Having considered the gender portrayals and explored the extent to which they are stereotypical and then considered the issues this throws up for the programmes in isolation and then as a comparison between the two programmes, you can conclude by considering them in the broader context of both being BBC1 sitcoms in the late twentieth century. What conclusions can you draw about gender issues on television and in society from these two programmes at the time? Have later sitcoms (for example *Nighty Night*) subverted the female sitcom genre any further? Are these the sorts of sitcoms we can expect in our cultural context?

Above all, remember that the exam is testing whether you know what gender representations are employed in each of your texts and can analyse these in terms of stereotypes and social values as well as compare them. In particular the question requires detailed textual evidence from the episodes you have studied. Obviously you cannot write about the whole of *The Vicar of Dibley*, for example, given that there were several series of the programme and several 'special' episodes, but you could choose to study the Christmas 2004 specials and write about them in detail. Each point you make should be backed up with a reference to a specific part of the text that you have studied, so you can demonstrate that you are very familiar with the texts themselves.

SECTION 4
AUDIENCE AND INSTITUTIONS

Media Studies is not purely concerned with media texts; a thorough analysis of the media will include study of both the audience that consumes the text and the institutions that produce it. During your study of these areas you will need to consider the new media technologies used to produce and distribute texts, the production practices involved and the organisations that own media institutions. This section aims to improve your understanding by offering examples and analysis of these key areas. In the OCR examination, for the first two questions you will be asked to read a passage, similar to the Case Studies in this section, and then answer a selection of questions on the passage. You should use this section to increase your content knowledge and practise the skills that you will need for the exam.

Part One

New media technologies

Introduction

Media-related technologies have developed at an incredible rate even within the last ten years. The speed and capacity of computers have increased to such an extent that the standard 80 GB capacity of a computer today is considered the norm. Many home computers are now multimedia, allowing the user to access the Internet, play music or DVD films, edit video and manipulate images. The kind of technology we see in the home today would have cost hundreds of thousands of pounds fifteen years ago and means that many people are now capable of running businesses from a home computer.

The advent of digital technologies had an extremely significant impact on the media world. Television, radio, film and print text producers have all benefited from the speed and quality of digital processes. Again, this development is now available for home consumption, as well as being part of the production process, and means that the consumer has access to a greater choice of media reception types than ever before. We can, for example, receive our television programmes via traditional analogue means, via satellite or cable, or via digital transmission.

Means of access and modes of consumption are a particular issue when discussing new media technologies. We could watch a film, for example, on video, DVD, digital projection, on wide-screen technologies such as IMAX cinema, or we could look at clips from a film on cinema websites. Music can also be accessed through different formats, such as CD, mini disc, DAT, MP3 and older formats such as tape. The developments in media technologies have meant an increasing number of contexts in which we can consume the media, formats that we can access and modes of consumption.

The technologies available to both the consumer and media industries are forming closer and closer links, with technologies converging in order to develop further. Mobile phones are now capable of accessing the Internet, as are games consoles. Home entertainment systems, which work as a network

of technologies with a centralised means of control, will soon be widely available. The necessary interrelation of technologies within these kinds of development has meant that media institutions are now converging in order to create all aspects of the new product. A home entertainment system, for example, will need TV, radio, music, computer and telephone manufacturers to work together.

The Internet

An important distinction you will need to acknowledge is that between the Internet and the World Wide Web. The Internet is an international computer network. It was created in the 1960s in the United States as a military-funded experiment in computer science. In 1969 ARPANET was created. This was a network of computers, which was a direct predecessor to the Internet we know today. It was not until the early 1980s that the Internet which we use as part of our everyday lives came into existence. The Internet is essentially a means by which data can be moved from one location to another.

The World Wide Web was created after the Internet. In 1990 a research physicist called Tim Berners-Lee developed a system for the Internet via which he could publish physics papers for his colleagues to read. His idea was to construct a democratic means of information sharing, which would allow a free passage of information on the Internet. In 1991, Berners-Lee developed his system further and then gave it away to the world. The World Wide Web, which stores information and can be accessed globally, came into existence.

The Internet and the World Wide Web which we have today have an incredible number of uses, for both the media consumer and the media producer. Connection speeds are improving all the time, as is the sophistication of the average home computer. Multimedia capacity has become commonplace and ever-increasing computer capacity means that many activities that would previously have been impossible at home, such as film-making and web distribution, are now possible. For the media producer, the uses of the Internet are many and varied. The film industry can advertise films by showing trailers on websites, radio stations can broadcast via the Internet, and newspapers now have online editions of their daily papers. Media industries can also use the Internet for audience-related research, analysing message boards, fan sites and 'hits' on particular websites to gauge consumer trends.

For the media consumer, the uses of the Internet are increasing at an amazing rate. As a forum for discussion, the Internet has always been popular with those who wish to avoid censorship or challenge dominant ideologies. For example, blogging (a diary log 'homed' on the Internet) has been used for a range of personal purposes, from presenting the world with an individual's personal taste in music to documenting events in Iraq which are not being reported by the main news channels. The freedom and democracy of the World Wide Web envisioned by Berners-Lee in the early 1990s seem best evidenced by this kind of Internet use.

It is not solely as a means of opinion presentation that the Internet can be used, however, and the opportunity for individuals to present their own media products to an audience is also an important use of the Internet. Whether the product is a short piece of digital film-making, a news article or a podcast, the Internet has provided an arena within which the amateur media producer can present his creations.

All of the above points indicate the benefits of the Internet and the World Wide Web, but you will also need to make yourself aware of the potential problems and issues surrounding the Internet. As you will have found when attempting to do research using the Internet, it is often difficult to distinguish between useful sites and those which contain either wrong or not very useful information. The sheer volume of different domains (73,000,000 and counting!) and the accessibility of the Internet for anybody who wishes to write about anything, can mean that information searches are quite frustrating. Finally, the issues of censorship of the Internet and those who seek to manipulate it for their own ends should not be forgotten.

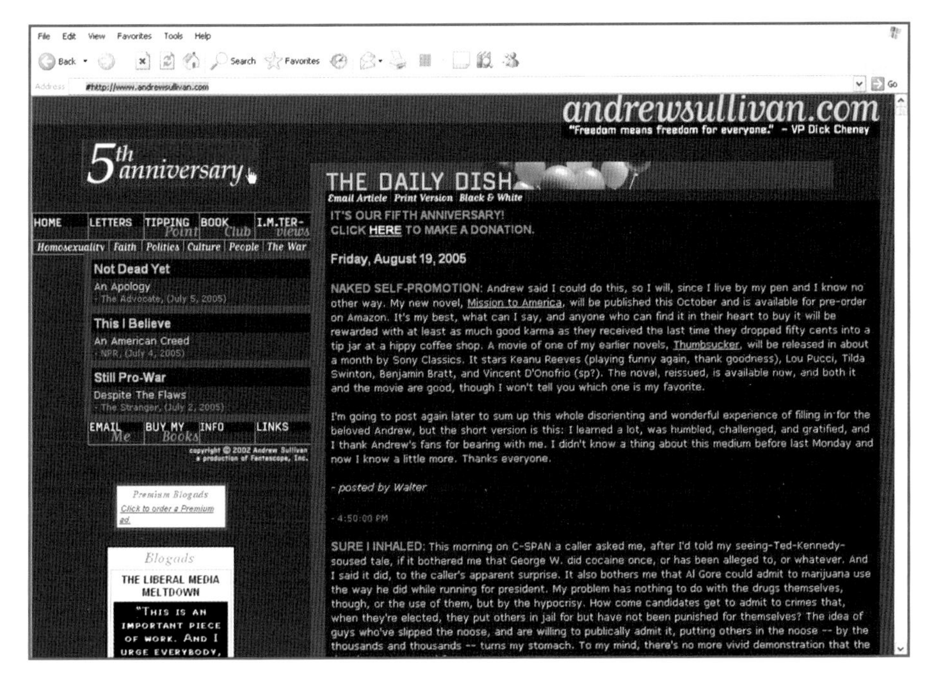

Andrew Sullivan's blog

DISCUSSION

Make a list of all of the ways in which you use the Internet. Then, in a small group, discuss the similarities and differences between the lists you have made.

With your small group, discuss the ways in which media industries might use the Internet.

CASE STUDY

Read the article carefully and answer the questions below:

The Blogging Revolution
Weblogs are to Words what Napster was to Music

By Andrew Sullivan, from *Wired* magazine, May 2002, www.wired.com

In the beginning – say 1994 – the phenomenon now called blogging was little more than the sometimes nutty, sometimes inspired, writing of online diaries. These days, there are tech blogs and sex blogs and drug blogs and onanistic teenage blogs. But there are also news blogs and commentary blogs, sites packed with links and quips and ideas and arguments that only months ago were the near-monopoly of established news outlets. Poised between media, blogs can be as nuanced and well-sourced as traditional journalism, but they have the immediacy of talk radio. Amid it all, this much is clear: The phenomenon is real. Blogging is changing the media world and could, I think, foment a revolution in how journalism functions in our culture.

Blogs do two things that Web magazines like *Slate* and *Salon* simply cannot. First off, blogs are personal. Almost all of them are imbued with the temper of their writer. This personal touch is much more in tune with our current sensibility than were the opinionated magazines and newspapers of old. Readers increasingly doubt the authority of *The Washington Post* or *National Review,* despite their grand-sounding titles and large staffs. They know that behind the curtain are fallible writers and editors who are no more inherently trustworthy than a lone blogger who has earned a reader's respect.

The second thing blogs do is – to invoke Marx – seize the means of production. It's hard to overestimate what a huge deal this is. For as long as journalism has existed, writers of whatever kind have had one route to readers: They needed an editor and a publisher. Even in the most benign scenario, this process subtly distorts journalism. You find yourself almost unconsciously writing to please a handful of people – the editors looking for a certain kind of story, the publishers seeking to push a particular venture, or the advertisers who influence the editors and owners. Blogging simply bypasses this ancient ritual.

Twenty-one months ago, I rashly decided to set up a Web page myself and used Blogger.com to publish some daily musings to a readership of a few hundred. Sure, I'm lucky to be an established writer in the first place. And I worked hard at the blog for months for free. But the upshot is that I'm now reaching almost a quarter million readers a month and making a profit. That kind of exposure rivals the audiences of traditional news and opinion magazines.

And I have plenty of company. The most obvious example is Glenn Reynolds, a hyperactive law professor who churns out dozens of posts a day and has quickly become a huge presence in opinion journalism. This is democratic journalism at its purest. Eventually, you can envisage a world in which most successful writers will use this medium as a form of self-declared independence.

Think about it for a minute. Why not build an online presence with your daily musings and then sell your first book through print-on-demand technology direct from your Web site? Why should established writers go to newspapers and magazines to get an essay published, when they can simply write it themselves, convert it into a .pdf file, and charge a few bucks per download? Just as magazine and newspaper editors are slinking off into the sunset, so too might all the agents and editors and publishers in the book market.

This, at least, is the idea: a publishing revolution more profound than anything since the printing press. Blogger could be to words what *Napster* was to music – except this time, it'll really work. Check back in a couple of years to see whether this is yet another concept that online reality has had the temerity to destroy.

Questions

1. **Name four different types of blogs mentioned in the passage.**
2. **What two things can blogs do that web magazines like *Slate* and *Salon* cannot?**
3. **Why does the writer think that 'you can envisage a world in which most successful writers will use this medium as a form of self-declared independence'?**
4. **What, according to the writer, could individuals potentially do within their blogs?**
5. **Can you think of any uses of blogs which have not been mentioned in the article?**

Digital television

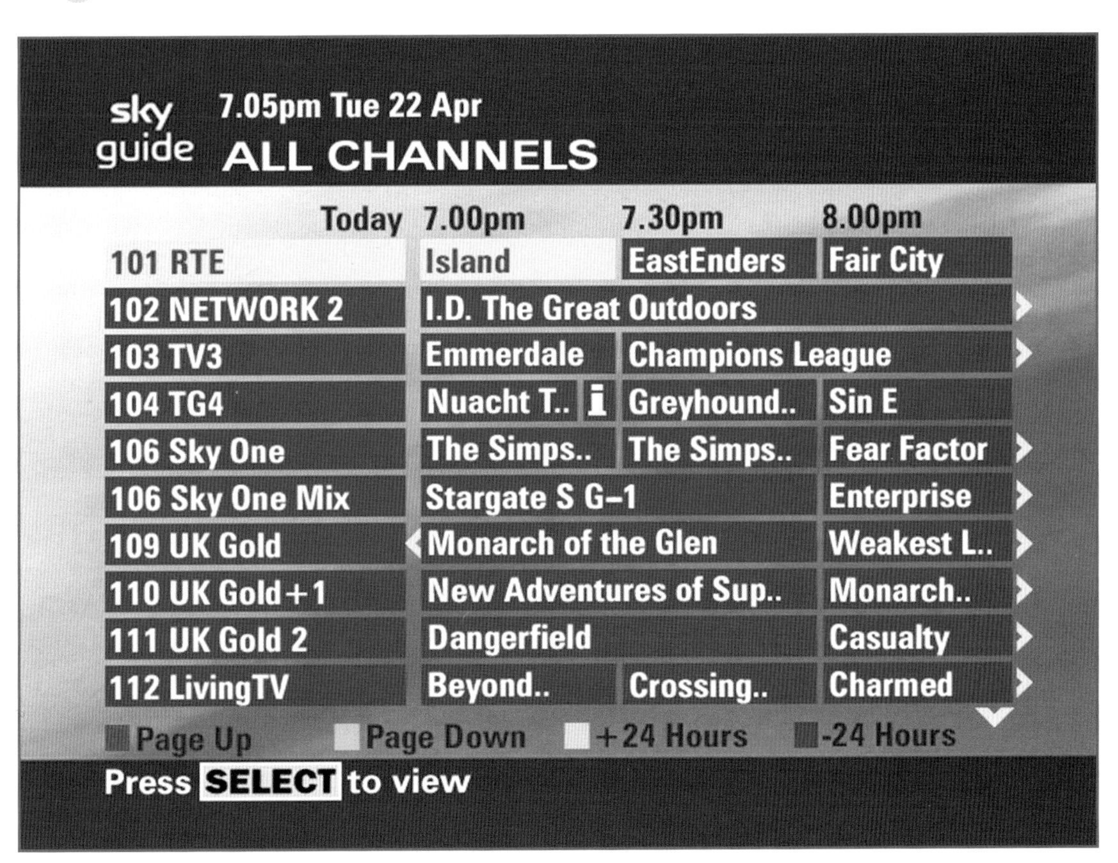

A digital TV menu

Digital television uses computer technology rather than standard systems to transmit signals. Unlike an analogue mode of transmission, digital television sounds and images are converted to computerised digits before being sent through the air. These digits can be received by aerials, satellite dishes or via cables, but need either a set-top box or a built-in decoder in order to process the signal for your digital television set. All of this means that pictures and sounds can be transmitted much faster than before and will retain a much higher quality. Interactive television is also possible using digital signals and we are, for example, already able to choose camera angles when watching live sporting events or music concerts.

In 1996, the Digital TV Group was established in order to work towards the launch of terrestrial digital television in 1998. There were eight founder members of this group, including the BBC, and the common aim was to establish an effective digital broadcast, providing also a forum for discussion of issues involving broadcasters, transmission operators and receiver manufacturers. Once digital was launched, the market quickly expanded. There are now three 'platforms' through which it is possible to obtain digital TV: satellite (via, for example, Sky Digital), terrestrial (via Freeview, which includes non-subscription digital BBC channels) and cable (via, for example, NTL).

Digital television has seen many new types of programme and, by extension, programme consumption. Interactive television offers the viewer greater control over the images being received. Video conferencing is also possible using digital transmission and may have a significant impact on the ability of businesses to communicate, as well as an individual's choice of communication means. 'Pay-per-view' television is also a feature of digital channels where the viewer is asked to pay a fee before being able to access, for example, a sporting event. This type of television is extremely problematic, however, and opponents argue that it will encourage the organisers of large events to allow only pay-per-view coverage, thus excluding those who do not have access to the appropriate technology.

Recent television technology developments, such as flat screens, have already hit the general markets and interactive television is already in evidence on digital channels in the form of TV shopping and 'choose your camera angle' style sporting event coverage.

The main recent advancement has been the move from analogue to digital transmissions, but the technology surrounding television is developing constantly – 3D and holographic televisions are in development, as are plasma screens which use small packets of glowing gas, rather than tubes.

Video recorders may soon be outstripped by DVD as a means of viewing films at home, but the latest in Personal Video Recorders (PVRs) allow personalised recording. TiVo, which is made by Thomson and marketed by BSkyB and ReplayTV, is marketed in the USA and uses a hard drive to store programmes recorded from the television. The system has the ability to 'learn' the viewing habits of the household and record programmes accordingly. This kind of recording technology takes the analogue signal from your TV aerial and converts it into digital codes that can then be stored. When you want to watch the programmes that have been recorded, an MPEG decoder translates the signal from digital back into analogue so it can be read by your television. This translation of signal is not necessary with a digital TV set-up.

What will also be extremely significant for television in the future will be the convergence of both the industries and the technologies they produce in an attempt to provide more advanced and integrated systems. Part 2 of this section will look at the institutional importance of convergence in more detail, but in terms of technology, we can construct three areas of product that seem to offer natural convergence. These areas are telecommunications, media technologies and IT technologies.

Telecommunications technologies, such as satellite TV and telephones, may provide one area of convergence. Television broadcasting, the film industry, book publishing and newspaper technologies seem to offer another logical group of related industries that would benefit from more integrated systems. The last area of potential convergence is within the realm of IT technologies, and we may see increased links between Internet providers, computer software and hardware manufacturers, and other IT service providers.

DISCUSSION

1. What do you think are the main benefits to the consumer of digital TV?
2. What do you think are the main benefits to the media industry?
3. What has been your own experience of digital television? What do you think are the potential drawbacks of this kind of technology?

CASE STUDY

Read the article carefully and answer the questions below:

(Adapted from www.pcmag.co.uk/news)

Digital TV switchover to cost £6bn: Set-top box power usage to bump up electricity bills

Daniel Thomas, *Computing*, www.computing.co.uk, 21 Jan 2005

The switchover to digital television could cost Britain in excess of £6 billion, with set-top box receivers leading to a rise in household electricity bills, industry analysts warn.

Financial analyst firm Enders Analysis predicts that £3.5bn of this public cost will result from greater use of electricity by set-top boxes in the next twenty years.

Some £865m will also be needed to upgrade or install new aerials if households are to receive digital reception, with at least one per cent of UK homes not being able to watch digital TV unless satellite receivers become available.

Another £2.1 billion could be required to fund regulator Ofcom's proposed public service publisher which would provide new digital content for UK citizens, said analyst Chris Goodall, speaking at the Oxford Media Convention, yesterday.

An additional £250 to £400 million could be required to help the old and vulnerable access digital TV, assuming that voluntary services will provide services free of charge.

But Goodall said the planned 2012 switchover to digital would recoup some funds and improve services when the government sells off the current radio spectrum used by analogue TV.

'Analogue broadcasting is extremely broadcast inefficient and if we freed it up then telephony on mobile phones would be much better than it is now,' said Goodall.

But Ian Moss, head of communication policy at the Treasury, told *Computing* that the financial benefit from a spectrum sell-off will be 'pretty low'.

'It's more about the economic value that can be gained from new services launching when the spectrum is made available,' he said.

Questions

1. **Why, according to the article could 'digital television cost Britain in excess of £6 billion'?**
2. **What needs to be done in order to ensure that all households can receive digital installation?**
3. **How would the government 'recoup some funds' in 2012?**
4. **Why do you think that 'analogue broadcasting is extremely broadcast inefficient'?**
5. **What do you think the main pros and cons will be of a digital changeover in 2012?**

Digital radio

Until digital technology became available to radio, all programmes were broadcast using analogue transmissions (either AM or FM). Analogue processes present the listener with the actual sound which is being generated (during a radio play, for example) and thus tend to recreate any interference or distortion which may occur in the studio. Analogue signals can also be affected by hills or tall buildings that might impede their movement. Digital radio signals are translated into digits and carried by the radio waves in a way that stops interference or distortion. Digital radio provides not only a clearer signal but a greater 'air-space' for programmes, thus aiming to provide the consumer with a bigger range of programmes from which to choose.

DISCUSSION

Imagine that you were being asked to 'sell' digital radio to your grandparents' generation, i.e. people who are used to analogue radio technologies. What would you outline as the main benefits to this technology? With a partner, you have 200 words in which to outline the main benefits of digital radio. You will then be asked by your teacher to read out your summaries to the class.

CASE STUDY

Read the extract carefully and answer the questions below:

(Adapted from the information at www.bbc.co.uk/digital radio)

What does DAB digital radio have to offer?

There's more choice with DAB. DAB technology means that broadcasters can transmit more stations than ever before. On average, the DAB listener will have double the choice they had with FM radio. The BBC launched five new digital radio stations in 2002, offering:

- **exclusive live sports**
- **the best of rock and pop**

- **all-day entertainment including kids' programmes**
- **music and speech for British Asians**
- **hip hop, R 'n' B, garage and drum and bass.**

And all your favourite BBC radio stations are already broadcasting on DAB.

One-touch tuning is easy to use. A DAB digital radio will tune to a station with one touch of a button. Simply scroll through the list of stations, then press the 'select' button to tune in. No fine tuning, no fiddling ... no fuss!

DAB means better reception. The annoying effects of interference on analogue broadcasts are a thing of the past. DAB digital radio has super-clear reception and pure sound, as long as you are within the coverage area.

Plus, the BBC's national digital radio stations are broadcast on the same frequency all over the country. So if you're listening to DAB digital radio in the car, you'll never need to re-tune, wherever you go. However, availability of BBC local radio services and some commercial stations varies in different locations and may require an 'autotune' to make them accessible in a particular area.

And brand-new features. Have you ever heard a song on the radio and wanted to know what it was? DAB digital radio sets have a small screen which carries information about the programme you're listening to. It could be:

- **track and artist details of a song**
- **plot summary of a drama**
- **instant sports results**
- **competition details**
- **news headlines.**

This service is expected to develop even further in the future, giving you even more free, useful information to make listening to DAB digital radio an even better experience.

Questions

1. **What is 'one-touch tuning'?**
2. **How might 'scrolling text' be an advantage to the radio listener?**
3. **What are the improvements in reception that the BBC promises with digital radio?**
4. **Why don't you need to re-tune an in-car DAB digital radio when you're on the move?**
5. **What are the benefits of digital radio to media producers such as the BBC?**

MP3s

The latest source of music that has opened up for music consumers is the Internet. Using free MP3 software, which derives its acronym from MPEG (Motion Picture Experts Group) 1, Audio Layer 3, an Internet user can convert a song from a CD into a computer file and post it on the net. Another user can then download the file and play it. This means that the music being transferred from one consumer to another is free. This is a significant issue that is causing a great deal of debate within the music industry. Fan sites and music industry official sites have fragments of tracks available to listen to or download, but they do not allow complete albums to be downloaded, and they do not release singles/albums on to the Internet before their official release date. Some artists are not concerned that the consumer may be able to download an album free, possibly even before release. They enjoy the fact that their music is being listened to by an increasing number of people. They don't consider MP3s a threat to sales: David Bowie, the Beastie Boys and Fatboy Slim are firm supporters of MP3s. Other artists, such as Metallica, The Corrs and Eminem have been fierce opponents and consider this type of access to their music to be undermining and illicit.

MP3 is not the only software that enables the consumer to 'stream' and store music files. WMA, or Windows Media Audio, was launched by Microsoft in April 1999 and offers a compression system which provides better quality than MP3. Copyright protection is provided by Windows Media Digital Rights Management (DRM).

DISCUSSION

With a partner, discuss what impact you think MP3 technology has had on the music industry and the music consumer.

CASE STUDY

(Extract from *iPod – therefore I am* by Stephen Moss, *The Guardian*, 2 January 2004, www.guardian.co.uk)

iPod – therefore I am

The iPodlounge website has 1,741 pictures of iPods, submitted by iPod-lovers all around the world. An iPod flying over the Swiss Alps; an iPod on the roof of the Australian parliament building in Canberra; a dog listening to an iPod in New Jersey; a man running the Washington marathon while listening to an iPod; an iPod on Mount Rushmore; iPods at the Grand Canyon, outside St Basil's Cathedral, in front of the Eiffel Tower and gleaming beside Sydney Opera House. Coming soon – an iPod on Mars.

Poddies will admit it, too: this is a cult that dares to speak its name. 'I'm in love with this machine and I may start sleeping with it,' announced Dominic Mohan recently in *GQ*. *Stuff* magazine placed it first in its list of 100 greatest gadgets, hailing it as 'the coolest thing to come out of California since the Beach Boys.' It even appears to have reached Wales. 'Just as any self-respecting Maoist would not step out in public without a copy of the Little Red Book,' said the *Western Mail* in a splendidly off-target metaphor, 'anyone in step with the zeitgeist will be clutching an iPod in 2004.'

Some people, adorers of technology, are labelled 'early adapters' (or 'adopters' – there seems to be some dispute and dictionaries have yet to adapt/adopt). They are the ones who had breezeblock-sized mobile phones in the mid-80s; their laptops are always half the size of anyone else's; they know you don't listen to Radio 2 on a BlackBerry Wireless Handheld. These people were importing iPods from the US at the beginning of 2003; upgrading them when they finally went on sale here in the spring; are probably laughing at us now as we struggle to catch up. I am a 'posthumous adapter': had I been a caveman, I would have doused the fire, refused to pick up a pick-axe and failed to see the point of the wheel. Huh, they call that progress?

Multiple iPod buying seems common. Tony, a large man with a sarf London accent, is buying two – one for his wife, the other for his 18-year-old daughter. Just 10-gigabyte models – the lowest spec – but sufficient to hold 2,500 songs, 250 albums. 'That's enough for anyone,' he says sagely. He has timed his arrival at Procom Electronics well – coming in just as a fresh batch of iPods shows up. The manager is tearing open the packaging as a reasonably orderly queue forms. Will Tony buy one for himself, too? 'I don't think so – I'm too streetwise for that. You become oblivious to what's around you.' I assume he is a boxer or a debt collector – always looking over his shoulder – but he says he has an interior design company.

Poddies radiate joy – the joy of first love or true belief. 'I love my iPod,' says Gareth. 'It's changed my life. Mine's a 30-gigabyte [already superseded by the 40-gig, note] and holds seven and a half thousand songs. I've downloaded 6,000 – the soundtrack of my whole life.'

Do you not feel a sense of loss, I ask Gareth, thinking of my collection of classical CDs, lovingly arranged by composer and opus number on an old pine bookcase. 'Not really,' says this hard-hearted modernist. 'All my CDs are under the bed now. I still buy CDs occasionally, but only in the way people still buy vinyl. It's nostalgia.'

CD sales are falling worldwide; record companies are panicking; the future of music is digitalised and downloadable; the Poddies are on the march.

'The iPod is the greatest piece of technology since the motor car,' says Paul, a music-loving, single professional in his early 30s who perfectly fits the iPod-enthusiast profile. 'Remember when the Walkman was launched in 1979 and people said this was fantastic – a moment that would change your life. Well, this is even more amazing. It's the first piece of kit that has convinced the philistine masses that Apple Macs are what we Mac users have known them to be all along – refined, easy to use, beautiful, cool.'

Is there anything wrong with the iPod? Not really. They are unquestionably small, compact, easy on the eye. But teasing questions do suggest themselves. Who really needs to carry round 1,000 hours of music, 102 songs by Madonna, the entire oeuvre of the Beautiful South? Is this really Nirvana? Gareth says it saves him having to listen to people 'yapping' on the bus, but is this not a technological pile driver to annihilate a nut? Paul says it is useful at parties because you can produce a play list that can't be tampered with; friends can't find that old recording of Wizzard's 'I Wish It Could Be Christmas Every Day'. But is that a reason to splash out £350, or a reflection of a bad choice of records – or friends?

And then there are the extremes to which Poddism can take you – the outer fringes of this new religion. Take Hannah. Hannah does not construct play lists – she lets the randomiser select tracks for her from the thousands she has downloaded. But, she says, the randomiser is not random. 'Sometimes I just know what's coming up – I can sense it. My iPod knows me and knows what I'm doing. The other day I was walking into a churchyard and it started playing Jeff Buckley's Hallelujah – it was an amazing moment.'

There are, however, still some unbelievers, clutching CDs, standing by their Discman, their shrill voices crying out in a desert of podlessness. 'I hate the idea of the iPod,' says music writer Caroline Sullivan. 'Why would you want to carry around 10,000 songs? Nobody needs that number. This is a complete Nick Hornby anorak's dream – middle-aged men will be buying it with joy. Models like it, too, but they don't have any brains. Ten thousand tracks are more than anyone has in their collection – you end up having to fill it with Hurricane Smith songs. What's wrong with a Discman or a Walkperson? It's just a gadget that appeals to men who want access to everything – all the indie schmindie stuff they think they should listen to, a rock critic's wish list of songs. They think it offers limitless potential, but our lives need editing, or it ends up like digital TV – hundreds of channels and nothing to watch.'

Questions

1. **What/who is an 'early adopter'?**
2. **What, according to the 'poddies' interviewed in this article, are the main benefits of the iPod?**
3. **What, according to the writer of the article and those interviewees who are not fans, are the main drawbacks of this kind of MP3 technology?**
4. **What does the article suggest has been the impact of the iPod and other MP3 technologies on the music industry?**
5. **From your own experience of MP3 technologies, what do you think are the main pros and cons?**

Computer-generated images (CGI)

Still from *The Incredibles*

Computer-generated images are evident in many media areas. Films, computer games, television commercials and programmes, amongst others, have all 'benefited' from this new technology. Ridley Scott's film *Gladiator* included a computer-generated Rome, for example. The ship and many of the characters seen walking on the deck in James Cameron's *Titanic* were produced on a computer, and the latest *Star Wars* instalment was littered with computer-generated images. These computer-generated effects are used either to approximate reality (to generate verisimilitude), as with the Rome of *Gladiator* or the ship in *Titanic*, or to give a sense of the unreal or science fictional, as with the numerous alien characters in the *Star Wars* prequels.

Computer-generated imagery of the type in evidence today was first brought to the attention of both the film industry and the general public in 1991 with James Cameron's sequel *Terminator 2*. The 'morphing' of the T-1000 robot was produced through improved hardware and software and was evidence to the film industry that this new form of special effect was popular with the viewing public. *Jurassic Park* proved to be another successful showcasing for this technology, as did the *Toy Story* films. As yet the main products of CGI have been settings and creatures; if human characters are computer-generated they are generally seen from a distance because it is extremely difficult to reproduce accurately the movements, gestures and skin quality of people on a computer.

The process of generating a computer image often begins with the skeleton of the shape to be animated. In *Jurassic Park* the ILM (Industrial Light and Magic) animators began by building dinosaur skeletons in their computers. They found pictures of bones, which were then scanned in to achieve a realistic dinosaur shape. Anatomically accurate models were also built and then scanned into a computer. The scanning was done using a Cyberware scanner, which focuses a revolving laser beam on its subject, thus obtaining information from all angles and from all depths. The next stage was to 'fit' the information from the scanner over the skeleton already created in the computer. The T-Rex dinosaur was produced in this way, and once its movements had been created in the computer, using knowledge of the T-Rex's shape and size plus the information gained through moving the models to predict how it would move, it came to life on the screen.

CGI elements are becoming more and more commonplace, especially in films. *The Incredibles* and *Shark's Tale* advanced CGI use further than ever before and the *Spiderman* films used extended sequences of CGI to represent the 'flying' sequences of the title character. As the technology used to create these effects advances, so do audience expectations and you will need to consider the impact of CGI on media audiences, as well as considering the part it plays in the marketing of media products.

DISCUSSION

With a partner, note down all of the examples you can remember of media texts which use CGI. Then, discuss what you think the role of CGI is in the experience of media audiences.

CASE STUDY

Read the descriptions of films using CGI below and then answer the questions that follow:

The Great Mouse Detective (1986)

The first major use of computer animation in an animated film – in the scene of the gears of London's famed bell tower Big Ben.

Luxo Jr. (1986)

A two-minute short from Pixar, noted as the first *fully* computer-generated, computer-animated film, about Luxo and his son – digital desk lamps. Oscar-nominated (the first computer animation to be nominated for an Academy Award), the film was directed by John Lasseter (of *Toy Story* fame) and William Reeves. Pixar's 5-minute *Tin Toy* (1988), the inspiration for *Toy Story* (1995), was the first computer animation to win an Academy Award. Billy, the baby character in the short film, marked the first time that a CG character had realistic human qualities.

Who Framed Roger Rabbit? (1988)

A co-ordinated effort produced by Disney, with live action directed by Robert Zemeckis and animated by Richard Williams. This was a remarkable blend of animated imagery and live-action human characters, and was filmed as a tribute to the entire pantheon of cartoon characters from Disney, Warner Bros., MGM, and other studios in the 1940s. The remarkable computer animation included sophisticated shading, lighting and shadows to make the characters appear very 3D and lifelike as they interacted with real-world objects and people.

The Abyss (1989)

Noted for its underwater visual effects, especially of the watery alien creature, a 'pseudopod,' this was the first example of digitally-animated, CGI water – and the first convincing 3D character animation. The water pseudopod replicates Mary Elizabeth Mastrantonio's face and appears to communicate by movements that resemble facial expressions.

The Rescuers Down Under (1990)

The first completely digital film from Disney Studios.

Beauty and the Beast (1991)

Featured integration of hand-drawn cells and computer-generated animation, especially in the ballroom scene in which Belle and the Beast dance – within a completely 3D-rendered background. The animated camera moves in 3D space. This new digital technology was tested in Disney's earlier films *The Black Cauldron* (1985), *The Great Mouse Detective* (1986), and *Oliver and Company* (1988). It was the first animated film to be nominated for Best Picture by the Academy of Motion Pictures Arts and Sciences.

Terminator 2: Judgement Day (1991)

Terminator 2 is the first mainstream blockbuster movie with multiple morphing effects and simulated natural human motion for a CG character. The lethal, liquid-metal T-1000 cyborg terminator, the first major digital character to be used in a film, morphs into any person or object. The morphing effect was first used in director Ron Howard's *Willow* (1988), but not to such an extent. Also, in post-production work, the truck crashing through the wall was flipped from left to right to create a better angle.

Lawnmower Man (1992)

This breakthrough film with groundbreaking special effects introduced virtual reality to films. In one CGI sequence, the two lovers become liquid metal, melding with one another and transforming into metallic insects flying across the computer-generated terrain.

In the Line of Fire (1993)

It was much cheaper to use footage of an actual 1992 Clinton campaign rally than to pay extras to rally, so computers were used to retouch the images digitally, and Bill Clinton was replaced with the faceless president that Clint Eastwood was protecting. Computers also took an image of Eastwood from his earlier film *Dirty Harry* (1971), made it look even younger (gave him a digital haircut, shaved off his sideburns, narrowed his tie, and gave his jacket a digital lapel), and then implanted it into newsreel footage from JFK's 1963 Dallas airport arrival, taken with a 16-millimeter camera of JFK and Jackie Kennedy at Glover Field on the day the president was assassinated.

Jurassic Park (1993)

This film from Steven Spielberg mixed animatronic and computer-generated (CGI), photo-realistic dinosaurs. The scenes of the living, eating, and breathing dinosaurs, especially the attack of the T. Rex, used mechanical robots and miniature models in stop-motion, frame-by-frame processing.

Forrest Gump (1994)

The film features impressive computer-digitized effects: Tom Hanks's digitally-composited conversations with past Presidents; the ping pong game/ball (and the crowd watching); the fluttering feather (with the string it was attached to erased); and the removal of Gary Sinise's lower legs.

The Lion King (1994)

The wildebeest stampede scene blended 3D computer animation with traditional animation techniques.

The Mask (1994)

A live-action film combined with cartoons composited onto the frame – (the Mask itself; a cartoon-style gun etc.)

Casper (1995)

The translucent image of the 'friendly spirit' was computer-generated. This was the first CG character that took a leading role.

Toy Story (1995)

The first fully 3D, computer-animated feature film, from a collaboration between Pixar and Disney Studios. Followed by an equally successful sequel *Toy Story 2* in 1999.

Dragonheart (1996)

A 10th-century fantasy fable with state-of-the-art digital animation of a talking dragon named Draco (with the voice of Sean Connery). This 18ft-tall, 43ft-long creature was expertly produced by Industrial Light and Magic.

Titanic (1997)

At the time, this was the most expensive film ever made, at $285 million. Contains stunning digital effects – the passengers on the deck, the wide shots of the ocean and sky, even Kate Winslet's iris that was digitally inserted into one of Gloria Stuart's eyes.

Antz (1998)

Following *Toy Story* (1995), this was the second fully computer-animated feature, preceding the release of Disney's all-CGI insect epic *A Bug's Life* by seven weeks. This was also the first CGI film to feature over 10,000 individually animated characters in various crowd scenes (such as the Starship Troopers-like battle).

The Matrix (1999)

Amazing special effects – airborne kung fu, slow-motion bullet-dodging (the 'flow-mo' and 'bullet-time' effects), shoot-outs, wall-scaling and other visual effects, in the kinetic, sci-fi virtual reality film from the directorial writing team, the Wachowski brothers.

Star Wars: Episode I – The Phantom Menace (1999)

This film undoubtedly contained more computer animation and special effects than any previous film. It also featured a completely computer-generated (all digital) main character named Jar Jar Binks (voice of Ahmed Best), a widely derided aspect of the film. Jar Jar was a 'Gungan', an alien indigenous to the planet Naboo. The annoying character was reprised in *Star Wars: Episode II – Attack of the Clones* (2002).

Final Fantasy: The Spirits Within (2001)

A photo-realistic, science fiction tale by director Hironobu Sakaguchi (created in the style of the interactive video game) that took four years to make. It advertised itself as 'Fantasy Becomes Reality'. It was the first hyper-real, computer-generated feature-length film based entirely on original designs – no real locations, people, vehicles or props were used.

Shrek (2001)

A fully computer-animated, colourful fantasy film (from DreamWorks and Pacific Data Images), and the first Oscar winner in the newly created category of Best Animated Feature, by the Academy of Motion Picture Arts and Sciences.

The Lord of the Rings Trilogy (2001–2003)

CGI-imagery was combined with 'motion capturing' (of the movements and expressions of actor Andy Serkis, who also served as the voice) to produce the barely-seen, supporting character of Gollum (originally known as Smeagol). A motion capture suit recorded the actor's movements that were then applied to the digital character. A more laborious visual effects process digitally 'painted out' Serkis's image and replaced it with Gollum's. (The same technique was repeated in *I, Robot* (2004), with Alan Tudyk as the robot Sonny.)

Star Wars: Episode II – Attack of the Clones (2002)

The first feature film shot and exhibited in digital video (non-celluloid), with a 24fps high-definition progressive-scan camera. Also features an extensive use of digital matte paintings.

Sky Captain and the World of Tomorrow (2004)

The first movie with very photo-realistic, all-CGI backgrounds and live actors. This meant that human actors were completely filmed in front of a green screen with no background sets at all.

Sin City (2005)

This Robert Rodriguez-directed, violent B/W crime-film noir, is based on three of the 1990s graphic novels by Frank Miller (who co-directed). *Sin City* is a stylistic comic book adaptation (containing vibrant splashes of color), starring Bruce Willis and Jessica Alba, and was shot completely with high-definition digital.

Questions

1. **What have been the main changes that have occurred in the use of CGI within films in the last 20 years?**
2. **How many different ways has CGI been used within the films described above?**
3. **Do you think that the use of CGI is more applicable to particular genres of film?**
4. **Are there any films which are not listed in the description above which you consider to be important within the history of CGI in films?**
5. **Do you think that CGI elements significantly change the viewer's experience of a film?**

Big-screen technologies

The spectacle of viewing images on large screens is not a twentieth-century phenomenon. Audiences in the early nineteenth century had access to a Diorama experience, and one of the most dramatic of the Diorama productions was *L'Arrivée d'un Train en Gare,* filmed in 1896 by Louis Lumière. Large landscapes were painted onto a huge transparent canvas and an audience would watch the image as variations in lighting projected through the canvas made it appear to move. Because of the size of the canvas, the audience had the sensation that they were being pulled into the image, thus taking part in the experience represented on-screen. This form of early visual spectacle was an attempt to approximate reality by creating a complete viewing experience. Because even the peripheral vision of those watching the Diorama caught what was happening on the screen, the experience was much more realistic.

Cinema continued to experiment with wide-screen technologies and the advent of sound and colour offered even more exciting audio-visual experiences for the audience. The next stages of development saw Fox projecting films in 70mm Grandeur. Paramount's equivalent was Magnafilm, and Warner Brothers' format was VitaScope. None of these proved to be particularly successful, partly because of the advent of an alternative new viewing experience in the form of television. It wasn't until the 1950s when Cinerama was introduced that wide-screen technologies became popular with audiences again. Films in this format tended to be of real events and the realism of the viewing experience caused some members of the audience to run from the cinema! CinemaScope was to be the next major advancement for the big screen and was developed by 20th Century Fox to deliver an even more realistic and exciting film experience.

Modern big-screen entertainment is perhaps best represented by IMAX cinema, a fully integrated system of film production which uses cameras, film stock, screens and projection equipment especially designed in order to recreate a live experience. IMAX digital sound recording is also used and is projected through the screen in order to enhance the live feel of the shows. The Expo event in Montreal, Canada in 1967 saw the first showcasing of IMAX cinema technology when film-makers Graeme Ferguson, Roman Kroitor and Robert Kerr presented their preliminary ideas for IMAX-style films. They offered their ideas for an integrated IMAX system that would use one powerful projector, and introduced the latest and most realistic wide-screen experience. At the Osaka EXPO in 1970, having worked with the backing of a Japanese consortium, Ferguson, Kroitor and Kerr revealed their first, finished, IMAX film and the technology which had created it. They also formed the IMAX Corporation in this year to produce, market and distribute their new system. After this introduction, IMAX cinemas quickly sprung up and are now to be seen all over the world. In 1994 the Sony IMAX cinema opened in New York City and in 1997 the BFI (British Film Institute) IMAX cinema was started in London.

The BFI IMAX uses Britain's biggest screen. It is more than 20 metres high and 26 metres wide. The projector weighs about two tonnes and the sound comes from an 11,600 watt digital surround sound system that has 44 speakers positioned in seven clusters throughout the auditorium. The verisimilitude (approximation to reality) offered within a big-screen cinema experience, generated by both the image and the sound, is different from that of a standard film. Big-screen productions saturate the senses of the audience and place them firmly within the world that is being portrayed on the screen. Whether this enhances the viewer's experience or limits it is something that you will need to debate.

DISCUSSION

What do you consider to be the advantages and disadvantages to film producers of creating a film using IMAX technology?

What are the differences between viewing a film in a big-screen format and viewing it in a standard format?

CASE STUDY

(Adapted from www.imax.com)

IMAX Technology

IMAX technology offers spectacular images of unsurpassed size, clarity and impact, creating a film-viewing experience unlike any other.

The IMAX projector uses 15/70 format film, ten times larger than a conventional 35 mm frame and three times bigger than a standard 70 mm frame. The film frame is projected onto giant rectangular IMAX screens as much as eight storeys tall, and in IMAX Dome theatres onto domes up to 27 m in diameter. This sheer size, combined with unique IMAX projection technology, is the key to the astonishing sharpness and clarity of 15/70 format films.

IMAX projectors are the most advanced in the world, more precise, powerful and reliable than any ever built. The unique feature which makes this possible is the 'Rolling Loop' film movement. The Rolling Loop, originally invented by Ron Jones, and developed by IMAX Corporation, advances the film horizontally in a smooth, wave-like motion. During projection, each frame is positioned on fixed registration pins, and the film is held firmly against the rear element of the lens by a vacuum. This provides picture and focus steadiness far above the standards of other systems.

The IMAX experience is completed by our state-of-the-art six-channel, multi-speaker sound system, designed specifically for IMAX theatres. The IMAX Theatre Network consists of 220 affiliated theatres, of which roughly 60 per cent are located in North America and 40 per cent spread across 30 countries. Approximately half of the theatres are part of commercial cinema complexes, and half located in institutional venues such as museums and planetariums. More than 100 of our affiliates are now equipped with IMAX 3D technology for a more immersive audience experience than ever before.

IMAX Corporation makes IMAX cameras available for rent and also offers many other customer support services to film-makers who want to take advantage of this superb technology. Our camera rental inventory includes 3 compact dual-strip IMAX 3D cameras, 2 lightweight IMAX MK II cameras for steadicam work and more than 20 other cameras to suit different requirements.

Questions

1. **What are the differences presented here between IMAX cinema technologies and those of standard cinemas?**
2. **What is 'Rolling Loop' film movement?**

3. **What help does IMAX say it offers to film-makers?**
4. **Why do you think roughly 50 per cent of the theatres are located 'in institutional venues, such as museums and planetariums'?**
5. **What do you think will be the next stage in big-screen film making?**

Video games

There is a vast market for video games and the present global market is said to be worth around £17 billion. The market is split between the games available for a PC and those which are played from a games console, with the latter type holding the bigger share of the market. Over a third of homes in the United Kingdom own an advanced games console, some of the most popular of which in the last five years have been the Sony PlayStation™, Microsoft's XBox and the Nintendo N64.

The first types of games from Sega and Nintendo used a cartridge system to 'feed in' the games, but with the arrival of the extremely successful CD-based Sony PlayStation™ in 1995 the technology shifted. In 1997 Nintendo launched the N64, which went into competition with Sony for the console market. With the number of people using the Internet reaching figures of nearly 200 million in 1999, the scene was set for a games console with Internet access, and in October 1999 Sega launched the Dreamcast games console.

Games consoles also have the potential to provide a central control mechanism or conduit for other types of entertainment system. Developments in this area have embraced the idea of technological convergence and have focused on the ability of the console to do more than just offer games. PlayStation™ 2 extends the capabilities of the first PlayStation™ in more than just its games capacity. It has a range of digital inputs and outputs that, in time, will mean that it can be connected to other entertainment systems within a household. The potential interactivity and convergence of future home entertainment systems is something that the developers of the new PlayStation™ have incorporated into their design. PlayStation™ 2 is based on a DVD drive and can play films and music, as well as games. What converges with this type of technology is not just formats and technologies, but different branches of the Sony organisation, such as its website, music and film production, which will work more closely together and will all be accessible through PlayStation™ 2.

The advances in this sector of new media technology have been dramatic and will continue to be so. What is interesting, however, is that the new consoles that are brought out by different companies have little or no compatibility. Unlike a television and video recorder/DVD, for example, a games console does not allow for use with other consoles or even with those from the same manufacturer that have gone before. Rarely are products offered which extend the capabilities and capacity of an existing console; new products are sold as entire units, which means that revenue generated is extremely high.

One of the most heated areas of debate concerning games consoles is the content of the games themselves. The violence of games such as *Carmaggedon* and *Street Fighter II* has caused some critics to blame the games for copycat violence. The issue seems to be whether or not those playing the games are prompted to violent actions. Does a world saturated with violent computer game images encourage players to become desensitised to the effects of violence, and if it does, do they then act out their aggression without conscience? The other side of the argument suggests that we have an ability to disentangle what is real and what is fictional; that the kinds of violent acts that we are shown on computer games may be unpleasant, but are kept (by the players) in the realms of fantasy and not acted upon.

DISCUSSION

With a partner, make notes on and discuss your own experiences of video and computer game playing. How have your experiences and expectations changed over the years that you have been playing these games?

CASE STUDY

(Article from BBC News Online, news.bbc.co.uk, 7 April 2005)

PSP™ embraced by DIY technicians

More than two million PSPs™ have gone on sale.

DIY software and hardware experts have been quick to embrace Sony's PlayStation™ Portable console

A glut of 'homebrew' features for the device have already been released, many of which were not part of Sony's official plans for the machine.

The PSP™ is a handheld console, which has wireless capabilities, and can play music as well as video games.

Tools for web browsing and online chat are among the first to appear since the console launched in the US and Japan.

The developments are not sanctioned by Sony but the firm has not commented on the homebrew tools.

Messaging platform

The $249 (£130) PSP™ handheld video game player went on sale in the United States on 24 March and within 24 hours one man had a working client for Internet Relay Chat (IRC), an older online messaging platform.

'I was on IRC, and someone mentioned how cool it would be to use their PSP on wi-fi at Starbucks to talk to people over IRC. I said, "I can do that", so I began working on it immediately,' said Robert Balousek, creator of PSPIRC in an e-mail interview with news agency Reuters.

Mr Balousek said about 100,000 people had visited the IRC client, and he is starting work on a new project that would let PSP™ users chat on the AOL Instant Messenger network.

Hacking new video game hardware is not new but the speed at which people have started to produce their own applications for the PSP™ is impressive.

Other 'hacks' include a way to transfer TV shows recorded by the Tivo digital video recorder to the PSP™, a program for reading e-books and a viewer for comics downloaded from the Internet.

Racing game

While many of the tools are probably in development by Sony in an official sense, some PSP™ owners just could not wait to get started.

Much of the new PSP™ functionality comes from using the web browser built into the racing game *Wipeout Pure*, which was meant to go to a Sony site.

By changing some of the PSP™'s network settings, the browser can be pointed to an Internet portal.

A number of people have already set up such portals, formatted to fit in the PSP™'s screen and offering links and a place to enter web addresses.

Other hacks include getting the PSP™ to play all games wirelessly over the Internet and playing multiplayer games with only one copy of the game.

Questions

1. **What do you think is meant by the phrase 'homebrew' features?**
2. **What are the 'hacks' possible with the PSP™?**
3. **What are the differences between the PSP™ and the PS2™?**
4. **Can you think of any disadvantages to this kind of game-playing device?**
5. **Do you think that the size and portability of the PSP™ will be important factors within its potential success? Why/why not?**

Mobile telephones

The first mobile telephones were large and cumbersome. Few people owned them, so mobile-to-mobile communication was not common. Mobile phone technology has advanced at an incredible rate in recent years and now wide-ranging and compact mobiles are a common sight. The lucrative and expanding nature of the mobile phone market means that competition between different networks, handset manufacturers, PDAs (personal digital assistants) and software companies is fierce.

The data-handling capabilities of many phones available at the moment means that the consumer can gain web access, explore the Internet and send emails, and it is this market space which is being competed for most intensely. Plans for mobile Internet services are being offered by AOL, BBC, Orange and Vodafone, to name a few. At the moment, the Internet can only be accessed via mobile if you have WAP (Wireless Application Protocol) technology installed on your phone, but with so many different providers coming into mobile phone technology, the next few years should see many different means of access. When phone display screens increase in size, it will be possible to add audio and video to the present mobile phone services.

In the context of Media Studies, mobile phones are an interesting piece of technology. Because of their developing multimedia capacity, they are being used within the media to speed up certain processes, such as the transfer of photojournalistic images from photographers to their newspaper, via the internet.

DISCUSSION

In a small group, discuss the different mobile phones you have had. What have been the technological advances you have experienced? What have been the pros and cons of the different phones you have had?

CASE STUDY

(Article by Richard Wray, *The Guardian*, 15 April 2005, www.guardian.co.uk)

Carphone boss says 3G 'will go mad'

Charles Dunstone, the chief executive of Carphone Warehouse, warned yesterday that unless Britain's mobile phone operators throw their marketing weight behind 3G technology this year, new operator 3 will run away with the market.

Europe's largest independent mobile phone retailer yesterday said it expected its annual profits to be at the top end of expectations. In calculating its figures, Carphone was not counting on a big pick-up in sales of handsets incorporating the new technology, which enables video calling and fast downloading of music and video clips.

But Mr Dunstone, who founded the business in 1989, said yesterday: 'If you want my personal opinion I think 3G will go mad in the second half of the year.'

He said 3, which is owned by Hong-Kong based conglomerate Hutchison Whampoa, has done well to grab more than 3 million customers since its launch two years ago.

He said O_2, Orange, T-Mobile and Vodafone are all going to have to start stimulating sales of 3G handsets 'or it's going to start running away from them'.

So far, only Vodafone and Orange have had large-scale launches of 3G in Britain. Sales of Vodafone's 3G handsets are understood to have been poor while Orange has been forced into a 'buy one, get one free' offer. T-Mobile is poised for a full launch of its 3G service, while O_2's main push is likely to be in the second half of the year.

Analysts had pencilled in profits for Carphone of £98m to £102m for the year to the end of March 2005, with about £122m for the current year.

Carphone also said Hans Snook, the founder of Orange, will be quitting as chairman in July, to be replaced by John Gildersleeve, former commercial director of Tesco and a Carphone non-executive.

Questions

1. **What, according to the article, does 3G technology allow mobile phones to do which they previously couldn't?**
2. **Why does Charles Dunstone think that other mobile phone retailers are going to have to stimulate sales of 3G phones?**
3. **Why do you think the sales of 3G phones have been 'poor' for Vodafone and Orange so far?**
4. **What do you consider to be the benefits of 3G mobile phone technology?**
5. **Can you think of any disadvantages of this type of technology?**

New media technologies: key terms

- Digital
- Analogue
- Convergence
- Interactivity
- Connectivity
- Portability
- Miniaturisation.

Part Two

Media ownership

Introduction

As is the case with new media technologies, media ownership is in a state of constant flux. Companies merge or are taken over and what was once an autonomous company might now be a branch within a much bigger corporation. Convergence (the coming together of two previous separate media technologies or companies) is greatly in evidence within the area of media ownership. In Media Studies, the integration of products or institutions for mutual benefit is called synergy, implying that what is born out of the newly forged links is more effective than what had gone before. Synergy is in evidence, for example, in the release of certain products simultaneously. For example, a film may be released alongside an associated CD to produce maximum revenue. The advent of many of the new technologies outlined in the first half of this section has meant that production practices within media institutions, such as marketing and distribution, have become ever more wide-reaching and advanced. We now have the technology to consume our media in a dizzying number of ways, but it is also important to consider how our consumption is affected by who owns the companies behind the products we consume.

Media ownership is becoming more and more concentrated, with vast companies being created in the place of many smaller ones. This concentration is brought about in two ways. First, a larger company may take control of a smaller competitor in the same market or in a market into which the larger company wishes to expand. The second mode of concentration is brought about when a company wishes to buy into a particular 'branch' of another of equal size, in order to utilise the technology and expertise already held by that other company. For example, a company that manufactures hardware programmes may buy into one that produces appropriate software. For media institutions, convergence, in whatever form, has an effect on the products produced and the ways in which the audience consumes them. We may have a product suddenly drawn to our attention because a new parent company has the financial power to market it effectively. We may buy a product that we would not have considered before because of the reputation we perceive a new parent company to have.

Any discussion of media institutions should include analysis of those companies which are involved in cross-media initiatives, those which have a public service remit, those which are purely concerned with one aspect of a product such as production, and those which have been formed as alliances. This part of Section 4 will offer you case studies based on different ownership issues and will also help you to understand the effect that all of this has on the audience/consumer.

The BBC

The BBC is an example of a company that holds a public service remit. Revenue is generated from the license fee paid by the consumer and also from the sale of its products, not from advertising. Originally a private company set up by a group of radio manufacturers, the BBC was then nationalised to become a state broadcasting corporation. The BBC state service was set up in order to provide both radio and television broadcasting, but was intended to be independent of government interference. It was not established to provide a vehicle or means of expression for the ruling political party, and indeed the Royal Charter, which set up the BBC, stipulates impartiality of presentation, particularly in news and current affairs programmes.

Public service broadcasting (PSB) was seen as a way of reflecting the needs of the viewing public by offering programmes that were of interest to a cross-section of society. The impartiality of the BBC is often tested through coverage of such news items as strikes and elections, and as a student of the media you should look carefully at the ways in which events are reported and consider whether or not the BBC remains a 'voice of the nation' rather than a political voice.

Another important fact to consider in any discussion about the BBC and public service broadcasting is the shifts in programming which have occurred because of a widening of the television channel marketplace. With the advent of Independent Television on 22nd September 1955, Channel 4 in 1982 and Five in 1997, as well as satellite and cable, the BBC has been increasingly placed within an intensely competitive marketplace. Given the fact that there is now more competition for viewers, we must consider whether BBC programming has had to change in order to face that competition. It is argued that the BBC schedules contain too many soap operas, chat shows, comedy programmes and lifestyle programmes, and the channel has lost its distinctive nature. Its news coverage has to compete with terrestrial and satellite alternatives. The BBC now has digital channels for the consumer, such as BBC3 and BBC4, which means even more programme options. BBC3 provides entertainment, comedy and drama aimed at the youth market, while BBC4 contains programmes focused on the arts and culture. It is essential to consider whether the BBC has maintained its original remit to offer balance, impartiality and a reflection of a wide range of viewers' needs.

DISCUSSION

What are the differences between public service broadcasting and the independent TV channels?

What have been the main changes within BBC programming over the last 50 years?

CASE STUDY

(Article by Daniel Thomas, *Computing*, www.computing.co.uk, 2 August 2004)

BBC uses Athens Games to showcase graphics system
Broadcaster uses Linux to improve speed and accuracy of real-time results

The BBC will use Linux-based graphics software to improve the speed and accuracy with which it can process real-time results at the Athens Olympics.

The broadcaster will use this month's event to showcase the graphics system before using it at other major sporting events.

A portable PC system has been installed at the IBC Media Centre in Athens, which will receive real-time results in XML format from the Athens Organising Committee, and then use SQL databases and HP ProLiant servers to store the information.

Red Hat 8 Linux desktop applications on Apple eMac computers will then produce moving '3D' graphics, cutting down on the need for manual data input and graphics production.

'BBC One will be broadcasting in a live environment, where millions of viewers will be waiting for the latest information, so accuracy, integrity and reliability are incredibly important,' said Andy Townsend, design systems manager at BBC Broadcast.

'Our software makes it easier for the production team to receive and interpret results, which means they can find the most interesting stories as they emerge.'

Townsend says by using open standards technologies such as Linux, Java, SQL and XML, the BBC will be able to provide a more cost-effective, high-performance and high-availability computing system, 'suitable for the rigorous demands of Olympic schedules.'

The system includes a wide range of graphic design templates, so results tables can be created automatically from the data feeds.

'Producers can browse the database for templates they are interested in and then create graphics,' said Jon Hanford, senior systems analyst, BBC Broadcast.

'It means producers can choose graphics for any event they want, as soon as they like, so they can create them quicker without any errors,' he said.

Hanford says if the system is successful at the Olympics, BBC Broadcast plans to roll the technology out to other sporting events.

'A lot of new broadcast technology gets tried out on the Olympics and they are then rolled out for future BBC programming,' he said.

Questions

1. **What do you think the phrase 'real-time results' means in the opening paragraph of this passage?**
2. **What do you think the benefits to the TV viewer are of this kind of graphics system?**

3. **Why did the BBC use this kind of technology to show results within the 2004 Olympics?**
4. **Why do you think 'A lot of new broadcast technology gets tried out on the Olympics . . .'?**
5. **From your own experience of watching the Olympics on the BBC in 2004, can you remember the use of these new kinds of graphics? What did you think of them? Did they enhance your viewing experience?**

News Corporation

Rupert Murdoch's company, News Corporation, is an example of a multinational player in the media ownership debate. It has constantly expanded, both geographically and technologically, to become one of the most powerful media companies. News Corporation is the parent company for 20th Century Fox films and television, BSkyB, Sky Digital and Star TV (which operates in Asia) and, under the British press 'wing' of News International, Murdoch acquired the *News Of the World*, the *Sun*, *The Times* and *The Sunday Times*.

Rupert Murdoch

Expansion into Internet technologies came through the purchase of Delphi On-Line Internet that operates in America and the United Kingdom. There is also a book publishing section to News Corporation – it owns HarperCollins in the USA and the UK. Rupert Murdoch has built a multimedia and multinational organisation that works to allow him to promote a product from one particular section of the organisation through a company or product within another. Films to be released by 20th Century Fox, for example, can be marketed and promoted through newspapers, television stations, magazines and the Internet.

Because of the vast range of media products within News Corporation, Rupert Murdoch can afford to take risks on new products. If they are unsuccessful there will still be an extremely successful product somewhere else in the corporation to fill the deficit – one product can, in effect, subsidise another. At the moment, News Corporation products are targeted at the US, British, Western European, Asian and Australian markets, but Africa is sure to be of increasing focus.

As with other huge media corporations, fears have often been expressed concerning Murdoch's expansion plans and potential monopoly of the media market. In 1995, a government White Paper on cross-media ownership expressed concerns about Murdoch's bid for the Channel 5 franchise. This was credited with limiting the extent of News Corporation influence within British terrestrial television markets. As with many other media companies, News Corporation is expanding, not just through the countries in which it operates or the products which it offers, but by merging with other companies. Its potential consumer group is therefore ever-increasing.

DISCUSSION

Using the information above and your own knowledge of News Corporation, how many different News Corporation products can you name? How many different types of media text are included in your list?

What do you consider to be the impact of News Corporation on the media marketplace and the media consumer?

CASE STUDY

(Article by Dan Milmo, *The Guardian*, www.guardian.co.uk, 9 April 2004)

Murdoch's Italian pay-TV venture is on course

Rupert Murdoch's Sky Italia yesterday said it would reach subscriber targets for the end of the year after reporting a 20% increase in customers.

Tom Mockridge, chief executive of the pay-television broadcaster, said Sky Italia would meet its target of three million subscribers within the period. The News Corporation subsidiary has added 900,000 customers since its launch in July last year, giving it a base of 2.5 million subscribers.

'Of course, yes, it's a challenge, but the market has been very welcoming. We've already got a public target to be at three million by the end of the year, and with a lot of hard work and some good programming, I think we can hit it,' Mr Mockridge told Reuters news agency.

Sky Italia, which has a subscriber target of five million by 2007, was born following the $920m (£608m) takeover of Vivendi Universal's Telepiu service by News Corporation's Stream. Mr Murdoch's media group owns 80.1% of the new venture, with Telecom Italia holding a 19.1% stake.

News Corporation anticipates losses of $300m (£163m) at Sky Italia in the current financial year but expects the operation to be profitable by the end of 2005. The group's second-quarter figures were adversely affected by a $106m loss from the Italian pay-TV venture.

Guy Bisson, a TV analyst at research firm Screen Digest, said pay TV had a much stronger chance of succeeding in Italy after the Telepiu takeover pushed down costs and left the market in the control of a single player.

Piracy was the only issue that could pose a serious threat to the business, he added. More than 3 million Italian homes access pay-TV services through illegally manufactured decoder cards, according to the latest estimates. Sky Italia claims it has thwarted piracy after introducing technology from encryption firm NDS, a News Corporation subsidiary.

'If they can crack piracy they certainly will be on to a winner, because estimates for piracy in Italy run into the millions on satellite alone,' Mr Bisson said.

Mr Mockridge added that Sky Italia would not suffer from the rollout of digital terrestrial TV to the same degree as free-to-air broadcasters. But digital terrestrial remains the biggest threat after piracy to a multi-channel provider, as shown by the success of the UK's Freeview service.

The Italian government is pushing legislation through parliament that will accelerate the implementation of digital terrestrial services in Italy.

A crucial part of Sky Italia's defence against newcomers is its football offering, but its commitment to the sport has sucked it into the financial crises afflicting Italy's top clubs. Sky Italia made an advance rights payment to AS Roma last month to allow the club to submit its qualification for next season's Champions League. But Mr Mockridge said that was a one-off bail-out and for a month only.

'It was something we were happy to do, but not something we would consider generally.'

Questions

1. **Why does News Corporation not seem to be concerned about the anticipated 'losses of $300m'?**
2. **Why does Guy Bisson think that pay-TV has a much stronger chance of succeeding in Italy now?**
3. **What are the two biggest threats identified to a multi-channel provider?**
4. **What does Sky Italia have that it thinks will be a defence against newcomers into the pay-TV market?**
5. **Do you think that the introduction of Sky Italia is typical of News Corporation's global media strategy? Why/why not?**

Sony

The Sony Corporation was founded in 1946 and has expanded at an astonishing rate. It is not purely concerned with media-related activities and products (there are some non-media subsidiaries, such as Sony Life Insurance Co. and Sony Assurance INC), but the majority of its operations do have a media focus. It is a global corporation and, as such, has a major influence on the production and purchase of media-related products.

There are few households now that do not either own or use something produced by Sony. Its major products can be split into the following categories: audio (e.g. mini-disc systems, CD players, hi-fi components, recordable mini-discs), video (e.g. VHS and digital video players, DVD players, digital stills cameras), televisions (e.g. projection TVs, flat panel display TVs, personal LCD monitors), information and communications technologies (e.g. computer displays, satellite broadcasting reception systems, cellular phones) and electronic components (e.g. semiconductors, LCDs, Internet-related business in Japan). This diversity of media-related products means that we may use more than one in a particular household. Sony has also been at the forefront of the development of media technologies (although not all of them have been successful).

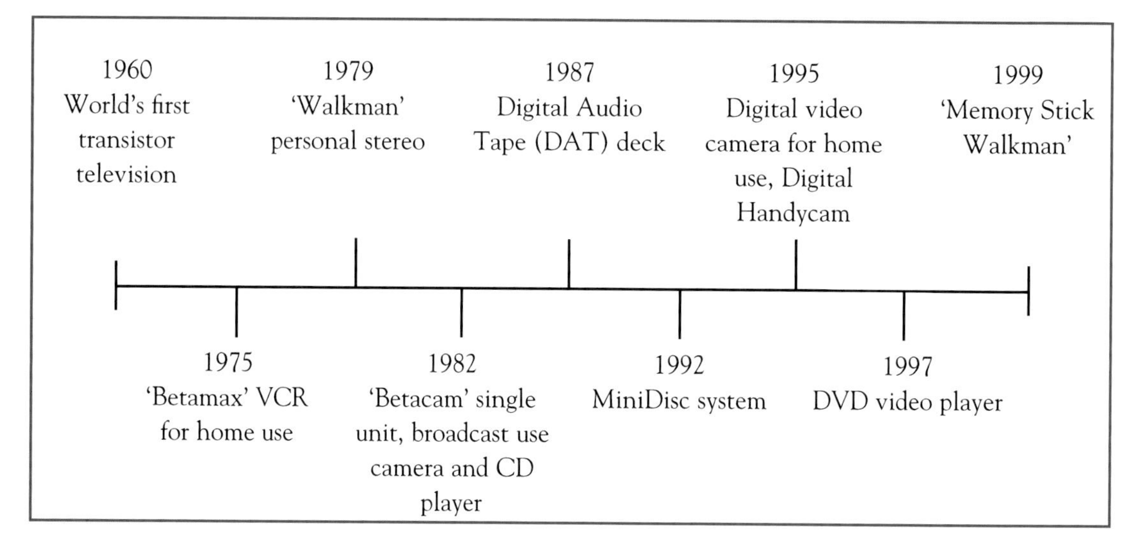

From a Media Studies perspective this is an interesting list of events because it charts trends in media technology development. The movement towards digital technologies is evident, as is the translation of industry-standard equipment into a home context.

The Sony Corporation has six main business areas: Electronics, Games, Music, Pictures, Insurance and Others (includes credit card business), which means that even if you do not have a physical product in your household, it is likely that you will have access to one via, for example, the Internet. The potential for internal synergy is enormous. Sony Pictures could join with Sony OnLine Games to produce a 'tie-in' game/film, for example, and in this way create a much greater market exposure for both products. Sony Music could then release the soundtrack of both. The breadth of the corporation also enables developments to be gambled upon. 'Betamax' was obliterated by VHS as the domestic standard for home video technology, in spite of being able to provide superior picture quality, but the success of other divisions of Sony were able to stop this from becoming cataclysmic.

DISCUSSION

With a partner, list the number of Sony products you each have in your household. What kinds of products are these? Do you think that Sony is the dominant company in any particular types of media product?

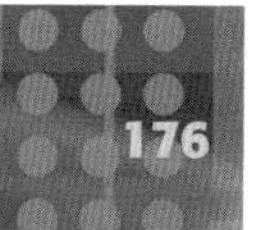

CASE STUDY

(Extracts from a Sony Computer Entertainment America Inc. press release dated 3/02/05, from www.usplaystation.com)

PSP™ (PLAYSTATION™ PORTABLE) SET TO RELEASE ON MARCH 24 ACROSS NORTH AMERICA

Sony Computer Entertainment America to Retail Single SKU PSP Value Pack for $249.99

Sony Computer Entertainment America Inc. announced today the North American launch details for its highly anticipated PSP™ (PlayStation™ Portable) handheld entertainment system. Available through retail outlets on March 24, the company continues its consumer-centric legacy with the release of the PSP Value Pack for a suggested retail price of $249.99 US/$299.99 CND. In addition to the revolutionary PSP™ hardware, the PSP Value Pack contains an unprecedented added-value package of accessories and entertainment content, including 32 MB Memory Stick Duo®, headphones with remote control, battery pack, AC adaptor, soft case and cleaning cloth, movie/music/game video sampler UMD™ disc including multiple non-interactive game demos, and for the first one million PSP Value Packs shipped, a special UMD video release of the feature film *Spider-Man™ 2* from Sony Pictures Entertainment.

Sony Computer Entertainment will manufacture one million units for sale in the North American market by the close of its fiscal year ending March 31. This figure is part of the company's total three-million-unit worldwide PSP™ system shipment estimate within the same time period. PSP™ released in Japan on December 12, 2004 and is already a hit, with more than 800,000 units shipped, including a 200,000-unit allocation that sold out on day one.

PSP™ sets a new standard as the first truly integrated portable entertainment system designed to provide consumers with a comprehensive entertainment experience including games, music, movies, communication, and wireless networking. Featuring graphics rendering capabilities comparable to the company's leading in-home console, PlayStation™ 2, PSP™ brings an unparalleled gaming experience to a portable platform, allowing users to enjoy 3D games, with high-quality, full-motion video, and high-fidelity stereo audio. PSP™ also allows for digital photo display and supports digital music playback in both MP3 and ATRAC formats.

'PSP will evolve and elevate portable entertainment, giving users the freedom to play full 3D games, watch movies, listen to music and connect wirelessly on their terms, their time and their place,' said Kaz Hirai, president and chief executive officer, Sony Computer Entertainment America Inc. 'More than ever, today's consumer demands access to entertainment outside the home without compromising quality. With more than 100 PSP game titles currently in development world-wide, and the ability to download and listen to digital music and view feature films with breathtaking screen quality, PSP lets users control their entertainment options, all in one package.'

PSP™ features an unmatched 4.3-inch, 16:9 wide-screen TFT LCD that displays full color (16.77 million colours) on a 480 x 272 pixel high-resolution screen. PSP™ also comes complete with built-in stereo speakers, exterior headphone connector and diverse input/output connectors such as USB 2.0, and 802.11b (Wi-Fi) wireless LAN, enabling users to connect to the Internet and play online via a wireless network. Up to 16 PSPs™

in the vicinity can also be connected to each other directly in ad-hoc mode, allowing for wireless head-to-head competition. In addition, wireless capabilities will allow software and data to be downloaded to a PSP™ and saved onto a Memory Stick Duo®.

PSP™ also adopts a newly developed compact, but high-capacity, optical disc, Universal Media Disc (UMD®), as its storage medium. UMD is the next-generation compact storage medium, only 60mm in diameter but can store up to 1.8GB of digital data, more than three times the data held on a CD-ROM. A broad range of digital entertainment content such as high quality 3D games, music, movies, video clips and other programs can be distributed on UMD®. To protect this content, a robust copyright protection system has been developed for UMD®, which utilizes a combination of a unique disc ID, 128-bit AES encryption keys for the medium, and individual ID for each PSP™ hardware unit.

About PSP® (PlayStation® Portable)

PSP® (PlayStation® Portable) is a new portable entertainment system that allows users to enjoy 3D games, high-quality full-motion video, and high-fidelity stereo audio. With graphics-rendering capability comparable to that of PlayStation®2, PSP™ features a 4.3 inch wide screen, high-resolution TFT display. PSP™ also adopts a newly developed compact but high-capacity (1.8GB) optical disc, Universal Media Disc (UMD®), as its storage medium. With a wide range of accessories and connectivity options, including Memory Stick Duo®, USB 2.0, IR port and WiFi wireless LAN, PSP™ is the new entertainment platform from PlayStation.

Questions

1. **What are the main differences between the PSP™ and the Playstation™ 2?**
2. **Do you think that the portability of the product will be an important factor within its potential success in the media marketplace?**
3. **Do you agree with the statement 'More than ever, today's consumer demands access to entertainment outside the home without compromising quality'? Which other media products do you think are being marketed on this basis?**
4. **Is there any type of technology that you think is missing from this new entertainment platform?**
5. **Why do you think that Sony have brought out the PSP™?**

Cross-media ownership

Many media companies are involved in expansion processes and one of the areas we need to consider is cross-media ownership. This means that a company might have a significant stake in several different media organisations, such as films and newspapers. We have already looked at one example of this type of organisation in the form of News Corporation, and have also considered the restrictions that can be placed upon it – because Rupert Murdoch already owns 20 per cent of the British newspaper market, he is prohibited from holding a terrestrial TV licence.

In 1962, the Royal Commission on the press, using the language of the Department of Trade and Industry, stated that 'action should be taken to regulate the increasing concentration of newspaper

ownership which could threaten the freedom and variety of expression of opinion and perhaps even the unbiased presentation of the news'. There is a variety of restrictions on cross-media ownership in Britain that attempt to halt any movements towards monopolies, and perhaps the most significant piece of legislation to date has been the 1996 Broadcasting Act, which forbids any company that owns 20 per cent of national newspaper circulation from having more than a 20 per cent share of an ITV company or Channel 5. This was the legislation that halted News Corporation's move to purchase a larger stake in British terrestrial television.

Many media companies, however, believe that these types of restrictions are unhelpful when trying to compete for a share of the global media market. This is something that is beginning to be recognised also by the British government, which published a White Paper in Autumn 2000 that aimed to consider reforms of broadcasting and telecommunications regulations.

Cross-media ownership issues impact on the audience in a number of ways. First of all, we may consider the ways in which cross-media products owned by the same company or alliance of companies can become 'branded': in other words, they may begin to take on a group identity that is the construction of the parent companies. Is it possible for a product to retain its individuality within a market controlled by cross-media companies? The second area for consideration involves issues of bias and partiality. The more that companies expand and the more powerful they become, the more products are at their disposal through which they can communicate their own ideological viewpoint. We therefore need to consider whether media products that we study (and consume) can remain ideologically balanced and unbiased within a climate of ever-increasing cross-media ownership.

On its own, News Corporation is involved in cross-media expansion, but there have also been many alliances and mergers formed between media companies in order to expand the possibilities of cross-media ownership. One significant example of this is Viacom, which owns MTV and Paramount Pictures and has merged with USA television group CBS. The new company is now worth $66 billion. This produces a business generating sales of $21 billion, which is greater than any of its rivals except Disney.

DISCUSSION

With a partner, note down what you consider to be the advantages and disadvantages to media companies and organisations of cross-media ownership.

CASE STUDY

(Article by William Cederwell, from *The Guardian*, 19/02/04)

Disney's Magic Kingdom is still standing

For now, it looks as though the fight is over. The Walt Disney Company, the entertainment giant, has rejected a $54bn (£28bn) hostile takeover bid from Comcast, America's largest cable operator. Disney's board of directors said the offer was too low and that the deal would not benefit their shareholders. The directors also took the opportunity to endorse Michael Eisner, the controversial Disney chairman.

But many wondered just how long Mr Eisner could last in his post, regardless of what happens to Disney in the future. The *Wall Street Journal Europe* thought the company would be better served with a different man at the helm. Disney shareholders 'have been on a roller-coaster ride with Mr Eisner for 20 years now, and some want him to get off. While the Disney chief has pocketed hundreds of millions of dollars [from his remuneration packages], the company's earnings have been effectively flat for a decade and shares were recently trading where they were six years ago.' The paper hoped the threat of a takeover was incentive enough for Disney's board to 'finally ... address the company's failings'.

The New York Times had fun comparing the management styles at Comcast and Disney. At Comcast, there is less centralisation and authority is freely delegated to department leaders. But at Disney, where Mr Eisner is 'accustomed to being obeyed, acclaimed and despised in about equal measure', no creative decision is made without his approval, right down to the colour of the bumper cars in Disney theme parks. This tends to drive away Disney's talented executives, the paper said, thus 'dimming its creative spark'.

The US press also spent time guessing whether more hostile bids for Disney would follow from other suitors. The Disney name is 'enough to give pause to any media conglomerate', the *Los Angeles Times* noted. The paper thought Microsoft, with its 'stockpile of billions of dollars', was a likely 'wild card'. Forbes thought that Disney's shareholders were actually quite keen to see their company acquired for the right price. And the *Philadelphia Inquirer* suggested Disney's best defence against any future unwanted bids was 'to acquire another company in order to make itself too big or unattractive'. On Tuesday, Disney seemed to be heeding that advice, announcing 'it had acquired two of Jim Henson Company's best-known properties – the *Muppets* and the *Bear in the Big Blue House* – for an undisclosed sum' (*NY Times*).

The Sunday Times explains why Disney's fortunes have been in decline. This is 'no fairy tale ... it is the story of the relentless pressure for change placed on media and communications companies by the non-stop revolution in technology'. No matter if you control the rights to Mickey Mouse and Madonna, 'content alone is no longer enough'. The paper conceded Disney's woes were exacerbated after 9/11, when tourists stayed away from theme parks, triggering 'a vicious circle of falling revenues, cost-cutting and falling standards ... The financial crisis then spread to other parts of the empire.'

It didn't help matters that Disney's 'key relationship' with Pixar, the computer animation studio, had also ended, said the *Independent on Sunday*. It was all thanks to Pixar that Disney enjoyed its lucrative 'string of blockbuster films', including *Finding Nemo* and *Toy Story*.

The Lex column of the *Financial Times* thought it likely that Comcast would now 'sweeten its rejected bid'. Although Comcast needed to make more of the positive business 'synergies' arising from the deal, such as the combination of Disney's 'content' with Comcast's 'distribution', said Lex, the problem with hostile takeover bids such as these is that the parties involved are rarely 'talking to one another', which makes it harder to focus on the merits of the bid.

But David Harding and Sam Rovit, in the *Wall Street Journal Europe*, felt a Comcast takeover of Disney had only 'dubious strategic merit' and would 'end up destroying meaningful amounts of shareholder value'. The companies are incompatible, they said, and Comcast can't be expected to grapple with Disney's problems effectively.

Questions

1. **Why do you think Comcast attempted to buy The Walt Disney Company?**
2. **What have been the criticisms of Disney Chief Executive Michael Eisner?**
3. **What were the benefits to Disney of its 'key relationship' with Pixar?**
4. **Why do you think Disney has not been as successful as it used to be?**
5. **What are the main benefits to a company of cross-media ownership?**

Digital initiatives

One of the most significant developments in media technology has been the move from analogue towards digital systems. Media companies are, of course, aware of the benefits both to product quality and transmission processes that this affords, and are also aware of consumer demand for digital systems. We will now look at some of the current digital initiatives in the media and the companies/organisations that are involved in their development and application.

Within the realms of public service broadcasting, the BBC has been involved in plans to expand the number of channels available to the consumer by creating two new digital options. Earlier in this section the programme profiles of new channels BBC3 and BBC4 were discussed. Digital options, with their range of programme types and means of consumption, provide an interesting debate when they appear within a public service broadcasting schedule. The remit of the BBC, as we have stated, is to be impartial, but also to act as a distinctive alternative to commercial stations. It is important to consider whether this can be sustained within a digital format, which allows a far greater number of programmes and which the consumer may associate with particular types of programme. Sir Christopher Bland, the then BBC chairman, countered these concerns when questioned about the place of digital alternatives within the BBC by stating that 'The BBC is very clear about its future and will continue to offer a distinctive, valuable alternative to commercial services.'

The digital television market is extremely lucrative and therefore a very competitive area. In order to try and control increasingly large shares of this market, companies often develop commercial links. One example in 2000 was between cable operator NTL and film company Universal in an aim to expand further into the digital television market. The NTL/Universal digital channel, called The Studio, provides competition for Rupert Murdoch's Sky within British digital television. In its development it planned to transmit programmes including sports events and films, and, with the Universal archive at its disposal, provide an attractive alternative. It was the intention of The Studio to be available to basic entry-level subscribers at no extra cost, which would make it extremely competitive. This provides another example of cross-media convergence within the media marketplace.

Microsoft is another company involved in digital initiatives and it has recently sought to expand into interactive television through a partnership with News Corporation, in order to create a partner company within .net TV. The link between Microsoft and News Corporation will bring the type of new technologies developed by Microsoft alongside the breadth of media products created by News Corporation.

As is evidenced by these new initiatives and by what we have seen of new media technologies, digital processes and products are becoming more and more common. In order to receive all that is digitally

on offer, however, the consumer needs to have the products that can decode digital signals in the home. There has to be a process of updating existing home technologies in order to take advantage of what is on offer, and this has an impact not just financially, but in the way we view media technology in the home. It does not seem enough these days to buy a television set, a computer or a telephone, which will then be kept for years. We seem to be entering a time where our 'equipment' needs to be constantly updated in order to keep up with developments. Referred to as 'built-in obsolescence', this means that the moment we buy technical hardware it is out of date. How consumer-friendly is it to market expensive systems which may become obsolete or dated very quickly, when we exist in a time when access to the latest technologies is marketed as an almost essential requirement of everyday life?

DISCUSSION

What do you think will be the next media-related digital initiatives? Make notes (for a class discussion) of where you think digital technologies will take media producers and media consumers next.

CASE STUDY

(Extracts from 'How Pixar conquered the planet' by Oliver Burkeman, *The Guardian*, www.guardian.co.uk, 12 November 2004)

How Pixar conquered the planet

Behind an 8ft metal fence, deep within a faceless office complex near San Francisco, one of the 10 most powerful computers in the world hums and blinks in a dark glass chamber. The machine, known as the Renderfarm, represents the final stage in the making of a Pixar movie, taking the millions of equations that the studio's animators have created to control each character, and crunching them down into individual frames of film.

In Hollywood, though, figuring out Pixar's secret has become a matter of panicky necessity. Since 1995, when *Toy Story* became the first computer-animated feature film, the company has had an unbroken record of triumphs, as popular with critics as the box office, resulting in 17 Oscars and sufficient millions to make Pixar, movie for movie, the most successful studio of any kind in the history of cinema. (*The Incredibles* took $70.7m [£38m] in its first three days in America, more than the rest of that weekend's top 10 put together.) Other animation studios, saddled with a string of flops, have been left to glower from the sidelines – with the exception of Disney, the grandfather of them all, thanks to a deal under which it provided most of the financing for Pixar's hits.

Telling a good story in animated form, though, requires a particularly bizarre kind of personality – an equal mix of childishness and deep, very adult patience. Pixar's offices are carefully calibrated to nurture the requisite eccentricity. The animation team work not in cubicles but in miniature open-fronted wooden cottages, each individually furnished by their occupants with a clashing variety of leopard skin sofas and extensive toy car collections. (In a detail that epitomises Pixar's alchemical knack for turning freewheeling creativity into profit, the cottages were actually cheaper than standard-issue office cubicles.)

Pixar's quasi-religious focus on characters and story leaves its army of computer scientists in a curious position. Their technological expertise is emphatically relegated to second place. Instead, the

importance of traditional drawing techniques is impressed upon everybody – even the workers in the accounts and human resources departments – thanks to Pixar University, an in-house animation school presided over by Nelson, at which all employees are allowed to spend several hours a week.

'When we made *Toy Story*, almost all the reviews only had one line about the fact that it was the first ever computer-animated film,' says Ed Catmull, the soft-spoken computer scientist who founded the studio in 1986 with Steve Jobs, who at the time was in exile from Apple and desperate for a major new success. 'And the technical people here were immensely proud of that.'

Catmull's personal contribution to the modern science of graphics is sizeable: he invented texture mapping, the system that allows a texture to be 'poured' over the surface of a character in a realistic way; and he co-invented something called the Catmull-Rom spline, which space and a near-total lack of understanding prevent me from detailing here. But he is the first to insist that all such tricks are irrelevant in the absence of a compelling story. 'We used to be proud of ourselves for saying story is king, story is king,' he says. 'After a while, we realised everybody else was saying the same thing too. People repeat what you say. But what's nice, from a competitive point of view, is that they don't repeat what you do.'

Computer animation's best human characters, consequently, are strictly symbolic representations, not lifelike creatures. And in any case, profound human emotions are not always best conveyed by the characters who appear the most human at first glance. (If you need convincing of this, compare any single appearance by Charles Schulz's endlessly complex *Snoopy* – animated or in strip cartoon – with the entire cinematic output of Richard Gere.)

The way Catmull sees it, the choice is between realism and believability, and the decision was made for him at an early screening of *Luxo Jr*, the two-minute-long short with which Pixar made its name in 1986. The only characters are two Anglepoise® lamps – a small one and a big one, presumably child and parent. 'Here was this remarkable piece of new technology, and we showed it to our community, the graphics community, people well equipped to ask us all about the splines we had used, for example, or these other really technical details.' But most of the computer scientists in the audience only had one question as they left the screening: 'Is the big lamp a father or a mother?'

Every Pixar film has a message. But where *Toy Story*, *Monsters Inc.* and *Finding Nemo* explored themes of self-knowledge, or of growing into adulthood, *The Incredibles* is positively Nietzschean. Some people are just better than other people, it seems to say, and their resentful inferiors ought not to try to suppress them, but to let them shine.

Questions

1. **What have been Pixar's main film successes in recent years?**
2. **What does 'technical expertise' come second place behind at Pixar?**
3. **What, according to the writer of this article, is the main message of a Pixar film? Do you agree with this?**
4. **What has been your experience of Pixar films? Why do you think that these films have been so successful?**
5. **What are the benefits to a media company, such as Pixar, of research and development into a technology such as CGI?**

Production companies

Production companies have an important role within the media environment today. They provide programmes for television and radio stations, cinemas and, through the programmes they produce, may have an impact on the profile of the channel/station. Granada Television, for example, produces programmes for all major UK channels including ITV1, BBC1 and BBC2, Channel 4, Five and Sky One. It is responsible for *Coronation St*, *Emmerdale*, *Heartbeat*, *Agatha Christie's Poirot*, and *I'm a Celebrity, Get Me Out of Here!*, *Parkinson*, *Ant and Dec's Saturday Night Take-away*, *Tonight with Trevor McDonald* and *This Morning*.

Your focus should extend beyond merely noting the names of the shows produced by a particular production company; you should also consider the types of shows made. Are there any genres of programme that seem associated with particular production companies? Are the programmes made aimed at particular target audiences? Is it possible to detect 'house style' in the programmes produced?

DISCUSSION

Using Granada as your focus, discuss with a partner whether you think there are any similarities between the TV texts that Granada produces.

Promo shot for *Big Brother*

CASE STUDY

(Adapted from www.endemol.co.uk)

Company profile

ENDEMOL UK is one of the biggest independent TV producers in Britain. Endemol is dedicated to exciting concepts that work across a range of media beyond traditional television, including interactive TV, the web, mobile phones, radio and DVD.

Highly successful Endemol production credits include: reality series BIG BROTHER, THE FARM and THE SALON; RESTORATION; music entertainment from BAND AID 20 to UK MUSIC HALL OF FAME and FAME ACADEMY; THE GAMES; live events such as THE BAFTAS and FASHION ROCKS; CHANGING ROOMS; GROUND FORCE; and READY STEADY COOK.

Production brands include ENDEMOL UK PRODUCTIONS, INITIAL, BRIGHTER PICTURES and ZEPPOTRON, specialising in a variety of genres including reality television, live events, factual entertainment, documentaries, youth shows and comedy. Endemol UK also owns VICTORIA REAL, the award-winning digital media company, and HAWKSHEAD, one of Britain's foremost corporate production companies.

Endemol UK is based in London and has offices in Bristol (ENDEMOL WEST) and Glasgow (ENDEMOL SCOTLAND). The company employs up to 800 people at any one time.

Endemol UK is part of the ENDEMOL group, a global family of leading production companies operating in more than 20 countries. Endemol is 100 per cent owned by TELEFONICA, the largest provider of telecom and Internet services in the Spanish- and Portuguese-speaking world, with companies in 17 countries and more than 62 million customers.

Questions

1. **Why do you think the main Endemol company includes a number of different 'production brands'?**
2. **What are the main genres of programme which Endemol produces?**
3. **How would you describe the main target audiences for Endemol's products?**
4. **Is Endemol a self-governing company?**
5. **What percentage of the weekly TV schedule do you think is taken up by Endemol products?**

Media institutions: key terms

- Synergy
- Convergence
- Cross-media
- Digital initiatives.

Approaching the exam: tips and hints

Content revision is, of course, an essential part of revision and you should make sure that you have read through your case studies very carefully before the exam. The second key part of the revision and preparation process is practising with past exam papers. The more you hone your time-management skills and practise the different types of questions included in the 2732 exam, the better your answers will be. Your teacher will give you past exam papers with which to practise and you should go through these carefully.

The two sections of the 2732 exam have the same types of questions for you to answer. Obviously, the content required by section A and section B is different, but the skills needed to answer the different types of questions are the same. This section aims to give you tips and hints on how to approach the exam in general and how to approach each of the question types specifically.

One of the most important things you will need to remember for this exam is to answer only on the section for which you have been prepared. NEVER do both section A and section B, as this will halve your chances of a good mark. NEVER do section A if you have been prepared for section B and vice versa. Regardless of how tempting the other section looks, you will not have been prepared for it, so will not be able to answer the questions properly. This advice might seem obvious, but every year there is always a number of students who do either both sections or the wrong section.

Time allocation is of crucial importance with any exam. For the 2732 exam you have 1 hour in which to show your examiner your skills and understanding. Use that hour very carefully. The first few questions (1a, 1b, 1c and 2a) carry relatively few marks and if you take half an hour to answer them, you will not have enough time to answer the more 'valuable' questions. Within your allotted hour, you will need about 5 minutes to read through the passage. You will probably scan the passage again each time that you answer a specific question, so you do not need to spend too much time reading at the beginning of the exam. You should then use 25 minutes to answer questions 1a, 1b, 1c, 2a and 2b. Remember that the 2b question carries significantly more marks than those which precede it, and therefore needs more time and consideration. You will need at least 10 of your 25 minutes to answer the 2b question. Having answered these first questions, you will have your long answer left. Once you have chosen between questions 3 and 4, you should spend your final 30 minutes creating a comprehensive, well-referenced and well-argued essay. Some students choose to write their long answer at the beginning of the exam and this can prove a very useful strategy, as it allows the long question to be completed without the pressure of the final clock-watching which goes on at the end of an exam.

The content needed for each of the question types within the 2732 exam differs greatly. You may only need to write three words to get full marks for a 1a answer, but the 17–20 marks awarded for the 2b answer require paragraphs, examples and an argument. The 2b question also asks you to extend your answer outside the passage and you should avoid referring only to the examples used in the passage, as this will lose you marks. Take the opportunity within your 2b answer to show your examiner what your own knowledge and experiences are.

For questions 3 and 4 you will need to create an answer that is more like a traditional essay in its structure. In order to achieve the best mark possible for this question, you will need to:

- Write enough. You do not get 45 marks for writing half or even one side of A4!
- Create an argument that considers both sides of the debate you are analysing and also offers your own response to the two sides described.
- Refer systematically and in detail to your own examples. Each time you make a new point, make sure that you include an example.
- Make sure that your comments relate specifically to the question you are answering.
- Use media-specific terminology.

Keep all of this advice in mind when you are preparing for your 2732 exam. Those students who practise their exam skills, as well as revising content, invariably do much better.

Summary

Any discussion of new media technologies should include comment on the development of the technology, the organisation behind it, how it might have changed audiences' expectations of certain media experiences, and the developments that might happen in the future.

Analysis of media ownership issues should focus on the profile and role of different media institutions, the influence they have in the media market, and how an institution and the products created by it are consumed by the audience.

There are certain advances and ideas that are relevant to both technologies and institutions. You should remember to include analysis of the role of new digital technologies, in terms of both increased application and mode of consumption, the place of synergy within media debate, and the increasing evidence of convergence of product and institution within the media arena.

SECTION 5

KEY SKILLS AND A LEVEL MEDIA STUDIES

Introducing Key Skills

You will probably have heard the term Key Skills in your school or college, but might not have understood fully what it means in relation to your own study. Key Skills are not specifically related to a subject area but are **generic**, which means that they can help improve your learning and performance in all of your study areas. The Application of Number Key Skill, for example, is not only relevant within Mathematics, and the Key Skill of Communication does not exist solely within English. These skills allow you to show employers or academic institutions that you have basic skills in key areas such as Communication, Application of Number and Information Technology. You can study the Key Skills in isolation or practise and present your Key Skills knowledge through activities based around one of the subjects you are studying.

This section aims to provide you with activities you can use to enhance your understanding of A Level Media Studies and, at the same time, provide you with knowledge and practice of the core and wider Key Skills listed below.

Core Key Skills:	Communication Application of Number Information Technology
Wider Key Skills:	Working with Others Improving Own Learning and Performance Problem Solving

Part One

Key Skill: Communication

Topic of study: Representation

Representation is one of the key concepts within Media Studies. As we saw in Section 1, representation is the process by which images, sounds and words take on meanings beyond what they initially appear to include. The potential meanings within representational analysis may be the intention of the text creator or may be a product of the shifting contexts in which the text is viewed (or listened to). Representation is most commonly associated with both the positive and negative depictions of social groups. When you are commenting on the processes of representation, try to avoid restricting yourself to character analysis. Representation deals with the values, ideas and beliefs (or **ideology**) indicated by the depiction of an individual character or group of characters. The process of analysing representation may begin with a study of the gestures, mannerisms, attitudes, costume, associated *mise-en-scène*, narrative place and language of the character, but should extend to

deductions concerning the wider social group of which the character may be part, social attitudes towards that group and the attitude of the film or television programme towards that specific group.

CASE STUDY

Margie in the Coen Brothers film *Fargo*

Frances McDormand played Chief Marge Gunderson in the 1996 film *Fargo*. The character of Margie is of particular interest because she offers comment on both the representation of women and the police within the crime genre (we must remember, however, that *Fargo* includes elements of many other genres and should not be read solely as a crime film). Margie is the central figure in the film and is the character who solves the murders. She brings stability back to the narrative and re-establishes safety for the other characters within the film.

As a police officer she represents the law, and the progress of the film is towards her re-establishment of law and order. The way in which she does this, however, sets her apart from many other cinematic police characters. Her methodology and manner are a counterpoint to the violent world established by the criminal characters, Carl Showalter (Steve Buscemi) and Gaer Grimsrud (Peter Stormare). She is persistent, unflappable and peaceful in her approach. She solves the crimes through systematic police work, using procedure and deduction rather than dramatic action or sudden discovery of key evidence. The police officers around her are largely portrayed as slow and dependent on her greater powers of deduction. Her representation as a female detective differs from someone like Jane Tennison in the television drama *Prime Suspect* because the officers around her do not impede her. She is not a 'fledgling' detective like Clarice Starling in *The Silence of the Lambs* and neither is she under threat, as Jamie Leigh Curtis's policewoman is in Kathryn Bigelow's film *Blue Steel*. Margie represents organised, systematic, even dull, police work, but is effective. Law and order are not reimposed in a dramatic or maverick way in *Fargo* – they are the outcome of process and a desire to protect peace.

Possibly the most significant fact about Margie is that she is heavily pregnant throughout the course of the film. Her pregnancy is presented to us in scenes showing her constant need to eat and her morning sickness, as well as through her physical presence. She is not constructed as an object of desire for either the other characters within the film or for the viewer, but as a woman who balances the needs of her body with those of the situation she confronts. Her pregnancy de-eroticises her and the way in which she is represented promotes her as a member of a happy, developing, domestic unit. We are often shown scenes of Margie and her husband, Norm, which establish her home life as dull but peaceful and contented.

Margie differs from the other women in the film because she is not the victim of men (as with Jerry Lundegaard's wife, Jean) or there to provide them with a service (as with the prostitutes whom Carl and Gaer pick up). She uses her intelligence and calm to bring sanity to the madness that has been imposed by Jerry's plan and Carl and Gaer's violence.

The character of Margie offers an interesting dimension to the representational debates concerning women, the police and female police officers. Our response to her is complex because she avoids the usual stereotypes of female characters in crime-related films. She is not a victim, a *femme fatale*, a novelty maverick or a woman working in opposition to the officers around her. Margie's representation adds to the realism of the film. She refuses to be stereotyped and (gently and persistently, just as in her police work) challenges our preconceptions concerning the reading of female police officers in cinema.

DISCUSSION

Discuss in class groups how masculinity is represented through Margie's husband and one other male character.

Representing a specific group: the police

A useful place to begin when considering representation is a study of specific groups of people. If you consider the way a group's depiction changes over time, it is possible to make effective comments about the shifting attitudes towards them. The representation of the police has changed markedly over the years and we should see this as representative of changes in attitudes and beliefs. Remember, however, that representations can confirm established attitudes, as well as challenge them.

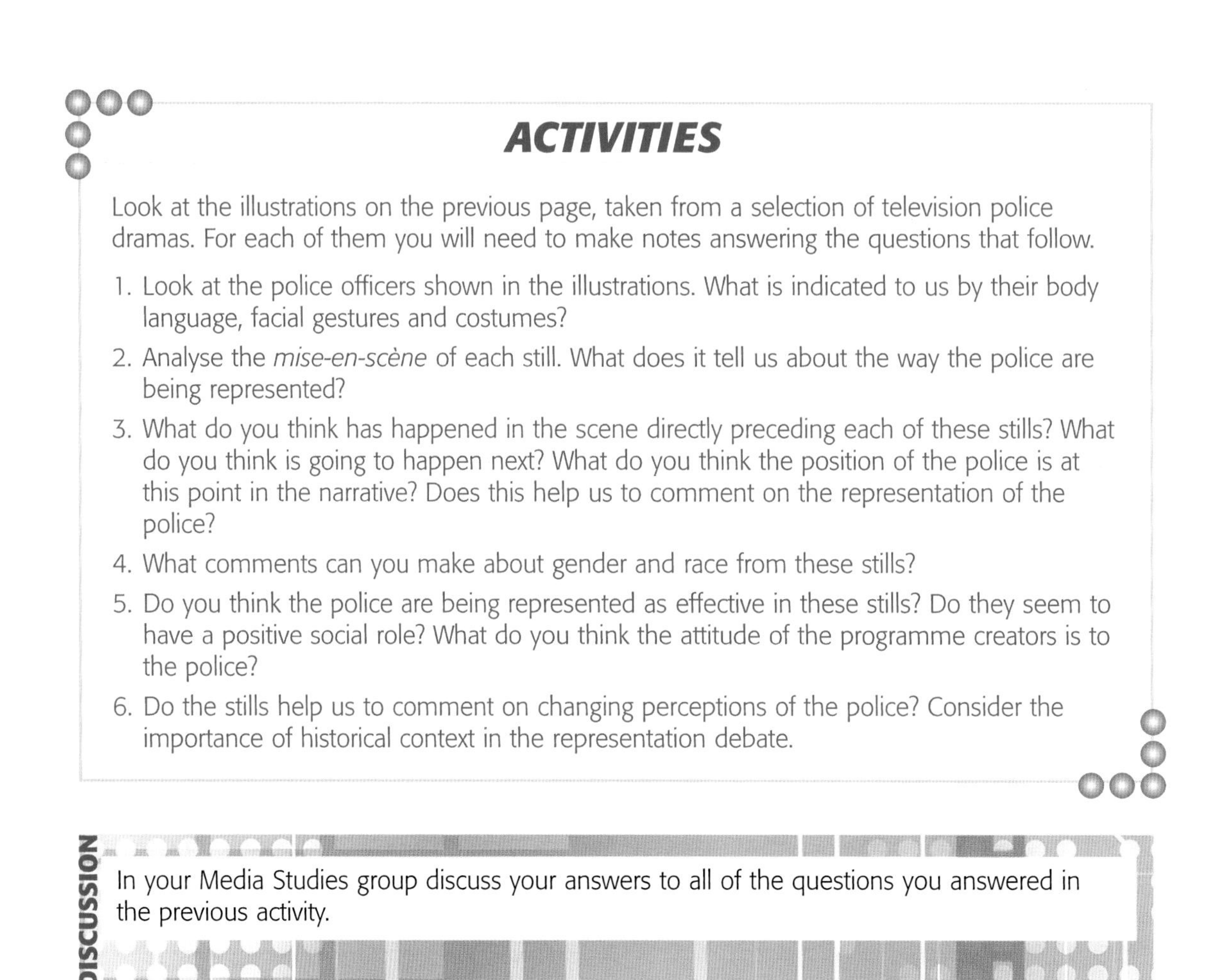

ACTIVITIES

Look at the illustrations on the previous page, taken from a selection of television police dramas. For each of them you will need to make notes answering the questions that follow.

1. Look at the police officers shown in the illustrations. What is indicated to us by their body language, facial gestures and costumes?
2. Analyse the *mise-en-scène* of each still. What does it tell us about the way the police are being represented?
3. What do you think has happened in the scene directly preceding each of these stills? What do you think is going to happen next? What do you think the position of the police is at this point in the narrative? Does this help us to comment on the representation of the police?
4. What comments can you make about gender and race from these stills?
5. Do you think the police are being represented as effective in these stills? Do they seem to have a positive social role? What do you think the attitude of the programme creators is to the police?
6. Do the stills help us to comment on changing perceptions of the police? Consider the importance of historical context in the representation debate.

DISCUSSION

In your Media Studies group discuss your answers to all of the questions you answered in the previous activity.

This discussion will provide practice for the Communication Key Skill C3.1a: Contribute to a group discussion about a complex subject.

Using character to generate representational debate

You do not have to focus on a group of characters in order to make comments concerning representation. The construction of an individual character is of equal use.

ACTIVITIES

1. Watch the scene from Hitchcock's *Rear Window* which introduces the character of Jeff. Make detailed notes on the way in which iconography (objects) and *mise-en-scène* help us to form a perception of this character.
2. Watch the rest of the film, making notes on the following:

   a) the position of Jeff in the narrative

b) his interaction with other characters

c) the era of the film and the gender politics evident at that time (you may have to consult history books or your teacher in order to answer this question).

3. Jeff has been described as representing a crisis in masculinity. He is confined to his chair and often seems afraid of a relationship with Lisa. Having made your preliminary notes on the character of Jeff, try to extend your comments to wider representational debate by answering the following questions:

   a) Do you think he represents a period in history in which many men had lost confidence?

   b) Why might this have happened?

   c) How does Hitchcock ask us to consider this debate through the character of Jeff?

4. Choose another film that you think asks us to consider the position of men in society (possibilities may include *Lock, Stock and Two Smoking Barrels*, *Deliverance*, *The Last Seduction* and *High Fidelity*).

   a) Watch the film and make notes on the way in which iconography and *mise-en-scène* are used in order to establish the central male character(s) and then later to develop them.

   b) Make detailed notes on the ways in which the characters' body language and costumes inform our ideas concerning their representation.

   c) What is the position of the characters within the narrative? Do they motivate the plot? How would you describe their role within the genre of the film?

   d) How is masculinity being represented through these characters? Does their role indicate a situation of crisis? What is being discussed about the place and expectations of men within the era of the film? Would you consider representations in the film to be radical or challenging to dominant values and beliefs?

The following activity should be done in class and the presentation will provide practice for the Communication Key Skill C3.1b: Make a presentation about a complex subject, using at least one image to illustrate complex points.

   e) When you have completed all of your notes, plan a presentation of your material for the rest of the class. You will need to select clips from your chosen film to illustrate some of your points. Make sure that you practise the presentation, and try to speak clearly. Organise your information in a way that is clear and systematic. You might also consider your presentation materials. You could produce handouts for the class that will consolidate any notes they take.

Using sound and words to inform representation

The majority of discussions surrounding representation deal with visual images, but sounds and words can also be instrumental in helping us to understand wider debates. The values and beliefs being discussed within media texts can be informed and expanded upon through an analysis of the aural (heard) part of the text. Sounds and words can help us to engage with debates about social groups, places and ideas.

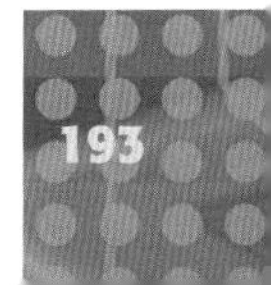

ACTIVITIES

1. Watch one of the scenes in *Taxi Driver* where Travis is wandering through the New York streets. Make notes on all of the sounds you hear in the scene – make sure that you note both the diegetic sounds (those which form part of the story world) and non-diegetic sounds (those which are part of the film's soundtrack). What do the sounds we hear tell us about:
   a) Travis as representative of social outsiders?
   b) New York as a place of chaos and confusion?
   c) Alienation and loneliness?
2. Choose a scene from *The Royle Family* where the whole family is together (including Nana). Make detailed notes on the following:
   a) The topic of discussion and the differing attitudes to it amongst the characters.
   b) The amount of time each character speaks, and who seems to have most focus within the discussion.
   c) The position of each character in the set and what this indicates about their place in the conversation.
   d) The attitudes of each of the characters to each other.
   e) The types of language each character uses to express their opinions.

   Once you have made your notes, work with a partner to make comments about how words and language interchange can inform us about the representation of the family offered in this programme. Does *The Royle Family* discuss stereotypes through its representation?

> The following two written activities will provide practice for the Communication Key Skill C3.3: Write two different types of documents about complex subjects. One piece of writing should be an extended document and include at least one image.

3. Choose a scene from a film or a television programme. You are going to create two pieces of written work that illustrate the importance of sound and words within representation. You should use the examples given above to guide your analysis.
   a) Your first writing task is a piece of critical analysis, which your teacher will assess. You should discuss in detail how the sound (diegetic and non-diegetic) and the words in the scene you have chosen represent social groups, places or ideas. Your analysis should be about 1000 words in length and should include a still from the scene you have chosen to illustrate your points.
   b) The second part of your task is to produce a worksheet for other members of your Media Studies group asking them to analyse the scene you have chosen. Try to construct a worksheet that begins with textual analysis of sounds and words, and builds towards questions concerning wider representational issues (use some of the questions we have already discussed in relation to *Taxi Driver* and *The Royle Family* for guidance). You will need about 30 minutes of classroom time to show the scene, ask your classmates to complete the worksheet and then chair a discussion.

Summary

As we have seen, media texts use images, sound and words to encourage us to move beyond technical textual analysis and consider wider issues of debate. The way certain ideas and groups are represented will change over a period of time and it is important to identify historical shifts in representation in your discussions. Don't forget that you are an active participant within this process and can challenge the way a social group or an idea has been represented by a media text.

Part Two

Key Skill: Improving Own Learning and Performance

Topic of study: Genre

Groups of texts that have similar elements or characteristics are described as being part of a **genre**. We may discuss horror films, cartoons, the news or soap operas, for example, and in doing so we are identifying genres. The producer of a media text may use the elements of a genre (its conventions) in a straightforward way, but they may also subvert conventions, mixing elements from two different genres to provide hybrid forms, or creating sub-genres by slightly altering the conventions used. The study of genre centres on the identification of conventions and the analysis of how they are used within a chosen text. The historical changes in the way a text may use the conventions of its genre will be dependent on the ideological climate in which the text is produced. For example, the 1950s science fiction film *The Thing from Outer Space* can be read as using generic conventions to offer a comment on the Cold War. The United States's military and scientific forces are pitted against an alien intruder (Communism) that seeks to disrupt the social order and jeopardise peace. Ridley Scott's 1979 film *Alien* reflects the fact that feminism has a more central role within current modes of thinking, offering us a female 'saviour' in the form of Ripley. It would be a mistake, however, to read *Alien* simply as a piece of feminist filmmaking – it merely offers comment within a wider debate.

DISCUSSION

Television commercials often use social groups to sell their products. Focusing on the use of the family within TV adverts, how does representation differ from product to product?

Through a detailed analysis of two newspapers, discuss the ways in which celebrities are represented in the tabloid press.

CASE STUDY

Horror conventions in Wes Craven's *Scream*

The horror genre includes many sub-divisions (or sub-genres). We could discuss slasher films, psychological horror or gothic horror cinema and identify horror conventions within all of them. Sub-genres and hybrid forms (films that merge more than one film genre, e.g. *Alien,*

Drew Barrymore in *Scream*

which may be considered to be a hybrid of science fiction and horror) take conventions and utilise them in a way that may be amended, subverted or self-consciously commented upon. Wes Craven's *Scream* provides an example of the slasher format, but also offers a commentary on the construction and consumption of the horror film.

The classic conventions of the horror film include: the final girl, a frightening place, brooding or ominous *mise-en-scène*, narratives that move from equilibrium to disturbance and back to a new equilibrium (although, according to structuralist critic Todorov, this basic structure is evident in all stories), a monster/monstrous human, themes of death and destruction, iconography such as knives and masks, and a disorientation/disturbance of the audience. In *Scream* these conventions are employed literally and at the same time self-consciously. The dialogue of the film includes detailed descriptions of the mechanics and effects of the horror film.

Sydney (played by Neve Campbell) fulfils the role of the final girl. Characters are being killed all around her and she is left at the end of the film having to confront the killers. This confrontation allows her to discover the true identities of the killers and find out the truth about her own mother's murder. The final girl re-establishes order by confronting her own past traumas and fears.

In *Scream* the frightening place is not a gothic castle or an isolated house, but the domestic home. From the first killing of Casey Becker in her middle-class suburban home, we realise that the place we would naturally consider to be safe is, in fact, not. Part of the threat and fear generated in this film is concerned with the invasion of the familial and domestic. These killers attack in the home, thus making the invasion that much more intimate.

The opening scene of Casey Becker's killing also provides examples of the ominous *mise-en-scène* characteristic of a horror film. She moves around a house lit by lamps which provide pockets of light and shadow. The darkened spaces are frightening for both Casey and the viewer because they provide places for a killer to hide. The lack of illumination in the scene is both literal and symbolic – neither Casey nor we know what lurks in the darkness. When Casey looks out of the window the mist over the swimming pool also provides an example of disorientating *mise-en-scène*.

In terms of narrative, *Scream* follows the equilibrium-disturbance-new equilibrium pattern of most horror films. The killing of Casey breaks the peace of the small town, and chaos ensues, as other characters become victims. The mid-section of the film charts the successive killings and the inability of the local police to solve the crime. It is only with the final confrontation scene that peace is reinstated. This equilibrium, however, is of a wiser and more cynical type.

The monsters in *Scream* are, of course, the killers who bring chaos and death into the world of the film. What is interesting about Wes Craven's version of this convention, however, is that they are not damaged victims who kill because of their own pain. These are bored teenagers with little or no motive (at one point in the film a character comments on the horror genre, proclaiming, 'This is the millennium. Motives are incidental.'), and for many viewers this is a far more frightening creation. Death and destruction are what the killers inflict upon the world of the film, but in *Scream* we are made to look further into this theme. We are also asked to confront an important question: Within a media-saturated environment where we are bombarded with images of death and pain, are we becoming desensitised to the reality of killing? Sydney lives with the horror of her mother's murder and, as a character, shows us the reality of what is seen on the screen, but those around her seem not to understand fully the impact of killing (until, of course, they become the killers' next victim). Through the character of Gayle Weathers (the news reporter), Craven debates this point; she has written a sensationalist book about the man accused of killing Sydney's mother. For many of the characters in the film, murder provides either a book deal or part of the horror film genre, and has ceased to be seen as a real threat.

Scream includes many classic icons of horror. We see knives and a mask in the opening sequence and these are used throughout the film to signify the killers. Knives are intimate and violent weapons. The killer must attack from close quarters and often stabs many times, heightening the fear and pain of the victim. *Psycho, Halloween* and *Nightmare on Elm Street* all include the use of knives, with the first two films also including disguises or masks. Horror films use disguise as a means of disorientating the viewer and obscuring the killer's identity until the end of the film.

As already mentioned, the position of the audience is important to the effectiveness of the horror genre. Often we are placed within a scene, and *Scream* includes many scenes in which we are positioned as Casey Becker or Sydney, waiting for the attack. This subjective (or point-of-view) camerawork forces us to enter a scene of a film and experience the character's fear. The dangerous situations we are sometimes forced to experience make the pleasure of the film's final peace and safety even more palpable.

Horror films often have a knowledgeable audience who are aware of horror conventions and have certain expectations of the genre. *Scream* is a film which clearly acknowledges that its audience will have seen previous horror films. It invites us to comment on the predictability of the genre and at the same time offers us a new, self-conscious, at times humorous but nonetheless frightening example of the horror film.

DISCUSSION

Look at the still. In small groups, firstly identify the genre of the film and then list the conventions of that genre, which are evident in the illustration. Have these films used the conventions in a literal, subverted or ironic way?

ACTIVITIES

This is an extended activity and should be completed over a period of about half a term.

Your task is to research the development of a particular genre over a period of four or five decades. You will be looking specifically at how audience expectations and current ideologies affect the production of films within your chosen genre.

1. Choose a film genre and list all of the conventions of that genre which you know of. When you have completed your list you should discuss it with other members of your Media Studies group and add any conventions they suggest.
2. Using IT resources and print-based materials, choose four or five films from your chosen genre from the same number of decades. For example, if you were to study the science fiction genre you might choose *Metropolis* from the 1920s, *The Thing from Outer Space* from the 1950s, *Close Encounters of the Third Kind* from the 1970s, *Blade Runner* from the 1980s and *The Matrix* from the 1990s.

> The following activity (3) will provide practice for the Improving Own Learning and Performance Key Skill LP3.1: Agree targets and plan how these will be met over an extended period of time, using support from appropriate people.

3. Write an outline of your research topic detailing:
   a) the resources you are going to use
   b) the genre and texts you are going to study

c) the reasons why you have chosen these particular media texts
d) what you aim to discover within your project
e) the interim deadlines you are going to set yourself and the work you will have completed at these points.

You should then present this outline to your Media Studies teacher and agree realistic aims and objectives.

You should refer back to your outline regularly to ensure that you are meeting deadlines and covering all of the areas you identified.

4. For each of the texts you have chosen, you should begin by watching them and making detailed notes on the conventions that are evident. You should be aware of how these conventions are used and whether they are being employed literally or in a subverted way.

Activity 5 will provide practice for the Improving Own Learning and Performance Key Skill LP3.2: Take responsibility for your learning by using your plan, and seeking feedback and support from relevant sources, to help meet your targets.

5. This activity requires you to research the attitudes and ideologies that surround the film. Use the following questions as a guide.
   a) When was the film released and what was happening at that time?
   b) How did the critics and public receive the film?
   c) Does the film offer any comment (either through the dialogue, the images or as an analogy) on the ideas or events current at that time?

   You may wish to survey older relatives, friends or teachers in order to discover information or use history books, CD-ROMs or the Internet.

Activities 6 and 7 will provide practice for the Improving Own Learning and Performance Key Skill LP3.3: Review progress on two occasions and establish evidence of achievements, including how you have used learning from other tasks to meet new demands.

6. At this stage in your research project you should review the progress you have made and decide whether you need to modify either targets or methodology. This is most effectively done in discussion with your Media Studies teacher.
7. Having analysed your films and researched their contexts, you will now need to create a presentation for the other members of your Media Studies class. You should use IT to create your presentation and include sequences from the films you have chosen to illustrate your points. You should include information on:
   a) the typical conventions of the genre you have chosen
   b) the conventions evident in the individual films and how they have been used
   c) the historical, social and ideological contexts of your chosen films
   d) the way the individual film text uses the conventions of its genre within a discussion of attitudes current at the time of its release

e) the resources you used to research your project, the problems you may have encountered, the extent to which you followed your initial plan and the overall success of your project.

8. Present your findings to the rest of your Media Studies class and answer any questions they might have.

FOCUS

1. Does the audience's knowledge of a particular genre affect their experience of a text?
2. In what ways is the study of generic conventions useful in an appraisal of the intentions of a media text?

Summary

The study of genre allows us both to categorise media texts and to understand their importance in relation to the world around them. Identifying conventions allows the student of the media to bring other texts from the same genre into any discussion. When analysing genre you should work with both the micro-elements (those implanted within the text itself, e.g. iconography, *mise-en-scène*, sound) and the macro-elements (those which 'surround' the text, e.g. narrative) of a text to identify conventions, using these to consider the effect of generic codes on the audience.

Part Three

Key Skill: Application of Number

Topic of study: Audience

Media texts all have a target audience. The target audience may be wide (**mass**) or specific (**niche**), but each media product will be designed to attract and engage that particular group of viewers, readers or listeners. There are many methods through which the producers of a media product can learn about the expectations and habits of their potential audience. In Section 1, The Key Concepts of Media Studies, it was suggested that you use the terms **qualitative** (connected with opinions) and **quantitative** (connected with numerical data) to describe the two main types of audience research.

The relationship between the audience and a media product is dynamic, which means that there is an interchange rather than merely a one-way deposit of meaning.

(For definitions of different readings of texts, see section 1 page 11.)

CASE STUDY

Stanley Kubrick's *A Clockwork Orange*

In 1972, Stanley Kubrick's *A Clockwork Orange* was released, causing immediate controversy. The film was a study of freedom and control and included scenes of sexual and physical violence. It depicted a world where violence was pervasive, and the only means of controlling this was deemed by those in power to be a harrowing method of brainwashing those who followed a violent path.

Still from *A Clockwork Orange*

For Kubrick, the film was a discussion and not an invitation to imitate. The almost cartoon quality to some of the violent scenes did not detract from the horror of the violence portrayed, but indicated the mindset of the film's narrator. There were many reviewers who sought to blame the film for copycat violence and argued that the audience was at times encouraged to sympathise with and even emulate the actions of the main character. If the central character was presented as a victim, then his crimes were perhaps a legitimate attempt to counter the confinement he experienced around him. This reading of the film would be considered to be so far from its preferred reading that it would be classified as an aberrant reading.

After *A Clockwork Orange*'s release, stories appeared in the press in which criminals blamed their actions upon the effects of watching the film. Moral panic ensued, and after Kubrick had received death threats and hate mail he decided to take the film out of general release in Great Britain, with the proviso that it could only be released here after his death. The British Board of Film Classification had passed the film for release, and it was not an institutional decision that forced Kubrick to act in the way he did. It was public pressure and the demonising of the film by some elements of the press.

If there is a preferred reading within this film, then it works as an invitation to challenge what we are shown and not accept dominant ideologies. Neither those in power nor the Droogs are depicted as having found an acceptable means of responding to the world around them. It is a film that demands a negotiated or oppositional reading. Within some studies of audience consumption, *A Clockwork Orange* is accused of encouraging copycat crimes, of helping to desensitise the viewer because of the cartoon, and yet extreme, mode of its violence. On the other side of the argument, we could look to researchers who believe in the audience's essential ability to distinguish between fact and fiction and remain active in the viewing experience.

DISCUSSION

Do you consider yourself to be a passive or active reader of media texts? Discuss examples of instances where you may not have challenged a text's preferred reading and instances where you have questioned what you have been offered.

Does your mode of response change from text to text or do you think you have a tendency always to respond in a particular way?

ACTIVITIES

For this exercise you are going to analyse the medium of radio.

Activities 1 and 2 will provide practice for the Application of Number Key Skill N3.1: Plan and interpret information from two sources, including a large data set.

1. RAJAR is the organisation that publishes data concerning radio consumption. Using either the RAJAR website or another available source, collect up-to-date data. Once you have all the available information, answer the questions below.
   a) What types of programmes are most listened to?
   b) On which radio channels would you find these programmes?
   c) What information is given on the profile of these programmes' audiences?
   d) How do you think radio stations use these figures?
2. Create a questionnaire which you can use in order to survey radio consumption. The target audience for your questionnaire will be family members and friends. You should include questions about programmes listened to, amount of listening time, contexts of listening, reasons for listening and changes in listening habits. After your questionnaires have been completed (a good sample will be of between ten and 20 people of different ages), you should make deductions concerning the different audience profiles you find.
   a) What are the similarities in listening habits amongst your sample?
   b) What are the differences?

The next part of the activity (3) will provide practice for the Application of Number Key Skill N3.2: Carry out multi-stage calculations.

3. In small groups, you are going to discuss and interpret your qualitative and quantitative data. Try to complete the following tasks.
   a) Using the group's qualitative research, create statistical data, perhaps in the form of percentages, to illustrate:
      - the genres of radio programmes most listened to and the profile of the listeners
      - the genres of programmes least listened to and the profile of the listeners
      - the amount of time that different audience groups listen to the radio and to specific types of programmes
      - the different contexts of listening you found

- the different reasons you identified for listening.

b) Look at the RAJAR data. How do these figures relate to those you have just calculated? What are the similarities and differences?

The next part of the activity will provide practice for the Application of Number Key Skill N3.3: Interpret results of your calculations, present your findings and justify your methods. You must use at least one graph, one chart and one diagram.

4. Still working in your small groups, you are going to present the information you have found to the rest of the class. The purpose of your presentation is to offer information concerning the consumption of radio, but you will also need an introduction to your presentation that outlines your research methodology and its effectiveness. You will need to organise your information systematically, using at least one graph, one chart and one diagram. You should also create a handout for the members of your Media Studies class, which includes the main points and data within your presentation.

Summary

Within any study of the audience you will need to analyse both the theories of audience consumption and the research methods used by media institutions to target the audience effectively. Audience members all have expectations, preconceptions and histories of consumption, which they bring with them when encountering a new text. What is interesting for the media student is how these things affect the consumption of the product and how media institutions attempt to discover and use them to try to ensure success for their product.

FOCUS

1. What methods of audience research do media institutions use in order to help them create effective products?
2. In what ways do American and British research about the audience differ?

Part Four

Key Skill: Information Technology

Topic of study: New media technologies

New media technologies are in constant development. The means by which we can consume the media around us are expanding and the processes of media production are developing with the advent of newer and faster technologies. As we identified in Section 4, most households are now saturated with media technologies. We can communicate through landline telephones, mobile telephones, the

Internet or even videophones. You might also choose to receive your radio and television stations through digital means, rather than analogue. We have more information available to us now than ever before but, as we have already discussed, this does not necessarily mean that the information is used effectively.

CASE STUDY

The Internet

Many homes now have access to the World Wide Web through the Internet. The web consists of more than a billion pages of information, which can be viewed all over the world. The Internet has provided global access to many types of information, which is being constantly added to or amended.

With the advent of the Internet, e-commerce industries have arisen that allow the consumer to purchase products without leaving the home. Media industries use the World Wide Web to promote their products and to transfer information quickly. Photographers, for example, can send newly taken images via the Internet to their newspapers, thus ensuring a speed of delivery which could result in the all-important 'exclusive'. Within the film industry it is now possible to send sections of film, via the Internet, to production companies. The music industry can build sound into websites and promote the latest releases.

The accessibility of information via the Internet means that information is 'democratically distributed'. The average user can access sites on thousands of subjects. Critics of the Internet cite this as one of the major problems, however, as accessibility means that information can be received by those for whom it is not appropriate. The availability of pornography has caused much debate and, because of the many millions of computers now in homes, it is difficult to enforce legislation on who should have access to it.

Another issue surrounds the quality of information offered by some sites. The vast quantities of information available do not ensure quality. It is left to the consumer to decide the appropriateness and accuracy of information they have found. Our ability to distinguish and differentiate is essential when dealing with large amounts of information and critics point to a lessening of our ability to discriminate, caused by a tendency to be overwhelmed by the volume of information available.

As a new media technology, the Internet has many positive uses and its development will make the potential transfer of images and information much quicker. It is also an effective tool within marketing campaigns and audience research. The problems surrounding the use of the Internet, however, are concerned with the access to and consumption of potentially problematic or inaccurate images and information.

ACTIVITIES

This activity will extend over a period of five or six lessons and will include homework time. The aim of your project is to research and present information connected with the range and application of new media technologies. You will need to work in groups of about four.

The following activities (1 and 2) will provide practice for the Information Technology Key Skill IT3.1: Plan and use different sources to search for and select information required for two different purposes.

1. Each member of the group should opt to research information concerning two from the following list of new media technologies:
   - the Internet
   - mobile telephones
   - digital television
   - digital radio
   - DVD (digital versatile disks)
   - games consoles
   - big-screen technologies, e.g. IMAX cinemas.
2. Once the selections have been made, each member of the group should aim to research the following:

   a) the development and history of the piece of new media technology

   b) audience consumption of each piece of technology.

   Research should be carried out using different research techniques (qualitative and quantitative) and sources. Possible research techniques might include: questionnaires given to different households, taped interviews with members of different households, making notes from multimedia sources. The sources for your research may include: the Internet, CD-ROMs, school/college Intranets, print-based publications.

The next activity (3) will provide practice for the Information Technology Key Skill IT3.2: Explore, develop and exchange information and derive new information to serve two different purposes.

3. Once each member of the group has completed the research section of the task you will need to arrange a time to meet in order to discuss your findings. Each member of the group should then present their findings and answer any questions. Information should be organised by using spreadsheets for data and other IT tools for other information. Individuals will need to give details concerning the sources they used as well as the information gathered. Once each individual has presented the information, the group should try to find links between the different developments and consumption of the new technologies.

The last activity (4) will provide practice for the Information Technology Key Skill IT3.3: Present information from different sources, for two different purposes and audiences. Your work must include at least one example of text, one example of images and one example of numbers.

4. This part of the activity requires the group to prepare a presentation of all of the material found. You will need to use visual images, text and data to create the presentation. Discuss together what would be the most effective way to organise your materials, decide who will be presenting which sections, and make sure that you have all of the equipment necessary. You might decide that the presentation can be split into the two sections outlined in question 2, or you might group certain new technologies together which have similar development and consumption profiles. Try to find two audiences or 'forums' for your presentation: one might be your Media Studies class and the other could be a subject such as Business Studies where students will ask different types of questions.

FOCUS

1. Do the media technologies that today's youth market have at their disposal enhance or inhibit their ability to challenge the world around them?
2. How do you think new media technologies will develop in the future?

Summary

The technologies evident within the world of the media allow us to gain information much faster than before, to communicate in many more ways and to produce media products that look much more sophisticated. They are in constant development. Your discussion of new technologies, however, should not only concern itself with development and use, but should also analyse what the impact will be on the individual concerning our response to the media and, indeed, to the world around us.

Part Five

Key Skill: Working with Others

Topic of study: *Mise-en-scène*

As we have already noted in earlier sections, *mise-en-scène* is a term we use to describe what is shown within an individual shot. Imagine that you freeze-frame a scene from a television programme or film: what are the elements you see which allow you to make comments about the various meanings generated? *Mise-en-scène* includes the study of character positioning and body language, lighting, settings, sets, colour, props and decor. A shot is composed in order to explain narrative or further character development or understanding, to define the film or programme generically, or to add mood and atmosphere.

CASE STUDY

Use of *mise-en-scène* in Tim Burton's *Sleepy Hollow*

Tim Burton's *Sleepy Hollow* is a cinematic version of Washington Irving's 1819 story *The Legend of Sleepy Hollow*. It is essentially a ghost story and in order to have his modern audience recognise it as such, Tim Burton was careful to create a very particular *mise-en-*

Still from *Sleepy Hollow*

scène, adding to it his own particular style of gothic/horror seen previously in films such as *Beetlejuice* (1988) and *Edward Scissorhands* (1990).

The town of Sleepy Hollow is often shrouded in mist and fog. It is vulnerable and threatened by potential attack from the headless horseman. It becomes an isolated environment, which makes both the characters and the audience feel disorientated and wary. The mists often seem to have a life of their own, curling around houses and, by their presence, often predicting the arrival of the horseman. Many of the scenes, both interior and exterior, are shot to appear darkened. Small pools of light are created by candles in the interior shots and we are left with an actual and metaphorical lack of illumination characteristic of horror. Ichabod Crane (played by Johnny Depp), the detective of the film, gropes around for answers, but the truth is hidden by both the mystery narrative and the disorientating *mise-en-scène*.

The heightened nature of some of the colour saturations in *Sleepy Hollow* adds to the gothic fairy-story feel of the film. The situation is unreal and mysterious. This is a world of nightmares and, as such, the *mise-en-scène* exaggerates shapes and colours to produce the strangeness of a dreamscape. The tree which provides the focus of the final scene is huge and knotted, like something from one of Grimm's fairy tales, providing the *mise-en-scène* with another piece of exaggerated Gothic iconography. The scenes with the horseman often frame him with mist, darkness and a blue colouring, which intensify the chilling nature of his crimes.

The set of *Sleepy Hollow* creates a world of nineteenth-century houses, muddy pathways and woodland; a once tranquil place which has been invaded by fear. As with many fairy stories this is an idyll made horrific by the forces of evil, and the *mise-en-scène* illustrates this through the silence, chill and mist that descend after dark. The houses and costumes of the film are part nineteenth century and part timeless gothic fairy tale. Ichabod Crane's scientific

equipment, for example, locates him in a particular period of forensic science history, but also gives his character a strange, almost childlike quality.

The *mise-en-scène* of *Sleepy Hollow* works to create atmosphere, period and genre, as well as indicating a characteristic style of the director. Tim Burton has said of his film, 'We wanted to keep the spirit of the horror movie but be fun with it'.

Gaining information concerning narrative through *mise-en-scène*

Looking at a still image, or **frame**, from a moving image will allow you to make certain assumptions about the place of the action depicted within the narrative of the whole text. You could consider the setting of the still, its lighting and the props used in order to decide whether you are looking at an introductory scene to the narrative or a climactic scene. Certain colours might be dominant that may give you a clue as to the tone and importance of what you are seeing. Consider the last frames of Ridley Scott's *Thelma and Louise*, for example: the Thunderbird is launched from the cliff in a blaze of sunshine, the colours are rich and bright, nothing is evident within the frame apart from the characters, the car and the Grand Canyon below. This is not an image that evokes doom, and therefore we are asked to view it as a climactic moment, a moment of liberation for Thelma and Louise.

Still from the last frames of *Thelma and Louise*

ACTIVITIES

This activity would provide practice for Working with Others Key Skill WO3.1: Plan complex work with others, agreeing objectives, responsibilities and working arrangements.

In groups of about four, each choose a moment that could be considered a turning point in a film. Try to choose films from different genres, and moments that have different significance: you could choose climactic, introductory or dramatic moments. Each of you should then freeze-frame your film and make detailed notes on the ways in which the *mise-en-scène* evident in the still helps to inform the audience about the place in the narrative where the still is found. It is important that you agree in your group to choose very different examples and that you also agree a clear and comprehensive way to make your notes – you could decide on spidergrams, for example. After you have analysed your particular still, present your findings to the rest of the group and together formulate some ideas as to how different types of film seek to motivate narrative through *mise-en-scène*.

Gaining information concerning character through *mise-en-scène*

When analysing character within the *mise-en-scène* of a particular still, you will need to consider the following:

- the position of the character within the frame
- the body language and posture of the character
- their relation to other characters within the frame
- the relationship of the character to their setting
- how the character uses the props that surround them
- how they have been lit.

From a still (a freeze-frame shot) we can make deductions about the importance of the character within the scene and the film, the emotions of the character at that time and their place within a particular genre.

DISCUSSION

Look at the still from *EastEnders* shown overleaf. With a partner, analyse the still for character construction within *mise-en-scène* using the six points listed above.

ACTIVITIES

The following activity will provide practice for Working with Others Key Skill WO3.2: Seek to establish and maintain co-operative working relationships over an extended period of time, agreeing changes to achieve agreed objectives.

In a group of up to six students you are going to 'track' a soap opera character and consider how their status and significance alters over a period of two weeks. Choose one of the soaps that is broadcast two or more times a week and select one character within it for analysis. Each member of the group should opt to record and watch a particular episode, making notes on the importance of the chosen character within that episode. Individuals should also find a still that contains the character, and analyse it for how *mise-en-scène* helps the

audience to understand better the character and their status within the episode. During the two weeks you will need to keep each other informed about the work you are undertaking. Don't forget to ask other members of the group for feedback during this period, in order to ensure that you are completing the task effectively. Once all of the individual viewing and note-taking has been completed, your group should meet to discuss how the chosen stills indicate the possibly changing position of the character over the two-week period. You should then present your findings to other members of your Media Studies group and ask them to discuss with you any shifts of character significance you have discovered and how the *mise-en-scène* you have identified illustrates this.

Still from *EastEnders*

Using *mise-en-scène* to aid with genre identification

We have identified the main elements that make up the *mise-en-scène* of a shot as character positioning and body language, lighting, props, sets, colour, setting and decor. Media texts can use these elements very effectively to indicate genre. Imagine a still from a film where the lighting created produces pockets of shadow, the character's body language is nervous and defensive, their face is crumpled with fear, the setting is isolated, the set is recognisable but, because of the lighting, takes on an ominous feel. It would be fairly safe to deduce from this that we are looking at a still from a horror film. A still from a fantasy film might be saturated with vivid colours and bright lighting, generating a surreal effect. A Western still might position a sole character amidst an arid and isolating setting to create the impression of questing and loneliness, characteristic of that genre.

DISCUSSION

With a partner, look at the illustration here, and discuss how the various elements of *mise-en-scène* allow you to comment on the film's genre.

Still from *Boogeyman*

ACTIVITIES

In small groups, brainstorm as many film genres as you can. Each member of the group should then choose two of these genres. Your task is to create a still for each genre that includes appropriate *mise-en-scène* elements. You could draw the still – use a cut-and-paste method or a computer program. Your still does not have to be elaborate and could include rough sketches or words to indicate a particular aspect of the *mise-en-scène*. Try not to draw your examples from an existing film, but create original ideas. When the tasks have been completed, present your stills to other members of your group and together discuss whether or not they evoke the chosen genre effectively.

Using *mise-en-scène* to analyse mood and atmosphere

The mood and atmosphere generated within a visual image are essential factors for both our enjoyment and critical appreciation of a text. The audience is more likely to be drawn into a visual text if it is engaging. Mood and atmosphere are effects generated by all of the aspects of *mise-en-scène* we have already identified. We discussed earlier how dull or shadowy lighting effects can create an ominous mood within films, and we linked this to the genre of horror, but this section does not concern generic identification, and indeed any film may need to express an ominous or portentous mood through its *mise-en-scène*. A visual text may need to express the feelings of a group of people before they enter the scene and this can also be effectively constructed through lighting, sets, props and colours. An atmosphere of confinement might be essential to the themes and intentions of a text and this too can be produced through careful construction of *mise-en-scène*.

DISCUSSION

In what ways can *mise-en-scène* be used to generate the following moods and atmospheres? Make specific reference to films or television programmes to substantiate your points.

Moods:	Atmospheres:
depression	confinement
euphoria	ominousness
loneliness	liberation.
uncertainty.	

ACTIVITIES

In small groups, look at each of the stills and comment on the *mise-en-scène* evident and how it works to create mood or atmosphere.

Still from *Psycho*

Still from *Schindler's List*

Still from *Alien*

Still from *Citizen Kane*

FOCUS

Having worked through all of the discussion points and activities in this section, you will now have a clearer idea of how *mise-en-scène* is used to give information to the audience concerning narrative, character, genre, mood and atmosphere. You should now be able to present the information you have found in a clear and comprehensive way.

ACTIVITIES

The following activities will provide practice for the Working with Others Key Skill WO3.3: Review working with others and agreeing ways of improving collaborative work in the future.

FOCUS

1. With specific reference to three films or television programmes, analyse the ways in which *mise-en-scène* can be used as a generic convention.
2. Write a detailed analysis of how *mise-en-scène* can enhance our understanding of the narrative.
3. Discuss the ways in which *mise-en-scène* has been used in two media texts to inform character development.

For these activities you will need to work in small groups (these should not be the same groups you have worked with for the other activities). You will need to have in front of you all of the work you have done so far in this section on *mise-en-scène*.

1. Discuss the effectiveness of working with your other groups and together come up with a list of points you think are important when working with others on a common task. You will need to try and implement this way of working within this activity.
2. Plan a way of presenting your findings to other groups which clearly shows the many ways in which *mise-en-scène* functions, and the meanings and effects it is capable of generating. You will need to consider the use of televisions and videos, white boards, overhead projectors and any other presentational tool you think is appropriate. You will also need to decide which member of the group is going to present which section of the material.
3. Present your work on *mise-en-scène* to other members of the group and answer any questions they might have.

Summary

Mise-en-scène, as we have seen, is not merely a cosmetic factor within a film. What has been placed within the frame is essential to our understanding not only of a specific moment, but of the text as a whole. You should consider *mise-en-scène* in two ways. First, as a set of elements through which you can analyse visual text moments extremely closely; and second, as a way of informing your discussions of macro-analysis issues, such as narrative and genre.

Part Six

Key Skill: Problem Solving

Topic of study: Photojournalism

A photojournalistic image is one that has direct connection to a news story, and has often been constructed in order to represent the story in a particular way. An image may be cropped in order to highlight specific sections, or it may be framed in a way that promotes a certain reading of the action or person depicted.

There are certain photojournalistic images which have become famous because of their power to represent certain attitudes to a specific event. The Vietnam War produced some powerful visual comments: for example, the burned Vietnamese girl running from a napalm attack, or the monk who had set himself on fire in protest against the Vietnam War.

What is important to consider within analysis of photojournalism, however, is not just the construction of the pictures or the event they depict, but the ethics surrounding the process of capturing the image. Intrusive or sensationalist photography, often associated with the tabloid press, prompts us to debate the desire for voyeurism surrounding certain pictures, and stark images of pain or death encourage an ethical debate about the responsibilities of the photographer: Should he/she

capture moments which will force the public to consider a difficult issue, or do they have a responsibility to help or intervene?

CASE STUDY

With a partner, look carefully at the images shown below. What 'readings' is the viewer being encouraged to form because of the way in which these pictures have been constructed?

Journalistic shots of the Vietnam War – young Vietnamese girl who had been burned by Napalm

Buddhist martyr burning to death after soaking himself in petrol

ACTIVITIES

The following activities (1 and 2) will provide practice for the Problem Solving Key Skill PS3.1: Explore a complex problem, devise three options for solving it and justify the option selected for taking it forward.

Your teacher will give you a brief description of three news items (they will include both political and human-interest stories).

1. In pairs, choose one of the stories. You should research the story and add detail to the brief description you have been given. You will then need to write detailed descriptions of

three images that you think would best represent the main elements within the news item. You should describe:

- the visual elements of the image
- the angles used to take the picture
- the framing you would use, i.e. how you would compose the picture
- which aspects of the news item your image would represent and why you think these are the main focus of the story.

2. Present your three possible images to another pair and, through discussion with them, decide which image you think would be most appropriate.

The next activities (3 and 4) will provide practice for the Problem Solving Key Skill PS3.2: Plan and implement at least one option for solving the problem, review progress and revise your approach as necessary.

3. Your task is now to create the image you have chosen. You could do this by taking a photograph using members of your class and appropriate locations to approximate the people and places suggested in the story, or you could construct the image from 'found' photographs using image manipulation software like Photoshop®. Once you have created the image you will need to present it to other members of your Media Studies group and your teacher for comment and review. You might decide at this point that the image is effective or you might amend it.
4. You now have to write the story, create a newspaper page and use the image you have created to illustrate the news item. In order to complete this task effectively you will need to make decisions concerning the following:
   - whether your story is destined for a tabloid or a broadsheet newspaper
   - the style of language most appropriate to the kind of newspaper you have chosen
   - the layout of the page and the positioning of your story. Do you think, for example, that your story is worthy of the front page?
   - the caption you will use with your image
   - the size of your image in relation to the text of the story.

   You may wish to word-process your story and then create a newspaper page through a cut-and-paste method, or you may decide to create the page using a desktop publishing program.

The next activities (5 and 6) will provide practice for the Problem Solving Key Skill PS3.3: Apply agreed methods to check if the problem has been solved, describe the results and review your approach to problem solving.

5. Before you present your page to other members of your class or your teacher, you need to create a means of assessing the effectiveness of your photojournalistic image to illustrate the story. You might produce a worksheet which asks questions about how the text relates to the image, what the image represents about the story, how the reader is positioned by the image and whether it effectively illustrates the news item.

6. Once the newspaper page and the assessment have been completed, you will need to present your work to both your Media Studies class and your teacher. You should photocopy your page for the class and discuss with them:
   - any problems you had in deciding on the components of the image you have created
   - your reasons for creating your image in the way you have
   - the methods you used to create it
   - your means of assessing the effectiveness of the image to illustrate the story, and the comments/suggestions you received
   - any changes you made during the task
   - the overall success of the image as a piece of photojournalism.

FOCUS

1. Is it possible to distinguish between tabloid and broadsheet photojournalism in today's press?
2. Are images more powerful than language as a means of commenting on news stories?

Summary

Photojournalism is, as we have seen, an area that provokes much debate, and the ethical considerations surrounding the capturing of certain types of images will need analysis. You need to consider both the technical means by which the image has been constructed and the intended readings of it which we are offered. Remember also that images have been selected by newspapers to promote a particular reading of a news article.

Part Seven

Key Skill: Communication

Topic of study: Sound

Sound is an integral part of a film and is delivered to the audience in two ways. First, there are the sounds of the story world: radios, street life, traffic and telephones, for example. This type of sound is termed diegetic. Second, there is the sound that is added to the film after shooting. This is not part of the story world of the film, but acts as a soundtrack. This is non-diegetic sound.

Without either diegetic or non-diegetic sound the audience would not be able to enjoy an aural dimension within their cinematic experience. The audience can link the visual elements of the film with what they hear. The linking of aural and visual also helps to shape how the audience interprets the images seen on the screen.

In order to explore how sound is used in film, it is necessary to identify some of the functions of both diegetic and non-diegetic sound. For the purposes of this section we will look at how sound works to generate setting, character and genre.

CASE STUDY

The use of sound in Alfred Hitchcock's *Rear Window*

Alfred Hitchcock's thriller *Rear Window* opens with a 1950s jazz soundtrack, which establishes the period of the film and also offers the only piece of non-diegetic sound evident in the film. The rest of the sounds we hear are generated in the story world. The use of sounds and music in *Rear Window* is sparing and precise and is used to propel the story world. (Interestingly, in Hitchcock's *The Birds*, no non-diegetic sound was used at all. In this instance the lack of background music intensified the tension enormously.)

The use of mainly diegetic sound gives verisimilitude (a feeling of reality). We hear radios, record players, children's games, piano playing, street noises and barely audible pieces of conversation, which establish the setting of a cityscape and the apartments that become the main arena of the action. The character of Jeff (played by James Stewart) is confined to his apartment by a broken leg. He is our focus throughout the film and our guide through the thriller narrative. The subjective viewpoint of *Rear Window*, which is evident within the many point-of-view camera shots, is also made clear by the subjective sound within the film. Hitchcock recorded much of the sound from the apartments across the courtyard from Jeff's. There are hollowness and distance in much of this sound, which places the viewer within the subjective aural viewpoint. We need to be positioned with Jeff in order for suspense to build. We are encouraged to make the same discoveries and mistakes that he does.

The characters in *Rear Window* are also given sound themes which help us to understand their position in the film. Miss Lonelyhearts, for example, is associated with the track 'Mona Lisa', and Jeff's signature sound is perhaps the cacophony of the cityscape – a confusing mass of sounds which he needs to disentangle (as he does with the thriller narrative within the film). Lisa (played by Grace Kelly) is a character who is gradually revealed to us during the course of the action and it is, therefore, appropriate that her character theme should be a piece of music constructed as the film progresses. The pianist across the courtyard finishes his composition and we discover at the end of the film that it is called Lisa.

Rear Window is an example of the thriller genre, and the sound within the film helps to define it as such. Our sense of suspense and tension is increased by the confusing fragments of sound we hear and it is only at the end of the final confrontation scene between Jeff and Thorwald that the tension is broken. There is virtually no sound within this scene except for the dialogue between the characters. Because of this hiatus the suspense builds to a pitch. We are relieved of tension only at the end of the scene when Thorwald ejects Jeff from the window (and, symbolically, from his voyeuristic tendencies) and is caught.

The sound in *Rear Window*, both the musical score by Franz Waxman and the diegetic sound, works to create character, establish genre, motivate narrative and illustrate atmosphere.

Sound and setting

Sound can be used to inform the audience of many aspects of setting. It can evoke historical period, country and character environment. The sound associated with a particular setting can inform us of its hostile, futuristic or idealised nature, for example. Diegetic sound may be used to generate effects such as a sense of chaos, establishing a frenetic setting which is inhospitable to the characters. Non-diegetic sound may be used to promote the idea that a setting is rooted in a particular period of history. As previously mentioned, Hitchcock's *Rear Window* opens with a jazz track, thus establishing its setting as 1950s America.

Still from *Blade Runner*

ACTIVITIES

These activities will provide practice for Communication Key Skill 3.1a: Contribute to a group discussion about a complex subject.

Non-diegetic sound

Look at the photograph from *Blade Runner*. Discuss in groups the following questions.

1. What kind of setting is presented in this still?

2. What kind of soundtrack do you think could generate a sense of the world you have just described?

Diegetic sound

Listen to the sounds of the city in the film *Se7en*. Discuss in groups the following questions.

1. What kind of environment is this?
2. How do you think the characters in this setting would respond to it or be affected by it?

Sound and character

Sound can be a major component in the creation of character. Non-diegetic sound can act as character theme and can either denote the physical presence of a character in a scene or imply their presence (perhaps in the mind of another character) when they are not visually evident. The soundtrack attached to a particular character may shift in key, pace or volume to establish a character's mood at a given moment within the narrative. As with diegetic sound, non-diegetic sound can also inform us of psychological state, whilst providing aural signifiers which we then associate with a particular character.

ACTIVITIES

1. Listen to the diegetic sound associated with Darth Vader in *Star Wars*. How is his role within the film confirmed by this sound?
2. Watch the opening underwater sequence in *Jaws*. The shark is not evident, but the soundtrack implies its presence. How does the soundtrack work to create a sense of the shark and its future role within the film?

The following presentations will provide practice for Communication Key Skill C3.1b: Make a presentation about a complex subject, using at least one image to illustrate complex points.

3. Find two more examples for both diegetic and non-diegetic character-related sound. You should prepare a presentation of these findings for the rest of the class. You will need to find clips from four films to exemplify your findings.

Sound and genre

Sound is an essential part of establishing genre. Both diegetic and non-diegetic sound can be used to signify the difference between, for example, a horror film and a Western. Bernard Herrmann's shrieking violins for Hitchcock's *Psycho* magnified the screams of Marion Crane in the shower scene, and immediately established the horror credentials of the film. Sergio Leone's use of the whistling pipe sound in his films evoked a hollowness, loneliness and conflict which established that type of sound as synonymous with the Spaghetti Western. Diegetic and non-diegetic sound can also be made to collide in order to establish signifiers within a film.

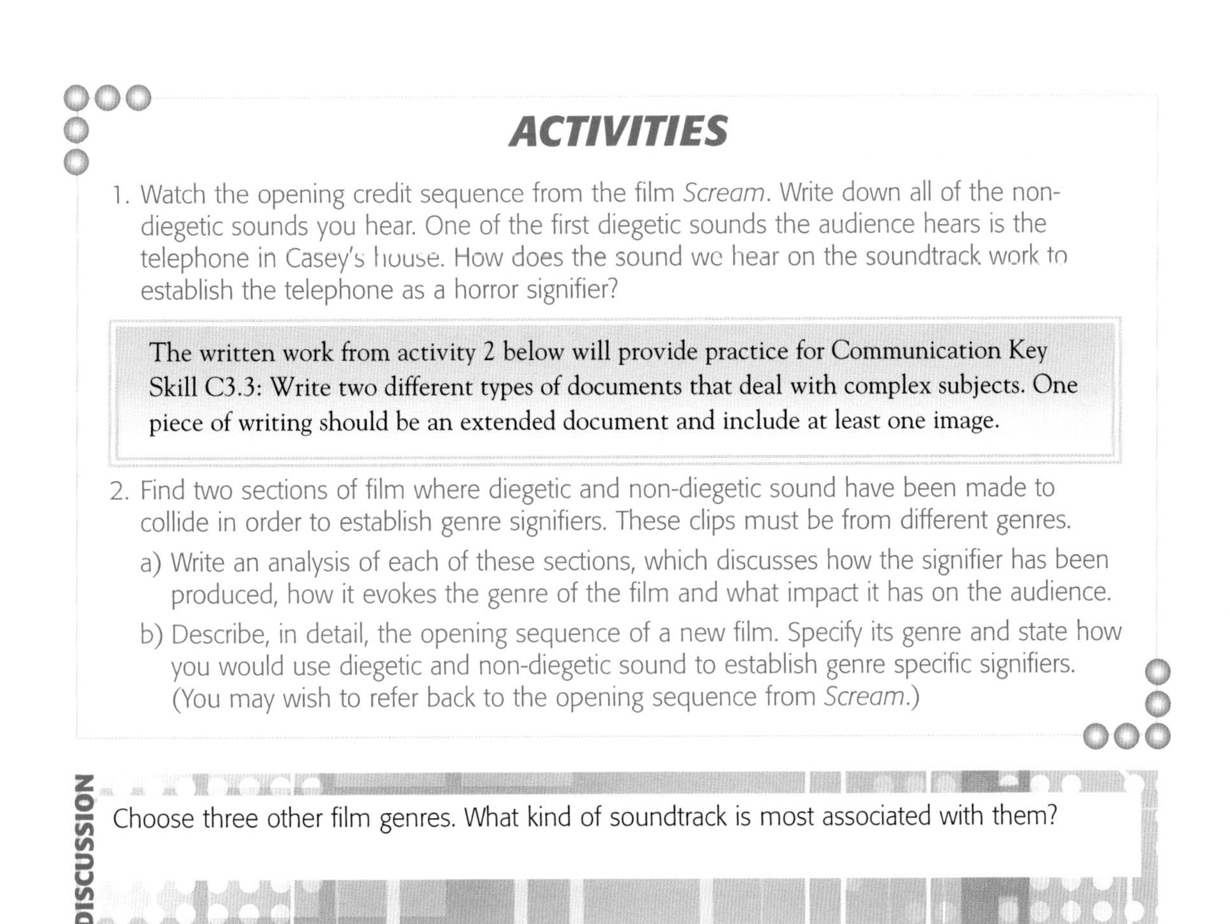

ACTIVITIES

1. Watch the opening credit sequence from the film *Scream*. Write down all of the non-diegetic sounds you hear. One of the first diegetic sounds the audience hears is the telephone in Casey's house. How does the sound we hear on the soundtrack work to establish the telephone as a horror signifier?

The written work from activity 2 below will provide practice for Communication Key Skill C3.3: Write two different types of documents that deal with complex subjects. One piece of writing should be an extended document and include at least one image.

2. Find two sections of film where diegetic and non-diegetic sound have been made to collide in order to establish genre signifiers. These clips must be from different genres.
   a) Write an analysis of each of these sections, which discusses how the signifier has been produced, how it evokes the genre of the film and what impact it has on the audience.
   b) Describe, in detail, the opening sequence of a new film. Specify its genre and state how you would use diegetic and non-diegetic sound to establish genre specific signifiers. (You may wish to refer back to the opening sequence from *Scream*.)

DISCUSSION

Choose three other film genres. What kind of soundtrack is most associated with them?

Summary

Sound, as we have seen, is an essential part of the fabric of a film. It can be used to increase the sensory experience and to shape meaning. Both diegetic and non-diegetic sound help to generate many aspects within a film. We have concentrated here on just three: setting, character and genre.

FOCUS

1. With reference to three films, write a detailed analysis of how sound is used to evoke setting.
2. Discuss the ways in which sound can be employed to inform the audience of issues of character representation.
3. Consider the ways in which sound is an integral part of our understanding of genre.

GLOSSARY

The following glossary offers short definitions of key terms and should be used in conjunction with the index and more detailed definitions of key terms within the book as a whole.

ABC (Audit Bureau of Circulation) – an independent organisation that provides circulation figures for magazines and newspapers.

Aberrant readings – when a reading of a text is very different from the intended reading. Such a reading may be mistaken or deliberate.

Aerial shot/bird's eye view – shots filmed from aircraft or helicopter, extreme high angle.

Advertorial – in a magazine or newspaper this is an advertisement that has the appearance of an article. The name 'advertising feature' will often appear in the margins of the page.

Ambient sound – natural background noise on television, film or radio, such as the sound of birds in a wood. In the same manner, **ambient light** refers to natural, available light that is not enhanced in any way.

American Dream – the belief that anyone in America can succeed and achieve their dreams and aspirations, regardless of their social background or financial starting point.

Anchorage – Roland Barthes suggested that all images are open to a variety of interpretations or meanings. He referred to this as **polysemy**. However, if an image is anchored by written text, or sound, then this 'anchors' or fixes the image to a particular reading.

Artificial lighting – any lighting that is used to light a film or television programme other than a natural source of light.

Audience – all those who receive or consume any media product. A **target audience** is the group of people at whom a product is particularly aimed. It may be identified as either **mass** (or **mainstream**) if it is targeted at a very large group of people, or **niche** if it is targeted at a smaller, more specific group of people.

Auteur – a French term meaning 'author'. It is used to refer to a film director who may be said to direct his or her films with distinctive personal style, such as Tarantino.

BARB – (Broadcasters' Audience Research Board) is an independent organisation that is used to measure the size of audiences for particular television programmes, for the television companies. BARB is jointly owned by the BBC and the ITCA (The Independent Television Companies Association).

Binary opposition – where texts are organised around sets of opposite values such as good and evil, light and dark.

Broadsheet – the term strictly refers to the size or format of the newspaper, although the term is frequently used to define certain newspapers. Newspapers such as *The Times* are often still called 'broadsheets' even though they are now published at a much smaller size.

Camera angle – this refers to the position of the camera in relation to the main subject. It could be a high angle, low angle, canted angle, worm's eye view or aerial view.

Character – the Russian critic and folklorist Vladimir Propp examined hundreds of folk tales and presented an analysis of character types and suggested that they had particular roles in narratives.

Chiaroscuro lighting – a term originally applied to painting and drawing, it comes from the Italian for light and dark. It applies to high-contrast lighting that gives deep shadows and bright highlights, such as is often used in film noir, for example.

Cinematographer – the person in film-making who is responsible for camera and lighting, more often referred to as the Director of Photography.

Connotation – Roland Barthes refers to this as the meanings that words, images and sounds suggest beyond the literal description or **denotation**. So a colour such as 'red' has **connotations** of danger or blood, i.e. meanings beyond the literal.

Continuity editing – sometimes referred to as invisible editing, this is the unobtrusive style of editing developed by Hollywood and still employed in most commercial productions. The basis of continuity editing is to cut on action so that the whole sequence looks natural. Elapsed time may be very different to edited time for a sequence.

Convergence – this is the coming together of different communications technologies and processes. Joined together by a modem, the telephone and computer **converge** to give access to the Internet and communication with many other computers. Convergence is often the result of alliances between or mergers of different companies, but alliances and mergers are not the same. Alliances are when separate individual companies work together in a business venture; mergers/takeovers are when separate companies become one larger organisation, as with the merger of AOL and Time Warner.

Cover lines – information about lead articles given on the front cover of a magazine.

Crane shot – a shot filmed quite literally from a high angle using a crane.

Cross-media ownership – is when corporations own different businesses in several types of media. For example, News Corporation has subsidiary companies involved in a range of media, including television, film and the press.

Demographics – demographic data refers to the social characteristics of an audience, described according to groupings such as social class, regional location, gender and age.

Denotation – is the simple description of what can be seen or heard (see **connotation**).

Depth of field – the distance between the furthest and the nearest points that are in focus in a shot. A wide-angle lens will have a much greater depth of field than a telephoto lens.

Diegetic/non-diegetic sound – diegetic sound is what appears to come from 'within' the narrative of a film, radio or television text, such as from a television playing in the back of a scene. **Non-diegetic** sound includes film music played over a scene, for example.

Digital – the conversion of sound and vision to transmit information in binary code using the numbers zero and one, which is recognisable to a computer. Increasingly a major way in which media texts are produced, distributed and consumed (e.g. CD, MP3, DVD, digital radio and TV, the Internet)

Discourse – the discourse of a text can be analysed to help identify the target audience, who are likely to use a similar register to that used in the text. Discourse can also refer to the ways in which a text is analysed. A feminist discourse about a text would analyse that text in a particular way, for example, using particular vocabulary and frames of reference, centred around the concepts of feminism. A Marxist discourse about the same text would analyse the text in very different ways, analysing the text in terms of commercialism and economic/political frameworks.

Dissolve – this is a fairly common form of **transition** in film or television when one image gradually fades out and a second image fades in to replace it. For a brief time the two images can be seen simultaneously. This is not to be confused with **fades** or **wipes** that are different forms of transition.

Dubbing – is a process whereby sound is added to film in the studio, after it has been shot. This may take the form of adding music or additional sound to dialogue, or it may refer to the addition of an entire soundtrack including dialogue.

Editing – is the selection of material to make a coherent whole. It may refer to the selection and amending of copy and still images for a print product, or sound for radio or images and sound for television or film. In film and television an editor will use a variety of methods of establishing the narrative of a text and will edit shots together in a variety of ways to communicate meaning to the audience.

Editorial – this may refer to a statement or article by the editor in a print publication, or it may also refer to any feature material in that publication which matches the ideology of the publication.

Enigma – is a question or puzzle that may be raised at the beginning of or during a text. It refers to one of Roland Barthes' codes of narrative that he called 'The Voice of Truth' (also called the **hermeneutic** code). These questions work to engage the interest of the audience and are there to be solved or to delay the pleasure of reaching the end of the story.

Equilibrium/disequilibrium/restoration of equilibrium – these are stages within a narrative associated with the narrative theorist, Tzvetan Todorov. A secure and balanced equilibrium is often used to begin a narrative (the happy opening) but this is soon disrupted by conflicts or events that cause disequilibrium. A typical happy ending will result in a restoration of balance and restoration of equilibrium.

Establishing shot – is a **long shot** or **extreme long shot** that establishes the location, general mood and the relative placement of main subjects within a scene. The ES of a Western often pans across the desert plain, for example.

Fade – is when an image gradually grows dim or faint and then disappears from the screen, leaving the screen blank. This form of editing **transition** is not to be confused with a **dissolve**. A fade is usually to a blank black screen and so is often referred to as 'fade to black' (FTB). This is the most common fade although fades to white or red are used for special effects. If an image gradually appears, having started from a blank screen, this is referred to as a **fade up** or fade from. Fade to and from black is commonly found as a standard feature in camcorders. These can be useful transitions at the beginning and end of a moving image sequence.

Form – this term means the structure, or skeleton, of a text and the narrative framework around it. For example, a feature film commonly has the form of a three-act structure. Some structures are determined by a genre and its corresponding codes and conventions. The form of a sitcom is largely defined by its genre expectations, for example.

Frame – as a noun this refers to the single area on a strip of film that holds a single image (or a single image on the timeline if you are using a computer to edit video). As a verb it means to change the position of the camera or to adjust the camera lens to compose the required image. You **frame** your image to construct a close-up, long shot or medium shot. If the framing of a shot is at an angle this is referred to as a **canted frame** or **Dutch angle**.

Gatekeeping – is the process by which news stories are selected or rejected. A gatekeeper is a journalist, usually the editor, who filters the news stories in order to present them in the most appealing way possible to the target audience. The term is also applied to other major decision makers in media industries who control output in a similar way.

Genre – this is the classification of any media text into a category or type: for example, news, horror, action-adventure, documentary, soap opera, docu-soap, science fiction, lifestyle. Genres tend to have identifiable codes and **conventions** that have developed over time and for which audiences may have particular expectations. Media texts that are a mixture of more than one genre are called generic **hybrids**.

Hegemony – the term given to the process by which **dominant ideology** is maintained. This concept was initially identified by the Italian theorist, Antonio Gramsci. It is a form of social consensus that is initially generated by institutions that wield social and political power, such as government organisations, the mass media, the family, the education system and religion. It is a form of consensus that is frequently re-negotiated between the powerful and the dominated. Hegemonic values differ from culture to culture.

High-/low-key lighting – high-key lighting is a lighting scheme that uses bright colours to generate a bright and happy atmosphere and is often used in comedies and musicals. Low-key lighting is where action is more dimly lit. The overall appearance is of darkness and shadow. This style of lighting is characteristic of thrillers, horror movies and film noir.

Horizontal integration – is when an organisation owns different companies of the same type. For instance, Rupert Murdoch owns several newspapers. This occurs when a company takes over a competitor at the same level of production within the same market sector (see **vertical integration**).

Ident – in broadcasting this refers to a jingle or logo that identifies the channel, station or programme, such as the animated BBC2 logo which appears between most programmes on that channel, or a jingle associated with a particular radio programme.

Ideology – an ideology can be seen as a system of ideas, values and beliefs which an individual, group or society holds to be true or important; these are shared by a culture or society about how that society should function. Ideas and values that are seen to be shared or perpetuated by the most influential social agents (the church, the law, education, government, the media etc.) may be described as **dominant ideologies**. A media institution will have ideologies which define and determine their products – a newspaper will have a particular political ideology which shapes its content, for example.

Intertextuality – often related to **post-modernism** and its culture and criticism. Intertextuality suggests that an audience understands texts by their relationship or reference to another text, or that a text is successful principally because of its intertextual references (e.g. *The Simpsons*, *Scream*). One of the effects on the audience of recognising intertextuality is that it flatters their ability to recognise references and feel superior, or to feel part of a group who share the same joke.

Jump cut – is a break in the continuity of shots in a film or television narrative. This may break the continuity of time by leaping immediately forward from one part of the action to another, even though it is clear that they are separated by an interval of time. Jump cuts can also break the continuity of space in the same way. This is the most common form of editing between shots used in film and television. The audience constructs the sequence of events between the two events as they are watching.

Lenses (telephoto, wide-angle) – a telephoto lens zooms in close to an object without moving the camera itself. It is the camera's equivalent to a telescope. A short telephoto is flattering for faces in close up. A long telephoto can also give crowded streets the appearance of being even more congested. A wide-angle lens offers a range of more than 60 degrees. It offers a certain amount of distortion, magnifying the foreground and reducing the size of images in the background. When used for close-ups, this lens will distort the image.

Masthead – the title of a magazine or newspaper, usually placed at the top of the front cover.

Mise-en-scène – literally everything that is put in the scene, or frame, to be seen on camera. This usually includes production design, set, location, actors, costumes, make-up, gesture, proxemics/ blocking, extras, props, use of colour, contrast and filter. Lighting is often included within *mise-en-scène*. Camera shot composition/framing/angle/ movement are sometimes referred to as *mise-en-shot*.

Montage – is taken from the French and means 'an assembly'. It has several meanings in the context of film:

(1) As a synonym for editing. Montage editing simply means constructing a narrative from a sequence of shots.

(2) In mainstream Hollywood cinema, to edit a concentrated sequence with a series of brief cuts with a series of transitions, creating the effect of the passage of time or movement over large distances, or for expressionistic moods.

(3) **Thematic** or **Soviet montage** was developed by Sergei Eisenstein by arranging deliberate juxtapositions of individual shots to suggest an idea that goes beyond meanings within the individual shots. He called this **collision montage**.

4) Any sequence that creates a particularly significant effect mainly through its editing. The shower scene in *Psycho* would be such an example, where the editing creates the horror although the actual event is never seen.

Narrative – the way in which a plot or story is told, by whom and in what order. Flashbacks/ flashforwards and ellipsis may be used as narrative devices. Tsvetan Todorov, Richard Branigan, Roland Barthes, Bordwell and Thompson and Robert McKee all analyse narrative structure and form in particular ways, for example. Texts may have linear or non-linear narratives.

National Readership Survey (NRS) – an organisation that provides information on the number and type of magazine and newspaper readerships.

News gathering – the process by which news is collected or found in order to be treated or packaged for presentation.

News values – the process by which news stories or features are selected and their priority and style of presentation decided (also referred to as gatekeeping). These are sometimes categorised as hard (real news, e.g. tragedies or important political events) or soft (e.g. celebrity news or news about new film releases). The news values are usually determined by the producers and editors to reflect the values of the target audience and what they are interested in reading about or looking at. These news values are likely to be different for different organisations. However, some theorists argue that they also determine and manipulate the agenda of the readers.

Pan and tilt – a pan is to turn the camera from a fixed position horizontally on the axis of its mount, usually while panning across a scene. Tilt is to move the camera from a fixed position vertically on the axis of the mount: for example, to show a character looking another character up and down. A **whip** or **zip pan** is the movement done rapidly rather than the usual slow and smooth movement.

Plugs – information about the contents of a magazine or newspaper given on the front cover to hook the audience.

Point-of-view shot (POV) – is a shot that represents the point of view of a character. This can often be shown as an over-the-shoulder shot looking at another character in a scene. A **subjective point of view** is when the camera functions as if it were the eyes of the character – a common device in horror films.

Polysemy – is the possibility of a sign to have several meanings. (See also **anchorage**.)

Pre-production – the entire range of preparations that take place before a film or television programme can begin shooting, including casting the production, drawing storyboards, planning shooting scripts, organising locations and fixing budgets, for example.

Production – is either a product itself or the actual process of filming, between pre-production and post-production.

Post-production – the period and tasks between the completion of production and the delivery of the completed film or programme. Post-production tasks include the editing of a film or programme, including creating titles, graphics and special-effects, etc.

Post-modernism – is a movement or phase in twentieth-century thought. The term is very difficult to define in simple terms. It is applied across all the arts and at its most basic refers to products that require knowledge of previous texts to appreciate fully form and function.

Preferred reading – this term describes the reading or meaning of a media text that follows the intentions, either conscious or unconscious, of the maker, or, in wider terms, the reading preferred by the dominant forces in society. (See **ideology.**)

Primary research – is information or data that you collect yourself when researching a text. This may include interviews, questionnaires, analysis of original photographs or other media texts that you undertake yourself, as well as watching/reading the text itself. (See also **secondary research**.)

Properties – are more commonly referred to by the abbreviation **props**. The term refers to any object that is carried and used by actors in a scene, as opposed to the larger items of furniture that are considered to be part of the décor of the set itself. In the singular, **property** is also used to refer to any copyrighted text – anything from a complete novel to a song title or synopsis of a plot.

Public Service Broadcasting (PSB) – broadcasting that is intended to entertain, educate and inform but does not have a primary commercial intent. The BBC has a PSB requirement in its Charter, so must ensure it produces products which meet this public service requirement.

Puff – words or phrases on the cover of a magazine used to boost its status and engage an audience, such as 'exclusive'.

Qualitative research – is research undertaken through observation, analysing texts and documents, interviews, open-ended questionnaires and case studies. It is reasoned argument that is not simply based upon statistical information. Qualitative research allows researchers to draw conclusions across large groups or make general observations.

Quantitative research – is primarily data obtained from specific responses to questionnaires or structured interviews. Quantitative research may estimate how many 15–25-year-old males watch *EastEnders*, but qualitative research is necessary to determine *why* they watch it. Quantitative research can draw detailed conclusions but these need to be substantiated with qualitative data before general conclusions can be drawn.

RAJAR (Radio Joint Audience Research) – this is an organisation involving the BBC and commercial radio (similar to BARB) that is responsible for calculating audience figures for radio programmes.

Ratings – ratings are the figures used when referring to the estimated size of audience for a particular media text. The ratings for weekly television viewings are published in most newspapers. (See also **BARB** and **RAJAR**.)

Readership – this does not simply refer to those who buy a newspaper or magazine, but to the total number of people who are likely to read the publication: usually considered to be three or four times the number of copies actually sold.

Realism – is the dominant mode of representation in contemporary media texts. The term usually implies that the media text attempts to represent reality in some way: a film or television programme is realistic because it accurately reproduces that part of the real world to which it is referring. Realism as a specific media form is more complex, involving expectations about particular narratives, constructs, editing and ideologies, for example.

Representation – the process of making meaning in still or moving images and words/sounds. In its simplest form, it means to represent someone or something in a media text in a way that communicates meaning to an audience. However, it is used to describe the process by which an image etc. may be used to represent/stand for someone or something, such as a place or an idea, and thus convey an ideology or perspective. Representation of social groups (such as women, asylum seekers or particular ethnic groups) can be stereotypical in the ideologies they convey.

Scheduling – is the planning of (usually terrestrial) broadcasting to ensure maximum target audiences for particular texts. Certain texts are scheduled at particular times of day; for example, children's programmes would not usually be shown at 11.00 p.m. Scheduling is perhaps less significant nowadays, with the vast range of cable and satellite channels now available.

Semiology/semiotics – the study of sign systems and their function in society. A media text comprises a sequence of signs; by deconstructing these signs and their interaction a reading of the text can be given.

Shot-reverse shot – is a standard technique for filming a conversation in which shots from one character's point of view are intercut with those of the second speaker, usually using jump cuts between the shots in the sequence.

Stereotype – is an over-simplified representation of people, places or issues, giving a narrow perspective or interpretation. Stereotypes can be a very useful way of establishing type or expectation quickly for an audience, as well as a tool for criticising or demeaning social groups or places.

Storyboard – the planning of a moving image text by using a series of drawings with written instructions for the methods of filming. Storyboards may be mostly sketches with instructions about camera angles, editing and so forth, or may be detailed artistic representations of each and every frame in a text. The storyboard is usually the first stage in pre-production, once a concept has been approved for production.

Stripping – (also occasionally referred to as **stranding**) is the form of scheduling on television whereby the same type or genre of programme (e.g. sport, soap opera, consumer programme) is offered at the same time every day, every week on a channel.

Style – this refers to the look of a media text. It can be identified (according to the medium), by the use of colour, typography, graphic design and layout, vocabulary, photography or illustration, *mise-en-scène*, lighting, music, camera angle, movement, framing, dialogue, editing etc.

Synchronous/asynchronous sound – synchronous sound is where the sound matches the action or speech in film or television. Asynchronous sound is when there is a mismatch – the most obvious example is when **lip-synch** is out; in other words, when the words spoken and the lip movement of the actor on screen do not match: for example, when a text has been dubbed from another language.

Synergy – is the establishment of the relationship between different areas of the media for mutual benefit. This may or may not be within the same organisation, although conglomerates such as AOL/Time Warner and News Corporation are able to make the most of such opportunities. An example might be when the launching of a new film is accompanied by the promotion of a wide range of merchandise, or a CD of the music and a series of magazine interviews. Synergy between films and music is quite common.

Tabloid – a tabloid is a half-sized newspaper. Strictly speaking, the term is related to size only, but is frequently used to refer to newspapers such as the *Sun* and the *Mirror* (these are also referred to as **red-top tabloids**). The *Daily Mail* and the *Daily Express* are referred to as mid-market tabloids. The term is used primarily critically these days since the broadsheets have moved to tabloid-size production.

Take – a take is a single recording of a scene or sequence of film (or video). In commercial film making several takes of the same shot are often made, until a satisfactory one has been achieved.

Teasers – short phrases on the front cover of a newspaper or magazine to tempt a reader to buy the publication or a teaser poster to intrigue audiences about a text which has yet to be released (e.g. a new film). **Teaser trailers** are short film or television trailers shown before a text is released, which serve to whet an audience's appetite for the text being promoted. **Theatrical trailers** are usually longer and more detailed. Generally, teaser trailers are released well before release date to excite interest and theatrical trailers released close to release date or even used post-first release (e.g. on DVDs).

Terrestrial – transmissions of radio and television that are from land-based transmitters rather than cable or satellite channels. In the UK, the terrestrial channels are BBC1, BBC2, ITV, Channel 4 and Channel Five. The cable and satellite channels can now be divided into the Free to View channels, such as BBC3 and BBC4, and the subscription channels, such as Sky Sports 1, 2 and 3.

Tracking shot (also referred to as a **dolly shot**) – originally when a camera was actually moved along on rails or tracks during a take, so as to follow the action. When the camera was removed from the rails and placed on a platform with wheels or castors the platform was referred to as a dolly, hence a dolly shot. These shots are also referred to as **trucking** or **travelling shots**.

Typography – the typeface or font that is used in printed texts.

Two-shot – literally a shot with two people in the same frame.

Vertical integration – is a term used to describe how one company owns all stages of production and distribution (and in the world of film, exhibition). The Hollywood Studio System from approximately the late 1920s to the 1950s was organised in this way. The Studios held the contracts for the actors and screenwriters, shot and edited the films in their own studios and then controlled exhibition and distribution.

In print publication it could refer to a company that owns all stages of production, from the paper mills that make the paper, through to chains of newsagents who sell the magazines and newspapers and the Internet service providers who have the servers which host the online editions.

Vox pop – opinions on current issues or topics recorded from members of the public. From the Latin *vox populi*, meaning 'voice of the people'. Vox pops are often used during news or documentary programmes: for example, obtaining a series of vox pops from angry commuters at a railway station when there is a strike.

Wide shot or **wide-angled shot** – is a shot that takes in more than 60 degrees of vision rather than the normal range of the camera at 45–50 degrees.

Wipe – a type of transition used in film and television, in which one scene appears to push another off the screen. In early film making the only possibilities were the vertical or horizontal wipe, but with developing technology a wipe can be in an almost infinite variety of patterns. This can be a popular way of moving between shots in music programmes, for example.

Wrap – (1) the conclusion of a day's filming or for the entire production. (2) An item in a news programme that begins with the newsreader, cuts to a location reporter and/or an actuality sequence and then returns to the newsreader.

Zoom lens – is a lens of variable length used to give the illusion of moving the camera closer to or further away from a subject without moving the camera itself. It does not usually take such close up shots as a telephoto lens. A zoom shot should not be confused with a dolly or tracking shot where the camera is physically moved. A zoom shot may sometimes be shown, i.e. the camera zooms in to a particular part of the scene as the action takes place – for example, zooming in on a character's face, to create tension as they respond to a piece of news.

BIBLIOGRAPHY

Useful websites

The British Film Institute: http://www.bfi.org.uk
Film Education: http://www.filmeducation.org
The English and Media Centre: http://www.englishandmedia.co.uk
BBC Online: http://www.bbc.co.uk
The Guardian and the *Media Guardian*: http://guardianunlimited.co.uk/
Adflip (contains a range of adverts to view): http://www.adflip.com
For everything you need to know about films – and often posters, trailers etc. as well: www.imdb.com

Books

Arroyo, J., 2000, *Action/Spectacle Cinema*, London: BFI.
Branston, G. and Stafford, R., 2002, *The Media Students Book*, London: Routledge.
Burton, G., 1997, *More than Meets the Eye*, London: Arnold.
Clark, V. *et al.*, 2002, *Key Concepts and Skills for Media Studies*, London: Hodder & Stoughton.
Edwards, M., 2003, *Key Ideas in Media*, Cheltenham: Nelson Thornes.
Gauntlett, D., 2004, *web.studies*, 2nd edn., London: Arnold.
Lacey, N., 1998, *Image and Representation: Key Concepts in Media Studies*, Basingstoke: Macmillan.
Lacey, N., 2000, *Narrative and Genre*, Basingstoke: Macmillan.
Lacey, N., 2002, *Media Institutions and Audiences: Key Concepts in Media Studies*, Basingstoke: Macmillan.
Martin, R., 2000, *Television for A Level Media Studies*, London: Hodder & Stoughton.
McLeish, R., 1999, *Radio Production*, Oxford, Boston: Focal Press.
O'Sullivan, T. *et al.*, 2003, *Studying the Media*, London: Arnold.
Peak, S. and Fisher, P. (eds.), annual publication, *Guardian Media Guide*, London: Guardian Books/Fourth Estate.
Stewart, C., Lavelle, M. and Kowaltzke, A., 2001, *Media and Meaning: An Introduction*, London: BFI.

INDEX